D0847459

THEOLOGICAL
INVESTIGATIONS

Volume XVI

THEOLOGICAL INVESTIGATIONS

THEOLOGICAL INVESTIGATIONS

VOLUME XVI

EXPERIENCE OF THE SPIRIT:
SOURCE OF THEOLOGY

by
KARL RAHNER

Translated by
DAVID MORLAND O.S.B.

CROSSROAD • NEW YORK

1983
The Crossroad Publishing Company
575 Lexington Avenue, New York, NY 10022

A translation of the first part of
SCHRIFTEN ZUR THEOLOGIE, XII
published by Verlagsanstalt Benziger & Co. A.G., Einsiedeln

This translation © Darton, Longman & Todd Ltd. 1979
First published 1979
Reprinted 1983

Library of Congress Catalog Card Number: 61-8189
ISBN: 0-8245-0392-9
Printed in the United States of America

CONTENTS

FOREWORD

THIS new volume of the *Theological Investigations* brings the series up to sixteen volumes (12 in the German). Once again this collection consists of a wide variety of essays, talks and writings, which the author was asked to produce on different occasions. From this one would expect a miscellaneous and random result, but in fact even a first, swift glance at the writings which originated in this way over the last few years and which seemed appropriate for such a collection reveals the quite clear emergence of a particular topic, namely the question of the Holy Spirit and his activity in the Church and in theology.

This is hardly surprising, since the charismatic movements in North America and in Europe have aroused interest in the gifts of the Spirit, in charisms and the guidance of the Spirit, and interest which came overnight to occupy the centre of the public, religious stage. It is indeed obvious that this type of experience of the Spirit raises a question which theology cannot and may not evade. For in the first place it seems as though a long forgotten Christian theme has once again taken on new life. But this brings with it the charge against theology that it has not been concerned with this important aspect of the life of faith. Today it is precisely non-theologians, the ordinary faithful, who must remind those 'responsible for Christian belief', i.e. theologians, of their neglect and forgetfulness, through the living proof of spiritual power. Furthermore the concrete expressions of this activity of the Spirit, such as speaking in tongues or healing, to mention only the most well known, seem to call in question the traditional theological enterprise, the whole way in which theologians think and reason. Effective Christianity would then detach itself from the realm of theology and find once more its original place in the charismatic faith of Christians.

vii

Without being able to investigate more closely the rights and wrongs of these charges, which, though mostly unspoken, are commonly felt, we may at this point simply note that they recall one of our earliest theological enquiries, from which an unbroken thread may be traced throughout our theological work. These enquiries have not been prominent for a long while in the German speaking world and have not, in consequence, received much attention. If they are now taken up in this volume, the purpose is to present the above mentioned theme in a somewhat clearer light, for it is from this concern that our writings over the last few years on the subject of the activity of the Holy Spirit have originated. In this way the collection presented here has acquired its unified theme and focus, which is expressed in the subtitle: 'Experience of the Spirit: source of Theology'. A few short remarks may at least indicate the exact meaning to be attached to this phrase.

As in earlier volumes of my *Theological Investigations*, the point of stress summarised in the subtitle should not be taken to suggest a systematic treatment of the topic. It may be said only to expose the underlying shape which is shared to a greater or lesser extent by the individual essays. If in the present volume that consists in the experience of the Spirit, then at least a theme is formulated, or rather a basic stance indicated, which extends beyond the particular texts which have been brought together here and is of crucial importance for the whole theological activity of the author. This implies not only the general truth that genuine Christian theology can only speak through the Holy Spirit and in that measure already presumes and includes the experience of his power. Rather it should point to that quite specific experience to which St Ignatius Loyola wished to guide and direct spiritual practice through his Exercises. This experience is characterised by discernment of spirits, by the process of choice, by the practical search for the will of God, to mention only a few aspects. Proper to such experience is the basic tendency, strengthened and stimulated by meditation on the life of Jesus which shapes and surrounds it, to seek for the appropriate theological expression by which the immediate experience may achieve greater depth and clarity. From spiritual decisions, which are essential for the life of faith, whether of the individual or of the Church, there follows an inevitable exchange between experience and reflection. This in turn permits the ecclesial and theological activity and structures to possess the necessary flexibility and reference to particular situations in the transmission of truth. This may be clarified more concretely if one recalls the author's earlier works, for instance the Quaestiones Disputatae, 'The Dynamic Element in the Church' or 'Visions and Prophecies', or the various utterances on freedom and on public opinion in the Church, on the task of the layman and his relation to the hierarchy. The attempts to find a solution to these and similar questions all involved the serious application of the same basic concept of the working of the Holy Spirit. This theme appears also in a more spontaneous and perhaps livelier form in the author's published papers on the subject of spiritual practice; one may mention here 'Spiritual Exercises' (1965) and 'Meditations on Priestly Life' (1970). In such practices the Christian attempts to lay himself open directly to the instinctual faith of the Church, to ratify and make his own those insights of faith which the Church has achieved over the centuries through the guidance of the Spirit.

In this context awareness of the Spirit is in no way restricted to the intense emotional experience of the individual; it is alive also in the broad stream of the Church's awareness of the Spirit. But this does not mean that on the basis of a sober, rational theology and psychology such intense experiences should without more ado be rejected or treated with sceptical doubt in every case. It is rather that men, who are still on pilgrimage through time and history, should never imagine that they have received an absolutely certain and final assurance of the Spirit. What better way, indeed, is there of maintaining a lively awareness of this state than to insert one's own experience into the activity of the Spirit in the broad mass of the Church?

One can see from these few remarks that on the one hand the reality of the Spirit in Christian faith confronts theological reflection with limit questions, with problems which Christianity is forced to face in order to come to terms with itself, its past, its present tasks and its power to fashion the future: namely, the foundation of faith, the experience of grace, living from faith, etc. The present era is not the first to raise questions like these, but perhaps the answers which belong to the Church's history of spirituality have in the meantime been partly buried and forgotten. But we can even today grasp with relative ease the theological statements on the topic. Naturally theology has always attempted in various ways to formulate its answers by listening to Scripture and this point of departure is one to which contemporary theology also remains bound.

On the other hand reflection on spiritual experience impels

Christian faith into the heart of the mystery from which arises the question of God and of Jesus Christ in his unity and difference with regard to the Father. And, since the Christian has to understand himself both in relation to Jesus Christ and at the same time in contrast to him, the question can at this point no longer be suppressed, the question, that is, which man is to himself. The ecclesial community should help to answer this existential question, for its claim and its ministry remain, as does man himself, under the influence not only of the purely divine activity of the Spirit but also of the operations of the world, if indeed this conceptual antithesis is here allowable. But the effects of the world are not at all so unambiguous, or so easily evaluated, for the contemporary Christian as appears to have been the case in the past. For in these effects, too, the Spirit can be at work; it can present signs of the times to the Church. Thus the scope of spiritual discernment is broadened almost beyond measure. There is today a widespread feeling of oppression, fear and insecurity, a sense of being lost. The countless variety of opposing questions and problems threatens to cripple the Christian. For however joyful and good the strict application of spiritual judgement may be in helping to solve this or that particular problem, it inevitably sharpens the perception of the relentlessly mounting number of similar questions. These the individual is no longer in a position even to survey by himself, still less to hope that he can make a substantial contribution to their solution.

In this sense what has been said so far, and indeed the whole collection of writings presented here, may leave the reader very dissatisfied. For the texts assembled here mostly deal with very specific problems, to which moreover the author has already addressed himself on various earlier occasions. So the volume may not appear to promise very much in detail, nor a great deal that is new. However the matter may be seen in quite a different light when the overall viewpoint, 'Experience of the Spirit: source of Theology', is allowed to coordinate and unify the contents and to offer a fresh perspective. This will bring to light connections and relations which scarcely come into view when the particular essays are read on their own. In wishing the reader to tackle this volume of the *Theological Investigations* in this way, the author is not so much concerned with the historical fact mentioned above that his own theological thinking sprang from the practice of the Ignatian Exercises and so in fact was fashioned in the light of reflection on the effective operation of the

Spirit. Rather he is moved by a consideration which is grounded in the very substance of theology. In every case theology must be built out of a living experience of faith which is given, in the author's opinion, when hope transcends particular expectations and is enveloped by a promise deeper than words, when responsibility is freely accepted and borne, even without the explicit ratification of utility or success, when freedom is lived and death is grasped as the entry into the unimaginable assurance of salvation. Everyone must dig out his own experiences of this sort from the rubble of his daily activity. In all these moments, so we affirm, God, and his liberating grace, is present and in them we experience what Christians call the Holy Spirit. And this awareness remains alive even at times of inevitable oppression. It is offered to us for our free acceptance, if we do not wish to barricade ourselves against it in a hell of freedom.

This experience comes to every man, albeit in an endless variety of forms according to the personal and historical situation of the individual. But the Christian knows that the Spirit of God, which is offered to him for salvation or judgement with continual urgency, has been guaranteed to man as finally victorious in the crucified and risen Jesus and has entered into a permanent and irrevocable covenant with the history of mankind. Thus the Christian is assured that this Spirit, which has been poured out on all flesh and is at work over the whole earth, is no longer to be driven from the world by the despairing rejection of the individual; it is indeed the Spirit of the Father of Jesus, the Spirit of Jesus himself. We trust in his effectiveness and in his victory, if we cast our gaze on Jesus and his victory in death and no longer do we overlook the government of the Spirit at work even in our own lives.

At this deeper and more fundamental level, we find that the particular questions and problems, which threatened to fragment, once more come together. Here Christians and theologians can discover the courage and the joy which they need in order to carry on. On this level, too, the intense charismatic experiences are to be grounded, so that they may transmit the power of Spirit intended by Christianity. If this collection should contribute to this progress, if it can in the best sense have theological repercussions in the world of spiritual experience and awareness of faith, if it can promote consciousness and awareness of a spiritual kind, and if finally it should encourage concentration on the pressing demands of particular problems, without thereby breaking the connection with the underlying framework, then these essays may continue the work which was intended as the purpose of the earlier volumes.

For the publication of this volume the author has once again relied on the assistance of Fr Karl H. Neufeld S.J., D. Phil. Because of many obstacles and numerous obligations, the author has scarcely had the chance to deal personally with the final draft and arrangement of this volume, in so far as the proposed texts required attention at various points, so as to avoid repetitions, remove superfluous material and add valuable notes. For this labour the author has his assistant to thank.

In conclusion I would once more express my joy in being able to dedicate this volume of *Theological Investigations*, even if rather belatedly, to my mother on the completion of the hundredth year of her life.

Munich, June 1975.

Karl Rahner

PART ONE

Faith and Spirit

1

THE FOUNDATION OF BELIEF TODAY

THE foundation of belief today is a large and difficult question and from the start one should expect only a few fragmentary remarks in the way of an answer.[1] Necessarily we cannot avoid being selective in our considerations and this may lead to some vital points receiving insufficient attention. In modern society, however, we become aware of various needs, requirements and desires which are relevant to the underpinning of Christian belief. This enterprise indeed always contains a risk and we need therefore to be convinced that it is *necessary* today to seek to establish some *grounds* for Christian belief.[2]

As long as Catholic theology exists – indeed we may assert from the very beginning of Christianity – apologetic has been undertaken and fundamental theology taught, even if in a variety of ways, with changing methods, points of departure and perspectives. But the conviction has always remained that Christianity, its faith and its theology must be missionary. Therefore appeal must be made to the unbeliever, the doubter and those on the way to faith. Catholic theology has never maintained the view that faith was a sort of leap in the dark into a world to which there was no other access except through the totally irrational decision to believe. The Catholic mind always included respect for human intelligence, for reflection and for

[1] On the question of the foundation of faith, cf. K. Rahner, 'Reflections on the Contemporary Intellectual Formation of Future Priests', *Theological Investigations* VI (London & Baltimore, 1969) pp. 113–138.

[2] The following reflections were written for a lecture given to preachers and catechists at the IVth Theological Conference at the Bildungshaus Stift, Zwetl in December, 1973. They have been revised and expanded for publication here.

intellectual reasoning and argument. Naturally such reasoning may proceed in a variety of ways depending on the exact topic under discussion and today, for example, it is rightly emphasised that Christianity has to find not only a 'rational' but also a 'narrative' or 'historical' foundation.[3] The Christian message that salvation is accessible in history cannot be expressed in terms of metaphysical reasoning alone, but must also be 'narrated' as the history of salvation. But even such 'narrative' theology is in fact rational, a point that the explanatory statements 'God became flesh', 'Jesus died on the cross', 'Jesus rose from the dead' themselves make plain. This in turn, of course, makes possible theoretical reasoning and metaphysical reflection in theology.

A first deduction follows from these preliminary remarks: whoever is to reach belief has the right to demand that the preachers of the Gospel 'give an account of our hope'[4], as we already find it expressed the New Testament. Such a grounding of faith has an external and an internal aspect; it is at the same time rational and spiritual. Certainly since the 19th century Catholic theology has not paid sufficient attention to the interior foundation of faith. Current apologetic and fundamental theology has been carried out in too rationalistic a manner. This point must be granted without further dispute.

It was said that, since revelation is evidently guaranteed by miracles, it follows that in the Old Testament, in Jesus Christ and in the Church derived from him, a historical revelation has been given. This fact was, as it were, proved as a whole and the intention was to extract specific truths of faith from divine revelation, demonstrated by such formal reasoning, and present them to the individual with the rider: this is revealed truth; you must believe it; it does not matter whether you understand it or not, or whether you find any interior, personal access to it. Even today it must be admitted that Church authorities still behave in a manner which appeals too exclusively to the formal authority of the Church and the magisterium. On the basis of this authority alone the individual is required to accept specific articles of faith without any effort being made to render such truths credible

[3] Cf. J. B. Metz, 'Erlösung und Emanzipation' in *Erlösung und Emanzipation*, Quaestiones Disputatae 61, L. Scheffczyk ed. (Freiburg i.Br., 1973), pp. 120–140, esp. 137–140; also J. B. Metz, 'A Small Apology for Narrative', *Concilium* 5/9 (May 1973), pp. 84–89 and H. Weinrich, 'Narrative Theology,' *ibid.*, pp. 48–56.

[4] 1 P 3: 15.

from within their own horizon of meaning.[5] What exactly is meant, however, by the 'internal' and 'external' aspects of the grounding of faith, or by its 'rational' and 'spiritual' side, must be more clearly indicated in the course of the following reflections.

THE SITUATION OF BELIEF TODAY

The *external* situation of Christian belief, of the possibility and duty of faith, is characterised by the crucial fact that Christianity and the Church are, in the expression of Peter Berger, a cognitive minority.[6]

What was the situation like in the past? For at least 1500 years the Church, and its theology and apologetic, existed in a historical and intellectual world formed by a more or less homogeneous Christian society. Faith constituted public opinion: it was accepted and taken for granted as self-evident. God's existence, for example, was regarded by St Thomas Aquinas as an assumption requiring no discussion for the ordinary mortal, for belief in God was an assumed fact in society to which everybody referred without question and with perfect right. Today the situation is quite different. Christianity and the Church are no longer publicly supported without question by society, or at least such backing is rapidly crumbling away. Thus Christian faith today is ever more plainly in a state of 'gnoseological' or 'mental concupiscence.'[7] This expression may seem to some an awkward, modish or odd description. Perhaps it should be briefly explained.

The fact of concupiscence, of that excessive desire which is a consequence of original sin, is already attested in ch.7 of the Epistle to the Romans as well as in the dogma of the Church and the teaching of the Council of Trent.[8] According to the Tridentine text, the state of concupiscence cannot be completely overcome, so that even the justified Christian must struggle 'ad agonem' with it in his Christian life. Until now it has only been considered and discussed with reference to the

[5] On the problem of 'Extrinsecism' cf. A. Lang and H. de Lavalette, *LThK* III, 1321–1323; also cf. K. Rahner, 'Remarks on the Importance of the History of Jesus for Catholic Dogmatics,' *Theological Investigations* XIII (London, 1975) pp. 201–212, esp. 203 sq.

[6] Cf. P. Berger, *Rumour of Angels* (London, 1971) pp. 12 sqq.

[7] For this expression, cf. K. Rahner, 'On the Relationship between Theology and the Contemporary Sciences,' *Theological Investigations* XIII (London, 1975), pp. 94–102; also in this volume, 'Faith between Rationality and Emotion'.

[8] Cf. the Decree of the Council of Trent on Original Sin, *Denz.* 1515.

ethical (or unethical) impulses in man. Man always feels himself driven by various forces and desires.[9] These impulses are not integrated and harmonised; they war one against another. In this state a man must live out his life. Even when he wishes clearly and freely to choose God, he will be impelled by quite different forces, that is, by egoism, or, as one used to say, by 'the flesh'. A man is unable in some measure to reach real peace and genuine integrity in his moral behaviour or to achieve the complete ordering of his life. He is and remains, as it were, two people: when he makes a wholehearted, personal decision in one direction, he is acutely aware that he cannot entirely reconcile the 'other' active within him to this commitment by means of his own choice of direction. But concupiscence, in the Christian sense of the term, is more clearly evident today in the realm of human knowledge as well as in the moral domain. In the 16th or 17th century a theologian, or even an ordinary Christian, could organise his knowledge into a more or less well-structured system. His questions and problems were open to solution. Moreoever it was known and recognised at that time that a unified, well-organised and comprehensible world picture could emerge in which everything found its proper place and nothing had to stand in opposition to anything else. Centuries earlier St Thomas Aquinas, in his *Summa Theologiae*, had already created such a system, in which the human knowledge of the day, the possible questions and answers, were all taken into account. The result of this unified synthesis was that each proposition was treated as an absolute and definite assertion. Either one accepted that God is a Trinity or one did not; tertium non datur. If one said no, then the denial possessed the same absolute and definite quality as the positive affirmation.

The present situation, however, is characterised by the above mentioned 'mental concupiscence'. Our minds are fed with disparate insights and pieces of information from a great range of sources of knowledge and these do not admit any longer of a positive and complete ordering into a coherent whole. When I began my theological studies forty years ago, I was far cleverer than I am today, if I take all the possible branches of knowledge and intellectual problems as my

---

[9] For this notion cf. Ignatius Loyola, *Spiritual Exercises* 'On the Discernment of Spirits' (313–336). The rules do not merely seek to create an awareness of the phenomenon; they also offer the individual practical help in dealing with it.

criterion of measurement. For today there is such a vast number of questions and areas of knowledge of a historical, metaphysical, philosophical, linguistic, sociological and religious kind that in the face of this mass of theological material I feel much stupider than I did then. Christian Pesch,[10] whose manual of theology I followed, could still be firmly convinced that he had dealt with all the relevant theological material in his 9 volume 'Theologia Dogmatica'. He had in some measure worked out a positive, theological synthesis in the then prevailing intellectual climate. Such a thing is quite impossible today. One would have to have some knowledge of, say, Aramaic, modern linguistic philosophy and sociology. To this must be added a thousand other things, so that a mass of phenomena, of whose existence we at least have some inkling, confronts us as questions to be answered and tasks to be undertaken. This enormous range of knowledge and intellectual possibilities, a range which can no longer be adequately covered, brings plainly to the fore that human limitation which I have tried to describe with the phrase 'mental concupiscence'. In the past men have been conscious of limits in the moral sphere imposed by concupiscence and in a similar way today the problem is felt in the realm of knowledge.

In this situation the individual is no longer in a position *adequately* and *positively* to organise in his mind all the knowledge which is important for his picture of the world. We ought not to behave as though a synthesis of faith and contemporary knowledge were still a possibility for the individual. We may rightly believe, however, that Christianity contains the final truth and meaning for man and the world. We may also be granted the conviction that ideally an ultimate synthesis must in itself be possible and that no data of knowledge exist which are so mutually opposed that one set must be accepted as true and the other rejected as false. Of course this ideal can only be approached asymptotically: it always lies before us and will presumably move away to an ever increasing distance. Limitations of time, strength, intelligence and memory remain even for modern man, despite all the available means of assistance, while the material to be gathered into any synthesis, coming from every branch of modern knowledge and from the whole range of human experience in history and in society, is ever on the increase.

[10] Chr. Pesch, *Praelectiones Dogmaticae*, 9 Vols. (Freiburg i.Br. 1914–1925).

THE CONSEQUENCES OF THE MODERN SITUATION

If we now turn to the question of the foundation of faith, the state we have described above forces us to concentrate first of all on the basic essentials of Christian revelation. The Second Vatican Council was justified in speaking of a hierarchy of truths even though it did not specify exactly what the expression meant.[11] It is immediately obvious that the individual articles of faith may be related either more closely to, or more distantly from, the fundamental centre of Christian faith. In this sense the idea of an objective hierarchy of truths is straightforward enough. But clearly we must reflect more carefully upon the subjective hierarchy of truths.[12] In fact the two are so closely intertwined that they share a common dependence upon the original revelation. What else can a man do if he is in a state of 'mental concupiscence', faced by an incomprehensible mass of knowledge which can neither be digested nor fitted into a synthesis, except to return to the original, central revelation? There must be such a centre which I can make my basic support and from which I can calmly accept the totality of Christianity. This I can do without having first achieved the perfect, but unattainable, synthesis of all Christian truths, even those of secondary importance, with contemporary knowledge and the modern mind. In today's world even the theologian who has spent a lifetime of study in his field has the right to say that, not being an exegete, he cannot give an exact account of how Mt 16:18 can be positively reconciled with the papal office as it exists and is conceived in the Catholic Church today. For this, particular specialist knowledge is demanded which is scarcely to be found in mind of one person. The earlier assertions of fundamental theology on this point certainly do

[11] On the notion of the 'Hierarchy of Truths' cf. Conc. Vat. II *Decree on Ecumenism*, Art. 11, commentary by J. Feiner in, *Commentary on the Documents of Vatican II*, II (London and New York, 1967), also K. Rahner, 'Theology and Anthropology,' *Theological Investigations* IX (London, 1972), pp. 28–45; 'The New Image of the Church', *Theological Investigations* X (London, 1973), pp. 3–29; 'On the Theology of Ecumenical Discussion,' *Theological Investigations* XI (London, 1974), pp. 24–67; 'The Faith of the Christian and the Doctrine of the Church,' *Theological Investigations* XIV (London 1976), pp. 24–46.

[12] The author has already discussed the problem of the subjective hierarchy of truths some years ago under the title 'Gestaltwandel der Haresie,' cf. *Gefahren im heutigen Katholizismus* (Einsiedeln, 1954); cf. also K. Rahner, 'What is Heresy?' *Theological Investigations* V (London and Baltimore, 1966), pp. 468–512.

not suffice as an objectively adequate answer to the question. They do no more than point in the direction in which an answer is to be found. But the Christian and the theologian must positively come to terms with truths of this sort, even if a direct synthesis of the kind outlined above is not obtained. So the only possible first step is for me to return once more in a conscious fashion to the innermost kernel of my faith.

In order to provide grounds for belief we can begin quite happily with man. There is no need to fear that this anthropological starting point necessarily leads to a subjective or reductionist version of Christian faith which is limited to one epoch. Certainly one thing is quite clear: the man who has no questions hears no answers, even though of course the question stays more plainly in a man's awareness if the answer is also heard, for question and answer hang closely together.

The more precise the question, the more care and attention will be paid to grasping the answer. Similarly the answer given in revelation clarifies the question a man asks. If one is aware from the start of the complementary relationship existing between the anthropological starting point and the theological answer, then one should not permit any further attack on the proposed point of departure. A man can say that he is only interested in answers for which he has a question; so God can only communicate with a person on a level which concerns that man's innermost core of existence. Why should this lead of necessity to an abridgement of Christian faith? Man is essentially a questioner; indeed he is an absolute question which does not stop at any given point. An objective curiosity is part of his nature, for a person is endowed, even before he begins to ask questions, with the grace of the Holy Spirit, which is rooted in the centre of his personal being. He is given the capacity to ask for infinity and to lay himself open to the infinity of God. If we do not hold back our questions, needs and desires from this natural right and this horizon of meaning, then we experience ourselves in the concrete situation of salvation as a question which can only find an answer in the self-communication of God in the Holy Spirit and in Christian revelation.

To the possible objection that I for my part have no interest in the trinitarian nature of God or that I cannot awaken any feeling for the Trinity in someone else who has questions of his own which I am trying to answer, then one may reply: examine the questioner more closely and at the same time reflect more deeply upon the meaning of the Trinity (original sin, purgatory, etc.). Bore down, as it were, into the depths of human existence and make a real effort to grasp the

meaning of the objective dogmas of the Church. Then it will become
apparent how the human, existential question and the concrete answer
of revelation come together and how the essential kernel and experience of revelation are brought to light. Out of this experience a valid
hierarchy of truths of faith is established. Of course the official teaching of the Church exercises normative power in directing the process
of grounding Christian faith, but today this must necessarily consist in
personal initiation and in arousing an inner experience of faith.[13] This
is even the case when someone asserts that he is unaware of any
experience of faith and has no interest in such a phenomenon. In fact in
his actual existence a man has a thousand experiences which he does
not reflect upon, which he even represses or pushes to the edge of his
consciousness and which he does not explicitly trouble himself over,
and yet they are still there. If they are brought to life in the right way,
they can illuminate the content of Christian faith, for a man is always
summoned by divine grace, which lies ever before him and is continually operative in his life. Naturally one cannot avoid a certain rift, a
certain tension between the doctrinal teaching, on the one hand, about
God, man and salvation history, which comes from without, and the
inner experience of faith, on the other, which is proper to each individual. One reason for this is the finite and subjective nature of human
consciousness, which is far from possessing the inner strength and
vitality to be capable from its own resources of developing the whole
content of Christian faith. There is the additional factor that human
subjectivity, raised up by grace, only achieves a sufficiently objective
level when operating in the framework of the *whole* of human history
and the total process of salvation and revelation. For this reason the
individual is always obliged, and justified, in referring himself to this
historical objectivity. The grace which is at work in man produces the
complete fullness of the reality of revelation and faith. Therefore grace
not only possesses an inner point of connection with human existence
but also a seed in every man out of which the whole history of human
salvation and revelation may grow, both in Christianity and in all the
great religions. To proclaim Christian faith, one must always be seeking for new ways to awaken to life this interior disposition and capacity. Christianity cannot be put over as indoctrination in the way

---

[13] Cf. K. Rahner, 'Die Notwendigkeit einer neuen Mystagogie', *Handbuch
der Pastoraltheologie* II/1 (Freiburg, 1966) pp. 269–271; also 'Die Rücksicht auf
die verschiedenen Altersstufen in der immer erneuten Glaubensmystagogie',
ibid., III pp. 529–535.

school children are taught that Australia exists, that is, by being told: you yourselves have not yet been there but others have travelled there and geographers have proved its existence. So you must accept that there is such a country. If one wants to communicate Christian faith in this way from the outside by appealing to the formal authority of the Church or to some generally accepted social institution, then one would not be preaching the message of God in the manner demanded by the present age.

At this point a second consequence my be briefly mentioned. Christians must be constantly brought to realise that, even apart from faith or theology, it is quite natural for people today simply to endure the fact of mental concupiscence. How much there is in our world that can no longer be gathered together into a positive synthesis! We may consider merely the enormous variety of conditions under which men achieve salvation. How many never reach the full use of their intelligence and are, as it were, taken up into a blessed fulfilment free and gratis. Others, on the other hand, seem condemned by God to have to work out their salvation in fear and trembling, with possible failure as the end result. Why do we not belong to the number of those who, according to the usual teaching of the textbooks, gain beatitude without any free decision? What can a man say in reply to questions like these except: I do not know? Here neither airy hypotheses and theological speculation are of any assistance, nor the view that all past assertions on the topic are now nonsense. It seems to me that one simply has to accept that in the present situation there are many things presented by both experience and knowledge which cannot be arranged into a neat pattern. Despite Küng's investigation, for example, I am convinced of the truth of the dogma of the First Vatican Council about the teaching authority of the Pope and hope to remain of this mind until the day I die. But I am equally aware that this teaching raises a thousand question marks. But that does not force me to the assertion that the doctrine of the papacy proposed up to now is simply out of date.

If one asks the average Sunday churchgoer whether he is convinced that the Pope is infallible, then perhaps only a fraction would reply, yes. So we are faced with the fact that only a few Catholics out of all those baptised really possess the mind of faith which is presumed by the Church as a matter of course: I believe everything which the holy, Catholic Church presents for belief. Now are the others, the great remainder, not Catholics? Two reasons militate against such a deduction. First a great proportion of these Christians base their lives on the essential substance of Christianity, even if perhaps they do not consciously reflect on it, and secondly they grasp, at least in some manner, the essential reality of faith. Now this appears decisive in the present case, for the outlook of mental concupiscence which is to be presumed today is not such that assertions which either really or apparently contradict the faith are held and proposed with *absolute* conviction. The religiously informed person does not in fact say: I am utterly and completely certain that the Pope is not infallible. If one interprets more carefully a statement which sounds like this, then it turns out to mean something like: I can't get a first grip on the assertion of papal infallibility; it does not seem to me at all probable; I am inclined to the opposite position, etc. If one tries to explain this outlook more clearly, one runs up against the pressure of mental concupiscence and its many-sided conditioning, which in practice excludes a *positive* and explicit commitment of faith to the statement of the First Vatican Council. In the present situation this ought not to be treated as a loss of faith. Whoever does see it in this way might be told: an absolute, all-embracing and final decision about the teaching authority of the papacy can be left aside. The difficulties and problems can be freely admitted but this too should not lead one to want to set up another absolute system. One should rather accept that it is in a certain sense impossible to acquire the requisite knowledge. Whoever agrees with this position can today in my opinion legitimately be and remain a Christian.

FROM THE EXPERIENCE OF FAITH TO THE ESTABLISHMENT OF BELIEF

A man desires to be free, to possess hope and understanding, to grasp his own freedom in such a way that it comes to fulfilment in the course of his life and realises the potential that lies within him; he wants to be a man of fidelity, love and responsibility. In practice the process of genuine, free self-determination comes about in all the opaque details, the doubts and obscurities, the incongruous events and apparently purposeless beginnings which flood into our life. For a man's biography is directed in freedom to a point of absolute decision and in fact already contains such a decision within it, since it is life as a single whole for which one is answerable and this life does not simply gutter out in the darkness of particular events.

Philosophers and other theoretical thinkers can of course reflect endlessly about concepts such as freedom, responsibility, love, altruism, etc. Indeed such notions are not clear and transparent to any of us. But they do nevertheless possess a meaning and give a direction to one's decisions in the thousand trivialities of daily life. The impression can force itself upon one that these words can all be explained away in psychoanalytic, biological or sociological terms, that they can be unmasked as the unavoidable superstructure of much more primitive realities which in fact constitute the real essence of human existence. But in all these endeavours one and the same subject is at work and is the responsible agent. Thus in the final analysis all these attempts to dissolve what is specifically human must be false. A man cannot and may not escape being a genuine subject and the freedom and responsibility this entails; I accept myself, I take myself on.

This self-affirmation is uttered without ultimate protest but still with full consciousness of the limitations and accidents of biological and historical existence, even if it is accompanied of course by the right and duty to alter and improve what is oppressive in these conditions. Nevertheless not all is open to such improvement; not everything which I must become is the result of my own decision alone. In the ultimate analysis I can either reject myself in radical protest or accept myself in the total and concrete reality of life, even though this remains opaque and oppressive and cannot be manipulated so that I have full and complete control over it. It remains full of pain and obscurity. However I can accept it in hope.[14] But the hope which embraces and sustains everything does not provide ultimate certainty that we possess it; rather it offers the promise that the incomprehensible element in all that is beautiful will in the end be made plain and that this meaning is final and blessed. That is my hope.

Can one be persuaded and convinced that such hope is a false and cowardly utopia and that to indulge in it is worse than letting oneself fall into a radical scepticism? But in fact this scepticism, however theoretically possible, cannot be sustained in the actual business of living, where I carry responsibility, where I love and am loved. An ultimate trust in the complete and all-embracing meaning of human existence is not simply a free floating ideology. It covers everything and is covered by everything which is encountered elsewhere in

---

[14] Cf. K. Rahner, *Meditations on Priestly Life* (London, 1973); 'Self-realization and Taking up one's cross,' *Theological Investigations* IX (London, 1972), pp. 242–259.

human life.[15] It is the free and basic act of human existence which can only find halting expression in human words. It reaches out finally to what we call God. Certainly the word 'God' is obscure but what is meant by it comes out in a man's life, or at least can do so, even when the word itself is absent. Today what is meant by it cannot easily be expressed within the frame of reference of the 'world architect', as was possible in the period of the Enlightenment. Furthermore we are acutely aware that great crimes have been committed under the banner of the word 'God' and that monstrosities and stupidities have been justified by appeal to it.

And yet the ultimate ground of my hope in the act of unconditional acceptance of my existence, this I can reasonably call God. God is far from being thereby made the projection of my hope into the void. For the moment I think of him as a projection, he becomes meaningless and ineffective in my life. On the other hand I can no more give up the ground of my hope than I can surrender the hope itself. So God must be what is most real, what embraces and sustains everything, for only thus can he be both ground and goal of my hope as I conceive it in the act of trust by which I accept my own existence. This God is an unfathomable mystery, for the hope in which freedom and reason form an indivisible unity reaches out beyond all expectations. Hope cannot provide a goal of its own making, since every individual item in life's reckoning is provisional and determined and threatened by another. The final destination of our hope in an unlimited existence must therefore be sought elsewhere.

The act whereby personal existence is accepted in trust and hope is therefore, as long as it is not the victim of self-deception, a letting go of oneself into the incomprehensible mystery. Christianity is far from being a clarification of the world and existence; rather it contains the prohibition against treating any experience or insight, however illuminating it may be, as conclusive and intellible in itself. Christians have less answers (at their disposal) than other mortals to hand out with a, 'now everything is clear'. A Christian cannot enter God as an obvious item in the balance sheet of his life; he can only accept him as an incomprehensible mystery in silence and adoration, as the begin-

---

[15] On absolute trust cf. K. Rahner, 'I Believe in Jesus Christ,' *Theological Investigations* IX (London, 1972), pp. 165–168; 'A Fragmentary Aspect of a Theological Evaluation of the Concept of the Future', *ibid.*, pp. 235–241; 'On the Theology of Hope,' *ibid.*, pp. 242–259.

ning and end of his hope and therefore as his unique, ultimate and all-embracing salvation.

From the innermost heart of his experience a Christian knows that he himself is sustained by this mystery in his trust and hope for the fulfilment of his being. So he calls this movement towards God at work within him, 'grace', 'the Holy Spirit', even if he does not necessarily have to reflect on it and may even repress it, although he cannot destroy it. The movement directed to the immediate presence of God he interprets as faith, hope and love. A Christian must grant every man who is faithful to his conscience this interior movement towards God, even when the other does not think of it in these terms and has not yet grasped its historical appearance in Jesus Christ in explicit Christian faith.[16]

A Christian is afraid that he is able to reject this inner movement of human existence in either open or hidden unbelief. But he is also hopeful, for himself and for others, that this movement will pass through every darkness and superficiality of life and reach its final and 'eternal' goal. Thus a man's existence remains in the last instance under the threat of his capacity freely to deny himself. This threat is continually overcome by the hope that the history of man's freedom, which is enveloped and determined by the freedom of the incomprehensible mystery, will, as a whole, achieve a blessed outcome through the power of God, even if no theoretical statement about the salvation of the individual person can be deduced from this hope.

JESUS CHRIST: THE SYNTHESIS

All that has been said up to this point is brought together in a mysterious way for the Christian in the encounter with Jesus Christ. The basic human hope and the experience of Jesus sustain and justify each other in an ultimately indestructible bond, which may be grasped by a man of integrity and reasonable conscience, as long as he assumes a stance of what Christians call humility in the face of the incomprehensible mystery.

The encounter with Christ is mediated both through the Gospel of

[16] Cf. K. Rahner, 'Observations on the Problem of the "Anonymous Christian" ', *Theological Investigations* XIV (London, 1976), pp. 280–294, where references to earlier publications and to the dicussion of this concept are to be found.

Christianity and of the Church based on the message of Jesus and also through the ultimate hope in God's grace.

What does a Christian see in Jesus? The answer may originate from various elements of experience and so the following considerations cannot represent the only possible description of the encounter with Jesus or one which is universally binding. On the other hand, the experience itself, for all its different aspects does possess a unity. The history of Christianity, which has its own unique importance, envisages one man who loves and is faithful even unto death, whose whole human existence, embodied in word and action, lies open to the mystery which he himself calls, 'Father', and to which he surrenders himself in trust even when his world is shattered. The dark chasm of his life is for Jesus the sheltering hands of his Father. He stands fast in his love for men; he is sure in hope, even when everything seems to collapse in the destruction of death. He was convinced that in him and his message the kingdom of God was at hand, that is, that God in direct love and forgiveness victoriously pledges himself to man, transcending all the good and evil forces which influence human existence. For the person who listens to the message of Jesus a new and decisive opportunity for man has come about, which is never to be surpassed. This experience also means that we are faced by a man who, in his life and death, does not fail to match up to the demands which are involved in being human. Thus Christianity is convinced that, despite every reason for scepticism in our experience of man, we may with innocent trust and total abandon surrender ourselves to one man in absolute dependence. Jesus' followers shared the experience of Good Friday without any illusions. And yet they then became aware, as a gift from Jesus himself, that his life is not in ruins, that his death is in fact a victory and that he is the one totally and finally accepted by the mystery of God. In a word they experienced the fact that he is risen. Of course one should not conceive of this resurrection as a return to the limits of a life restricted by space and time and the facts of biology; one should rather think of it as the ultimate salvation of the one complete man, body and soul, in God.

The mystery is the 'incomprehensible God' and so the manner of this acceptance cannot be given imaginative form. But whenever the absolute hope of man and the experience of the life and death of Jesus meet, we can no longer reckon with the destruction of Jesus without thereby denying this absolute hope and allowing the self-abandonment of man, whether willingly or not, to emptiness and futility. If on the contrary we search for the historical personality who permits us to trust that in him our hope is fulfilled, then we cannot find any other to name except the one presented by the witness of the apostles. The experience of Jesus gives us, in so far as we freely commit ourselves to our own hope, the strength and the heart to affirm from the centre of our own experience, and from the hope that lies within it, that he is risen. The basic human hope and the historical experience of Jesus are bound together for a Christian as a unity. Jesus of Nazareth is accepted by God and in Jesus God has answered the question which man constitutes in his unlimited, incomprehensible nature. Human existence is here finally and gloriously blessed and the sceptical human question, fashioned in guilt and futility, is transcended. The courage to hope is sealed. So Jesus is the ultimate answer which can never be surpassed, because every conceivable question is annihilated in death and he is the answer to the all-consuming question of human existence in that he is the risen one. As Word of God, he answers the question which we ourselves pose.

From this starting point there arise the statements about Jesus Christ contained in the traditional teaching and theology of Church, i.e. orthodox Christology. But the reverse is also true: whoever accepts Jesus as the insurpassable Word of God, as the final seal of his own hope in history, is and remains a Christian, even if he cannot follow the traditional Christological formulations or finds great difficulty in doing so, because they come from a framework of meaning not easily intelligible today.

Cross and resurrection belong together in the authentic witness to Jesus and in genuine and responsible faith in him. The *cross* means the stark demand for a man to surrender himself unconditionally before the mystery of his being which he can never bring under his control, since he is finite and burdened with guilt. The *resurrection* means the unconditional hope that in this surrender the blessing, forgiveness and ultimate acceptance of man takes place through this mystery.[17] It also

---

[17] Cf. K. Rahner, 'Frühe Bussgeschichte in Einzeluntersuchungen', *Schriften zur Theologie* XI (Zurich, 1973), where the author deals extensively with this aspect of the forgiving and saving will of God. This background should be taken into account if the reflections proposed here are to be properly understood. On the importance of the historical investigations into the sacrament of penance in the work of the author, cf. K.-H. Neufeld, 'Fortschritt durch Umkehr: Zu Karl Rahners bussgeschichtlichen Arbeiten', *StdZ* 192 (1974), pp. 274–281.

implies that if a man abandons himself to this movement, no further destruction lies in store. Cross and resurrection clearly show how this self-abandonment is taken up by God in the fate of Jesus and how the possibility of self-surrender, the hardest task of our life, is irrevocably promised to us in Jesus Christ. For the Lord is an absolutely concrete fact. A man need only involve himself with this specific individual in unconditional love and he then possesses everything. Certainly one must die with him; no man escapes this fate. Why not, then, utter with him the words, 'My God, my God, why have you forsaken me?'[18] or 'Into your hands I commend my spirit'?[19] In the destiny of Jesus every human philosophy receives for the first time a truly specific and concrete form. What exactly this philosophy looks like or should look like is not especially important. Once a man has reached Jesus, then it contains this simple message: just to be prepared to make the final act of hope and self-surrender to the incomprehensible mystery. Yet this covers everything because the fate of Jesus, a death which is life, has brought this philosophy into being, not of course in mere talk about death but in the actual experience and suffering of death.[20]

For us this moment still lies in the future. Our life is directed towards it without our knowing exactly when it will appear in our life. But only then has the essence of Christianity been grasped and conceived. A man can and should, however, prepare himself to be open to this event. The glory of our present existence is not thereby removed. Rather it gives everything its proper value and makes the burden light. Christianity is thus simplicity itself because it embraces the totality of human existence and leaves all the details to the free responsibility of man, without providing an exact recipe for them. At the same time it is the hardest thing of all, a grace offered to all which can and is received, even when unconditional hope has not yet discovered its seal in Jesus of Nazareth.

THE TASK OF THE CHURCH

Many people today seem to find Jesus more easily in anonymous hope without being able to call him by his historical name. But whoever has

[18] Mk 15:34.
[19] Lk 23:46.
[20] Cf. K. Rahner, *On the Theology of Death*, Questiones Disputatae 2 (Freiburg and London, 1961), esp. III 'Death as a Dying with Christ', pp. 64–88.

a clear enough encounter with Jesus must also recognise him for who he is; otherwise he would be denying his own basic hope. The raising of Jesus from the dead cannot be the victorious pledge of the presence of the divine mystery which forms the fullness of our life, unless the eternal validity of Jesus's resurrection were not also the object of the *faith* of many. Thus there comes into being the community of those who believe in him as the one crucified and risen. Within this community they discover the answer to the problem of their own existence and learn to become aware of the mystery in which he is both near at hand and far away, if we place ourselves in its presence. This community is called the Church. Those who believe in Jesus cannot be individualistic in their religion, if only because of their common relationship to the Lord. Moreover faith in Jesus can only be awakened through active witness and therefore demands the social structure of a community of faith which is gathered around Jesus Christ. Furthermore Christianity is ecclesial because man has a social nature, which means that the history of his freedom is worked out in the context of the community. Finally it seems contradictory today, at a time when there is growing emphasis on the need for greater human solidarity and social involvement, for individuals and groups to imagine that Jesus must be reached apart from his Church. This outlook reveals an out of date individualism which, even from a purely secular and historical point of view, has nothing to offer for the future. Also the most convinced individualist in matters of faith depends upon the Church for Scripture, tradition and religious language, even if he wants to sever his connection with the Church. In general truth has something to do with an open and at the same time critical attitude towards society and institutions. Without such an outlook even so-called personal truth would lapse into arbitrary whim and lose its meaning even for the individual. The precise value of the Church is of course assessed very differently by the various Christian bodies but Christianity universally recognises institutions and affirms an ecclesial orientation which is vital for its existence. Baptism is acknowledged by practically all Christians as the rite of initiation into the Christian community and this implies the recognition of the Church as a concrete and historical institution in society.

Every genuine Christian will certainly suffer as a result of the actual social form of the Church in history. For the concrete embodiment of the Church never matches up to its true nature. It preaches a message which questions its own empirical structure. It is, namely, a Church of sinners, whose members deny in actions what they affirm in words. The history of the Christian Church has plenty of horror and misery in it, and in the end there only remains the question: where else should we go if we leave the Church? Could we be more faithful to the liberating Spirit of Jesus if we, sinful egoists that we are, set ourselves up as the 'pure' at a distance from the poor, miserable Church? For our part the misery can only find a remedy through our sharing the burden of poverty for which each one of us himself bears the guilt. As a Christian in the Church a man carries the responsibility for changing it from within, for the Church always remains 'ecclesia semper reformanda', as the Second Vatican Council[21] emphasised. If we discover something genuinely Christian within us and really find out what it means, how can we then object to letting it benefit in a selfless way the community of sinners? By the power of Jesus Christ the Church will pass through its miserable history and come to the fulfilment which has been promised in the death and resurrection of the Lord.

Christians have had a basic awareness that the relation of hope and love to the incomprehensible mystery of their life which they call God can only be acknowledged, expressed and given credible form in an unconditional love of their neighbour, for this alone is capable of forcing open the hell of human self-centredness.[22] This love is not to be treated as something self-evident, otherwise it becomes corrupted into an expression of hidden egoism. As the liberating grace of God it stretches us continually beyond our capacity and is for this reason only really possible if a man, consciously or not, allows himself to surrender to the incomprehensible mystery. Then the Spirit of Jesus is at work, even if it is not explicitly acknowledged, as Mt 25 makes plain. Let us, therefore, hope that the grace of God performs this miracle in us too; everything depends on it.

At a time when there is of necessity a growth in human solidarity and social involvement, love of neighbour can only be authentic if it also takes a form which goes beyond the realm of private, individual relationships. Before all else love must today be expressed, though not exclusively, in Christian responsibility for the social sphere. The individual, groups and the Church as a whole has this task, each in its own

---

[21] Cf. Conc. Vat. II, *Lum. Gen.* Art. 8.
[22] Cf. K. Rahner, 'Reflections on the Unity of the Love of Neighbour and the Love of God', *Theological Investigations* VI (London and Baltimore, 1969), pp. 231–249.

way. To fulfil it requires hope in eternal life, the stimulus of the Christian spirit in the Church and the Spirit of Jesus himself. By recalling his death and resurrection the Church acquires a critical distance from its present state which prevents it from making into an absolute either the existing shape of things or some plan for the immediate future. Were the Church to dissolve into a humanitarian enterprise, it would betray its proper function, for it has the duty of declaring to the world the ultimate seriousness and the incomprehensible value of love of neighbour. This is, however, only possible through witness to the unfathomable mystery which the Son of man, Jesus Christ, has entered in faith, hope and love. But even today there seems great danger of not taking love of neighbour seriously enough, especially the neighbour who is encountered in secular society. And yet only in this love can a Christian find God, to whom he desires to surrender himself totally with Jesus Christ, *because* he is the incomprehensible mystery which Jesus did not resolve but rather accepted in faith and hope.

Christianity and the Christian churches also obtain in this way a new and balanced relationship to the non-Christian world religions, which in the past lay outside the orbit of Christian culture. Now Christianity cannot let go of the claim both to have received the definitive and all-embracing word of grace in Jesus, crucified and risen, and still to preach this word today. But this is not to deny that the liberating Spirit of God is active in all finite human affairs, within every perplexity and error. The non-Christian world religions witness in their own fashion not only to human limitation but also to the Spirit of Jesus. Certainly many of their major experiences can provisionally be included in the comprehensive answer of Jesus, because the history of the Christian message is far from complete.

Atheism has become a world-wide phenomenon, which affects millions today. But here too it should not be assessed by Christianity simply as an absolute human denial which expresses only the refusal to surrender oneself to the unsearchable mystery of God. It is rather to be seen as a stage in the history of the experience of God which clearly renders God a mystery more radical than a mere object of petitionary prayer, a mystery which cannot be manipulated by men either conceptually or practically, or fitted into any human frame of reference, but is solely to be trusted in hope.

Thought and action often tend to lead to a kind of bewilderment which admits of no resolution. At first glance it seems as though one.

had simply to carry on in the face of such perplexity, even without knowing where the path is leading. But the urgent question remains of what lies hidden beneath this silent, faithful and patient endurance. Here one runs up against the hope which human experience has formulated in two words: mystery and death.

Mystery means here that perplexity contains hope; death contains a veto against our masking or stifling this perplexity, or forcing it into a false optimism which is merely stupid and futile. If we gaze upon the crucified Jesus, we should realise that we are to be spared nothing. In hoping in his death, I dare also to hope that in a shared death lies the ascent to a blessed mystery. Despite every dark shadow such a hope permits life even now to emerge in its proper beauty and be filled with promise.

Christianity offers a simple task, a burden both heavy and light, as the Gospel asserts.[23] If a man carries it, then it begins to carry him. The longer life lasts, the heavier and the lighter the burden becomes. Christianity calls for a whole-hearted and straightforward profession of hope, amidst all the mysterious twists and turns of our life, and assures us that in this mystery there lies what we call God, eternal life, ultimate value and the salvation of our being. The message is proclaimed: look at the crucified Jesus who achieved eternal fellowship with God and not merely the validity of an ideology, and follow at his side the way into the unfathomable mystery. In this lies the whole of Christianity. Within our world and in our own life a mass of queries and tasks remain, for which there are no simple recipes or programmed solutions. For they remain our tasks, for which *we* are responsible. Christianity is straightforward and credible. For who can seriously forbid a man from fixing his gaze of Jesus and, even after 1500 years, prevent him from recognising in him today the seal of his hope? Whoever takes this step and holds firm to it despite every darkness in his life, that man is a Christian. No one can assert with absolute certainty that he in fact does this, just as no one can say that the whole business of Christianity is the result of external indoctrination and social support and is a mere facade behind which so-called Christians and messengers of the Gospel conceal their ultimate hopelessness and despair. I hope in my hope and in Jesus who seals this hope, that is, I hope to be a Christian. Certainly this is not harder to carry than the burden of existence which is laid on every man and which no one can

---

[23] Cf. Mt 11:30; 1 Jn 5:3.

shrug off. Christianity is a total whole, and therefore at one and the same time simpler and more mysterious, harder and easier than anything else. In this sense we can all of us merely say: I hope to be a Christian.

2

EXPERIENCE OF THE SPIRIT AND EXISTENTIAL COMMITMENT

I F we look closely at the topic of the experience of the Spirit and existential commitment, we find that the subject is in fact limitless[1], for even a first glance makes it clear that it is only a variation of the theme, 'Transcendence and History'. Although this fact is not yet taken as self-evident in the usual manuals of theology, it is nevertheless true that the gift of grace through the Spirit of God is in the first instance a genuine self-communication of God to the transcendent human self and not an internal or external categorial reality of human consciousness, material, as it were, for the free decisions of the human person. The topic of transcendence and history cannot receive complete clarification here; on the other hand we cannot simply presuppose it as a suitable theme for discussion. Only a few comments are possible at this point and these may only provide scant illumination, so that one must be content with their fragmentary character.

CHARACTERISTICS OF EXISTENTIAL COMMITMENT

The following comments, while especially important for subsequent reflections, should not give the impression that the essence of existential commitment is to be completely defined. Within Christian theology existential commitment signifies the free act of a human being in

---

[1] This study originated in an essay written for the Festschrift for E. Schillebeeckx. Since this essay is closely related to other studies found in this volume and partly covered the same ground, the text was revised to avoid tedious repetition; cross-references were also added.

which he has ultimate control over himself before God.[2] In the last analysis it is relatively unimportant whether in this decision the 'before God', i.e. the acceptance or rejection of God, is made explicit in words or not.[3] Since the exercise of freedom with respect to a purely categorial object and to a finite value, or one conceived as finite, is not possible without a prior, transcendent grasp of absolute being and absolute good – a thesis no Thomist would deny –, it therefore follows that every genuine, free decision must contain a reference to God on the part of the free subject. As stated above, the conscious analysis of this state of affairs is immaterial, because a man's behaviour with regard to the obvious and given categorial objects which always surround our historically conditioned use of freedom and through which that freedom is mediated, such behaviour can only be free if it occurs within the transcendent horizon of freedom, in the unlimited, prior grasp of absolute good, i.e. of God. In any case the basic tenet of Christian anthropology is to be formulated thus: a man's free behaviour is not limited to the categorial and finite object of his free choice or to a concept of God in his objective consciousness but extends to God himself. The transcendent nature of freedom not only enables us to make a *categorial* choice which has moral consequences, since it is assisted by various concepts bestowed by God as the guardian of that divine law of which we have an intellectual grasp; it is also its own object of freedom. For activity subject to categorial limits not only takes place within a transcendent horizon which is open to the absolute, it also radically alters this horizon itself. This means that such activity must be described as a possible, freely constituted acceptance of the self-communication of God, and so of salvation, or of damnation if and when this self-communication permanently comes to nothing.

In all this we have of course been speaking of the transcendent nature of man which is raised up by *grace* and which, through grace, is

[2] This notion should not be understood in the sense of a hypothetical decision as L. Boros proposes in *The Moment of Truth* (London, 1965). The author has never supported this hypothesis and his conception is much broader. Nothing is stated here about the historical moment in which a man actually takes this decision.

[3] On this cf. the study, 'Anonymous and Explicit Faith', in this volume and the author's earlier publication on the topic of the 'Anonymous Christian' with the ensuing discussion; references are to be found in 'Observations on the Problem of the "Anonymous Christian" ', *Theological Investigations* XIV (London, 1976), pp. 280–294.

ordered to the direct presence of God himself. This is not to attack the legitimacy of a limit concept of 'pure nature', that is, the idea of a transcendence of knowledge and freedom which does not bestow any promise of, or claim on, direct union with the ultimate goal of man, a goal which can only be approached in an asymptotic fashion. But this is really a question of a limit concept which cannot be used any longer as the starting point for any anthropological deduction. Now, however much the explicit notion of human transcendence raised up by grace may stem from Christian revelation, nevertheless it cannot essentially, and not merely historically, be drawn from the language of Christian revelation. If an experience of the Spirit occurs and if this appears, from a Christian point of view, to lie outside the explicit, institutional bounds of Christianity and even outside the range of its language, and if it is a genuine case of a revelation event, then the concept of 'graced transcendence' may be applied in an anthropological investigation, and not merely subsequently through an appeal to positive theological data. This is true even though the notion receives its best and purest expression in explicit Christianity and acquires greater clarity from this source. Nor is the truth of the above assertion affected by the fact that the meaning of graced transcendence implies that revelation is a genuine reality.

Whenever a man speaks of unbounded transcendence and does not stifle his spirit in the face of it but rather surrenders himself without reserve to the absolute reality of his transcendent nature and has some experience of it, then he is raised by grace to communion with the direct reality of God. This is true whether he reflects upon it or not, whether indeed he is capable of pursuing such reflections or not. It is also the case even if no reference is made to that event which we Christians call the explicit history of revelation.

Man's free control of his own transcendent nature, raised up by grace, either in acceptance or rejection, comes about through an existential decision which always involves historically limited, categorial material. This is where freedom is expressed and mediates the subject to itself.

How is the freedom which involves the categorial object related to the freedom of the subject towards himself and God? The relationship is a very complex one, but we should start from the fact, which is not immediately obvious, that there exist decisions which are objectively wrong but which do not destroy a man's positive relationship to God, so-called 'objective' sins which carry no 'subjective' guilt. An absolutely fixed relationship between the categorial content and the transcendental significance of a free decision cannot be given if by the 'content' of such a decision is meant the object of explicit, conscious awareness, i.e. all that can be put into words, empirically and historically comprehended and subsequently assessed. For this would be to ignore the transcendent element which is always involved in such an act and forms part of a man's awareness. With respect to this knowledge no discrepancy can exist between the evaluation of the act before God and by God and the act in itself. The alteration of the transcendental consciousness raised up by grace, mentioned above, is brought about by the categorial decision and does not, therefore, always correspond to the categorial content of the decision. Nor does it possess a univocal relationship to this content which can be determined by reflection. This is confirmed by the Catholic teaching that no one can form an absolutely sure judgement about himself and no one knows on the basis of reflection with certainty whether he is in a state of grace or not.[4]

One cannot deduce from the transcendent nature of man, raised up by grace, – in so far as it is open to explicit, thematic investigation – a determinate object of choice which is clearly differentiated from the goal of this transcendence. Conversely a particular, categorial object of choice, even if it is materially correct and conforms to the objective structure of man and the world, cannot guarantee for certain that its choice will bring about a positive relationship to human transcendence and its goal.[5]

SPIRITUAL EXPERIENCE

Before we begin a more detailed elaboration of our theme, something must be said about experience of the Spirit. Without offering further evidence here, we may propose the thesis as a basic assumption for our later exposition that the essential nature of genuine experience of the Spirit does not consist in particular objects of experience found in human awareness but occurs rather when a man experiences the radical re-ordering of his transcendent nature in knowledge and freedom

---

[4] *Denz.* 1534; 1540–1541.

[5] One should at least take note at this point of the highly controversial issue, whether a specifically Christian morality exists with regard to its material content. It seems to us that the reflections proposed here could be used at a starting point for such a discussion.

towards the immediate reality of God through God's self-communication in grace. In addressing ourselves to the question whether a man freely accepts this experience or rejects it, we must remember that experience of the Spirit is not constituted by a particular divine operation 'from without', working upon the human spirit conceived as an already finished entity. It comes about rather through God's self-communication to the human spirit ('uncreated grace')[6] by which God becomes a constitutive element of human transcendence.

Experience of the Spirit is, therefore, experience of the radical and permanent nature of human transcendence, which goes beyond itself towards God because it is constantly impelled by his self-communication. This innermost depth in man can be presented as 'nature' or in the form of free acceptance or the protest of rejection. Under 'nature' one should include everything which is presupposed for the existential self-determination of human freedom as the condition of its possibility. It is immaterial whether it is the simple, finite reality of creation or the unmerited gift bestowed upon this nature in its own proper way as the 'being' of man.

Like any other experience, the transcendent experience of the radical nature of the Spirit is mediated through categorial objects, for the finite, spiritual essence of man only comes to self-expression in relationship to what is other, and in the ultimate analysis this other must be *personal*. The above certainly applies to the normal case but does not touch the question whether a mystical experience may be imagined in this life in which the transcendent elevation of man by the grace of the Spirit is really grasped without the mediation of any categorial, a posteriori object coming from without.[7] In any case such a transcendent experience, in so far as it happens at all, can certainly be given objective form and, in this way, becomes a definite object of human awareness. Indeed transcendent experience as such is not the same as

[6] On the theme of grace cf. the article 'grace', *Sacramentum Mundi* II (London and New York, 1968), pp. 412–426. On the question of 'uncreated grace', cf. K. Rahner, 'Some Implications of the Scholastic Concept of Uncreated Grace', *Theological Investigations* I (London and Baltimore, 1961), pp. 316–346; see also under the heading 'The Self-Communication of God', *Sacr. Mun.* III, pp. 114–118; *ibid*, IV, pp. 297–305; *ibid*. V, pp. 348–355.

[7] On the question of mysticism cf. the other studies in this volume which deal explicitly with the topic, especially 'Religious Enthusiasm and the Experience of the Spirit'; 'Modern Piety and the Experience of Retreats'; 'Faith between Rationality and Emotion'.

the objective form in which it is conceived and the two should not be confused. Consequently it should not be tacitly assumed that the grace-filled experience of radical transcendence only occurs when an objective concept is also produced in the form of a categorial content of knowledge or when the experience is mediated to human consciousness through overtly 'religious' material.

Our thesis ultimately rests upon the view that every categorial object and the experience of it are finite and that no essential distinction can obtain between such objects, whatever may be the case in individual instances. To suppose the existence of such a distinction, by which a number of such objects appear as a result of a special, direct operation of God while the rest do not, is fundamentally to adopt a mythological understanding of the relationship of God to the world.

COMMITMENT AND THE SPIRIT

How are the experience of the Spirit and existential commitment related to each other? Existential commitment means in this context, for example, the choice of a particular career, a specific form of behaviour towards another person, the decision to marry, a particular religious act, etc. Of course such actions must bring into play a definite, positive relationship to the prior, transcendent nature, raised up by grace, and so to God in himself. But this raises the question how exactly the categorial object of an existential decision is connected to the basic significance of this decision, that is, the establishment of our actual transcendence in freedom, the acceptance or rejection of God, who communicates himself as the ultimate dynamic of our transcendent nature. Obviously this creates a difficult problem. A categorial object of choice can be in itself wrong and yet at the same time make possible the achievement of a positive relationship to God. On the other hand an object of choice which is right according to human criteria, in terms both of people and of things, and which lies within the objective norms laid down by God, such an object does not necessarily provide an absolute, unambiguous guarantee that by making such a choice a man really achieves a positive relationship to God, in which God communicates himself as God in grace. For one must not assume that psychological freedom of choice and its realisation with regard to a categorial object necessarily involves real, existential self-determination. Otherwise one could not make sense of 'venial' sin 'ex imperfectione actus'[8] and correspondingly of an 'impaired act of free-dom'.

Furthermore an object of choice which is correct by human stan-dards cannot guarantee the clear fulfilment of the existential commit-ment, since the latter refers to the transcendent experience of the Spirit and to God, while in a concrete situation of free choice several categor-ial objects can be presented at the same time. These may in fact appear under certain conditions as more or less equally possible in them-selves, but only one may seem to be willed by God as the necessary, concrete means which must be chosen here and now to achieve a positive attitude to the experience of the Spirit and of the existential relationship to God. It is not immediately self-evident in the case of a choice between several objects, in themselves legitimate and 'good', that it really matters, with respect to the relationship to God, which decision is taken. But we can take it for granted here that it does matter, since it is the view of those who possess genuine spiritual experience and knowledge that for something to be willed by God it is a necessary, though not sufficient, condition that it should be objec-tively right, i.e. conform to the 'Laws of God', be humane and in accord with the mind of the Church. But this condition is not in itself sufficient to establish it as willed by God. This view is not incompat-ible with the hypothesis that in some cases the subject may be thrown back *by God* in his decision upon the ambivalence and openness which is intrinsic to human freedom with regard to objects of choice. It is not possible to appeal to other experience in the face of such a spiritual experience, for this may be explained as the hypothetical case men-tioned above and offers no argument against the necessity imposed by God of deciding between objectively good alternatives.

THE PROBLEM OF CHOICE

How can a man come to an existential decision in the face of a number of worthwhile possibilities, if he is to proceed, not arbitrarily, but before God and in conformity with a choice willed by God? In daily life the ordinary man of piety usually experiences little difficulty and this simplicity should certainly not be disturbed. He has the personal

[8] Cf. the classical textbooks of moral theology, e.g. D. M. Prümmer, *Manuale Theologiae* I (Freiburg i.Br. 1923) no. 370 (Thomist); J. Aertnys, *Theologia Moralis I* (Turin, 1928), no. 258 (following Alphonsus Liguori); H. Noldin, *Summa Theologiae Moralis I*, (Innsbruck, 1956), no. 300.

impression that God 'tells' him what choice he should make out of those open to him; God 'enlightens' and 'inspires' him so that he knows quite concretely what is the will of God in a particular instance.

Now theology does not allow the possibility of 'new revelations' even for the most important decisions in the life of the Church and this rules out any regular intervention of God to determine which object of choice is here and now the right one. One cannot escape this conclusion by pointing out that in this case it is 'merely' a matter of the private sphere of human life, for this is just as important as the 'public' life of the faith of the Church. Such intervention would form a 'private revelation'[9] and while this can of course happen, it cannot be the presupposition for all such decisions, and that is what is at issue here. How, therefore, can the actual choice be made in an existential decision between various possibilities which are of the same, or similar, worth according to objective moral norms, but only one of which is willed and commanded by God? Given the above assumptions, a specific choice is only possible, unless one is to appeal to a mythological explanation, if one allows a synthesis of the transcendent experience of the Spirit and the encounter with the categorial object of choice freely offered here and now.

This synthesis allows for the experience of one morally possible choice in preference to others as God's purpose for us. Now the transcendent experience of God's self-communication in grace is not directed to a thing, or to a merely necessary being, but to a personal reality in freedom, to whom a man surrenders himself when he freely responds with faith, hope and love to God, who is present to him in what is necessarily a transcendent experience. Whenever human freedom is realised, it is experienced, whether this is thought out or not, as the free gift of God and as the continuation of his creative act in the life of the creature, for the creature owes both its essential being to God and also its free development. From this point of view a synthesis of the transcendent and the categorial is certainly conceivable. The categorial which is freely willed can be experienced as the fixed purpose creatively determined by God's freedom.

A word should be added about the meaning of the synthesis of the trancendent and the categorial, by means of which a *choice*, given by God, can be put into effect among various possibilities. First of all this synthesis is not to be ruled out where a categorial object of choice does not mask and disguise the transcendent experience but rather allows both the experience itself and the reflection which tests it to occur unhindered. This is not immediately obvious because it is assumed that the categorial object of choice is morally good and at the same time cannot be chosen by man on his own. A person may have the experience of being unable in a free and uninhibited way to fit a particular object of choice, even one that is morally good, into the movement of knowledge and freedom which is involved in the transcendent experience of the Spirit. He may reflect upon general principles and norms and seek to assess a particular object by reference to them. In doing so he may not come up against any objection to the choice of a particular categorial object, and yet somehow he has not *got it in him* to make the choice and this constrains and obscures for him the free impetus of the transcendent spirit in quite a different fashion from other cases where this experience does not occur. Of course a number of objects could be included on an equal footing in such a synthesis without there being only one which masks the transcendent experience of the Spirit. In this case all the objects would be possible not only on the basis of their human and rational legitimacy but with respect to God as well. This free selection would in fact be divinely intended and God's will would not have foreseen only one particular object. Here it is not of any particular importance either before God, or for the experience of the Spirit, which is in fact chosen among the various possible options.

Finally the synthesis intended by God between a particular categorial object of choice and the transcendent experience of the Spirit can and should be experienced in a more positive way. For the freely accepted transcendent experience of the Spirit is only possible here and now through concentration upon one distinct object of choice among others. This means that this object does not in any way lessen or distort the experience of the Spirit but rather provides a concrete and practical means of expression for it. According to what was said earlier an object of choice which by human standards is not in itself right, i.e. not in conformity with the norms of the moral law, can in practice mediate the free acceptance of the transcendent experience of the Spirit. Of course if this objective moral contradiction were clearly perceived and affirmed, then there would be no place for the experience of the synthesis of transcendent, spiritual experience and a categorial object of choice. To suppose otherwise would be to imply that the will of God, the creator, bore absolutely no relationship to the structure of the created world and was quite indifferent to it. In the last analysis, however, the will of God, together with his world, is precisely the object of transcendent experience. In a case where someone with full knowledge and consent willed what was objectively wrong by human, moral standards and wished in this way to attempt a synthesis of an essentially wrong object of choice and a freely accepted transcendent experience of the Spirit, his intention would remain unfulfilled and would not lead to spiritual experience. Such a synthesis simply cannot be achieved in this manner.

So far all that has been said about the connection and the complementary dependence of spiritual experience and existential decision has been on a very abstract and general plane. Certainly it could all be more clearly and precisely described, but the scope required by the topic has not allowed detailed consideration of the psychology of the transcendent experience of the Spirit in grace, of the logic of existential commitment or of the nature of freedom which cannot be neatly fitted into a logic proper to theoretical reason.[10] Nor can we deal with the various pieces of evidence offered by theological tradition which witness more or less clearly to the unity of the transcendent experience of the free spirit (of God and man) and existential commitment. In this connection, for instance, the Spiritual Exercises of St Ignatius could be adduced as evidence,[11] although this would require the treatment of texts whose exact meaning is still disputed today. My own view, however, is that they point to this unity of spiritual experience and existential decision.

This short study has contained not merely speculations and mental fantasies which have nothing to do with the concrete business of living. If this objection should be raised, the counter question must be put whether sufficient attention has been paid to the very real distinction between an unthought out transcendent experience which forms part of a specific object of consciousness, without itself being a categorial object, and the concept of such a transcendent experience which has been thought out, given objective form and expressed in words. If such a concept does not normally occur in daily life, this by

[10] Cf. K. Rahner, 'The Logic of Concrete Individual Knowledge in Ignatius Loyola', *The Dynamic Element in the Church*, Quaestiones Disputatae 12 (Freiburg and London, 1964), pp. 84–156.

[11] Cf. in the present volume the reflections contained in the essay entitled, 'Modern Piety and the Experience of Retreats'.

no means proves that the transcendent experience of the Spirit is also lacking.

Furthermore if someone were to maintain that he never experienced such a synthesis of transcendent experience of the Spirit and the objects of an existential decision, then again a counter question may be asked. Is it absolutely essential for the truth of the position outlined here that such a synthesis can frequently be experienced as a distinct, clear object of reflection? Or is not also conceivable that such basic options and commitments happen relatively infrequently and then directly determine the rest of a man's life?

3

RELIGIOUS ENTHUSIASM AND THE
EXPERIENCE OF GRACE

THE comments of a dogmatic theologian upon enthusiasm in the Church cannot take into consideration either exegesis and biblical theology or the phenomenology and history of religion, or church history, in so far as these are relevant to the topic.[1] However there are certain phenomena which merit our attention: experiences of the Spirit, glossolalia (speaking in tongues), the experience of a radical transformation of the 'old man' into a new person brought about by the Spirit of God, a radical conversion, and similar events which occur today in the various charismatic movements in the churches and which offer a real and concrete expression of Christianity.

We cannot give an exact description of such phenomena here nor can we assert with certainty that the comments we wish to make from a dogmatic viewpoint really bear upon their concrete and specific characteristics. We intend here to do two things. First we must

---

[1] The concept 'enthusiasm' requires some clarification. In the usual Catholic dictionaries, even in the 'Dictionnaire de Spiritualité' (Paris, 1932), it is not to be found. In Protestant circles it has been interpreted since Luther to mean emotional excess, cf. W. Trillhaas, *RGG II* (Tubingen, 3rd ed. 1958) and similarly Y. Congar, 'Enthousiastes', *Catholicisme IV* (Paris, 1956), pp. 262 sqq. From this background enthusiasm was seen above all in connection with prophetic proclamation, cf. Fr. Heiler, *Erscheinungsformen und Wesen der Religion*, (Stuttgart, 1961), pp. 274 sqq.; 281 sqq. In more recent times the positive aspects of religious enthusiasm have received more prominence, cf. W. J. Hollenweger, *Enthusiastisches Christentum. Die Pfingstbewegung in Geschichte und Gegenwart* (Wuppertal and Zurich, 1969). For the general concept cf. *Brockhaus Enzykl* V (1968) 562 and E. Fink, *Vom Wesen des Enthusiasmus* (Essen, 1948). Cf. also, R. A. Knox, *Enthusiasm* (Oxford, 1950).

delineate an area from the standpoint of traditional theology in which a phenomenon such as charismatic enthusiasm can be described and located in dogmatic theology. Secondly we must attempt to give some basic guidelines about the discernment of spirits. We must, that is, at least touch upon the question under what conditions a charismatic phenomenon can in any sense count as an experience of the Spirit, which, according to the dogma of the Church, is the grace-filled, divinising gift of God to justified mankind. In trying to provide at least the bare outlines of the 'locus theologicus', as it were, in which such enthusiasm can be rooted, we leave the question open whether the specific and concrete phenomena and experiences which are reported in the life of the Church today are in fact dealt with at all in our account. The question also remains open whether even the beginnings of an effective spiritual discernment can in fact be provided by such a dogmatic method or whether discernment of spirits,[2] if it is really to distinguish between the genuine and false elements in movements of religious enthusiasm, must supply much more specific criteria with greater human and psychological content than those offered from a purely dogmatic perspective.

We cannot simply proceed in our investigation from the definitive and infallible teaching of the official Church. In this area statements which are binding for a particular Christian denomination are not sufficient. Even if a complete theology of grace, whether Catholic or Protestant, were assumed, this would still be the case. If one restricts oneself to the Catholic theology of the Holy Spirit, the question still remains open according to the official teaching of the Church whether a direct experience of the Spirit can in fact occur in the sense determined by Catholic teaching on grace at the 6th session of the Council of Trent,[3] that is, the experience of the Spirit which gives justification, of sanctifying grace, and of the infused virtues.

Naturally Catholic teaching contains the doctrine of the indwelling of the Holy Spirit, the outpouring of the Spirit and its presence in men, justifying grace, the presence of the trinitarian God,[4] but unfortunately the question still remains unanswered in Catholic theology whether the Spirit enters the realm of human consciousness

---

[2] On 'Discernment of Spirits' see 'Discernement des esprits', *asc. et. myst* III (Paris, 1957), 1222–1291 (J. Guillet, G. Bardy, Fr. Vandenbroucke, J. Pegon, H. Martin) and H. Wulf, *LThK* X (Freiburg, 1965), 533–535.

[3] Cf. *Denz.* 1525; 1529–1530; 1553–1554.

[4] Cf. *Denz.* 3329–3331.

as the Spirit or is only accepted as a present reality through the external indoctrination, as it were, of Scripture and the teaching of the Church, but which we know lies beyond our own spiritual experience. Here we can leave aside the question of the exact manner and means by which the Spirit can be given to us at all. The discovery and establishment of such a basic division within Catholic theology may seem surprising. For the traditional Catholic theology of grace must obviously be familiar with some sort of experience of the Spirit. Actual grace which is declared to be absolutely essential, in the face of Pelagianism and semi-Pelagianism, for every saving action, is understood as an inner inspiration and illumination. Experiences of grace which help to overcome concupiscence are known as are ones in the sense of the 'Imitatio Christi'. Ignatius Loyola was familiar with such experience, a sense of consolation, and he regards it as beneficial for the whole' of Christian spirituality.[5] But a closer investigation of post-Reformation theology, at least since the Baroque period, reveals quite clearly that for a major school of theology, in which the Jesuits are also represented, a real experience of the so-called supernatural grace of justification, either habitual or actual, simply does not enter the picture; for this school the proper reception of the justifying Spirit of God, even when such justification brings about subjective human acts, lies beyond conscious awareness and is a purely ontological reality.[6] Obviously, given such an assumption, the whole problem which engages us here does not arise at all. For on this reckoning any form of charismatic enthusiasm, although it is not denied as a purely empirical phenomenon by this school and may indeed be cultivated in its spirituality, is something which in the last resort must be judged according to natural, human and moral criteria alone. Of course there may be talk in some sense of the experience of grace in such a school, but strictly speaking its conclusion must be that such experiences are natural events of a psychological kind which must be empirically investigated from a variety of viewpoints by different methods and judged according to human criteria. In addition one may say that these experiences fulfil the human and religious conditions for being 'ontologically raised up' by the grace of God but that this elevation by

[5] Cf. Ignatius Loyola, *Spiritual Exercises*, nos. 6–10, 313–336.

[6] It is essential to see these remarks in the general context of the theology of grace; cf. the author's article in *Sacramentum Mundi* II (London and New York, 1968), pp. 412–426; also F. Stegmüller, 'Molina' and 'Molinismus', *LThK* VII (Freiburg, 1962), 526–530.

the Spirit is a reality whose occurrence transcends human consciousness. According to the pre-suppositions of this school of theology, religious enthusiasm may be regarded as a very important phenomenon, perhaps even as absolutely necessary and indispensable for justification, but nevertheless as a phenomenon which, in the language of such a school, belongs to the pre-conditions required for acts of salvation. To put the matter more concretely: a supernatural act of faith which confers salvation consists for this school in objects of consciousness which are mediated verbally and doctrinally by the teaching of the Church. These objects can basically be heard, received and known by a purely natural act and can be related to human freedom of a merely natural kind. The only qualification added by this school of theology is to the effect that, when such acts are freely undertaken as acts of faith, then they are in reality 'ontologically' elevated by the Holy Spirit into an event which takes place beyond consciousness. This act of faith, in so far as it has been ontologically transformed by grace, is the bearer of *salvation*, which it would not be were it a purely natural occurrence. But from the point of view of human consciousness the credibility, meaningfulness and revealed character of the content of faith can be shown, according to this school of thought, without recourse to the supernatural assistance of the Holy Spirit which is necessary for salvation. Only in the moment when the act of faith becomes a saving act is it raised ontologically by grace beyond the scope of conscious awareness, so that in this sense it possesses an ontological character substantially different from that of a purely natural act.

All this, however, takes place outside the realm of consciousness. All the elements open to psychological comprehension which play a part in the occurrence of such an affirmation and decision of faith can indeed be spoken of as grace from the point of view of the actual providence of God, etc. But in the last resort this grace is essentially regarded as *natural*, medicinal grace which must be sharply distinguished from the properly pneumatic element, the purely ontological elevation of the psychological event which we call religious awareness, the experience of faith or the affirmation of faith.

If, then, we want to speak of Christian enthusiasm from the standpoint of dogmatic theology, we must from the start make a clear and definite break with this approach which has been traditional in the Jesuit school. We are convinced that both Scripture and a more representative and genuine theological tradition within the Catholic

Church point to a different understanding of grace. Grace, the Holy Spirit, the working of the Spirit of God in the proper sense of divinising grace which is radically new and really contains the Spirit of God, all this is something which in our view, to put the matter cautiously, operates within human consciousness. Pneuma means for us, in the strictly theological sense of grace which raises up and divinises supernaturally, a genuine *self* – communication of God in himself.[7]

Even if we set ourselves completely apart from the position mentioned above, which has an extensive following in Catholic theology, we must nevertheless clearly and realistically admit that at first glance the opinion of this school which we have rejected seems to have a great deal to recommend it. That is to say, if we consider the rather naïve and self-conscious wave of pentecostal enthusiasm which has appeared on the contemporary scene and get to work on it with the tools of the psychology, history and phenomenology of religion, then we might well be tempted to say: all this enthusiasm which has come to the fore in modern Christianity is psychological, an expression of natural, human capacities which appear elsewhere in the history of religion taken as a whole. One could say that the phenomena of the gifts of the Spirit, of charismatic enthusiasm are basically universal religious events and are perhaps to be found in a more or less pure, confused or distorted form in every religion. One might feel that, since they are present everywhere, they do not imply any peculiarly Christian phenomenon. They occur under various guises in different religious sects, both inside and outside Christianity; they appear within various Christian denominations, cultural groups and social classes; they may be found in a variety of psychological or cultural types, but in essence they point to purely human capacities, which in the last analysis have nothing to do with Christianity as such. From this perspective one might attempt to defend the basic position of the Jesuit school of thought outlined above by suggesting that only such a stand can rescue the specific essence of Christianity from the onslaught of charismatic enthusiasm, which, on psychological, historical and phenomenological grounds, would reduce it to the level of other religions. Only in this way can we locate the specifically Christian element firmly in the supernatural elevation of man by the

[7] Cf. K. Rahner, 'The self-communication of God', *Sacr. Mun*. III (London and New York, 1969), pp. 114–118; *ibid*. IV, pp. 297–305; *ibid*. V, pp. 348–355.

Spirit which lies beyond the scope of human consciousness. This would provide a safe refuge from the psychological and phenomenological scepticism of today. One could treat the whole phenomenon of religious enthusiasm either positively or negatively, with benevolence or scepticism. One might in certain circumstances regard such phenomena as very useful or as an inevitable concomitant of religion, but the exact elucidation of their origin would be a question in which dogmatic theology could happily declare itself to have no interest.

OUTLINE OF A CONTEMPORARY THEORY OF GRACE

First of all we must select and sketch out the theory of grace which we are to take as axiomatic, in so far as grace is regarded as the sanctifying and justifying self-communication of the Spirit of God himself. Obviously our remarks here can only take the form of a thesis proposed without further theological reasoning to support it. What justification there is for the thesis in this context consists in the usefulness which we hope it has for a theological interpretation of the phenomenon of religious enthusiasm, which is the concern of the present study.

I mean by the essence of grace the self-communication of God to the transcendent spirit of man. In virtue of this self-communication the transcendence of man is permanently and necessarily ordered to the direct presence of God, whether this be the object of conscious or thematic reflection or not. Furthermore God's self-communication is a dynamic force which transforms the inner, transcendent reference of the human spirit to God so that this transcendent, spiritual movement finds its fulfilment in the beatific vision, the direct knowledge of God face to face in love, in which God is possessed without the mediation of any created reality. Grace is thus understood as the radical transformation of human transcendence so that God is not merely the final goal of human striving which one may come nearer to but never reach. He is not only the ultimate objective which, asymptotically approached, opened up the whole spiritual movement and intellectual history of mankind and kept it in motion. Grace is also that which makes it possible for this movement to *reach* God in himself. Naturally, therefore, grace divinises man and bestows upon him a share in the holiness of God.[8] Such a preliminary understanding of grace in

[8] Cf. K. Rahner, 'grace' *Sacr. Mun.* II (London and New York, 1968), pp. 412–426.

relation to human transcendence makes it possible first of all to allow grace to operate in cases where apparently a directly Christian communication of justifying grace is not present, where the conscious interpretation of the elevation of human transcendence does not occur, or, if it does, is only expressed in a very obscure manner. The notion of the specific essence of grace outlined here does not in fact result in insoluble conflict with the problems and difficulties which the Jesuit interpretation of supernatural grace mentioned above sought to avoid. According to the latter view, grace is a divinisation of man which takes place ontologically beyond the realm of consciousness and which properly speaking, at least in normal cases, is present for the first time in human awareness only in the beatific vision. It takes as its starting point the problem that all other specific, categorial religious phenomena which can be described and empirically analysed are to be found outside Christianity and beyond the bounds of any spirituality proper to the Church. Now on this view it seems very difficult, if not impossible, to explain their existence through the operation of what in all seriousness we can call the Holy Spirit, the self-communication of God. Such an interpretation is based on the conviction, expressed in scholastic terms, that this grace essentially and properly consists in the *self-* communication of God, i.e. in what scholastic theology calls uncreated grace, in contra-distinction to any habitual or actual grace, however sublime, which is created in us by God. Uncreated grace is thus God himself, the goal and ground of those acts which are related to God in himself. According to our thesis no particular, categorial object of consciousness is assigned to this grace, which is present rather in transcendent experience. This latter can, however, subsequently be the object of historical and categorial reflection and in fact must be reflected upon, since no transcendent experience is to be found without some complementary historical expression. This account of the matter avoids a conception of divine grace which would make of it a particular, inner-worldly phenomenon which comes from without (a conception to be rejected on theological as well as philosophical and historical grounds). For the peculiar type of divine causality of grace that this assumes seems to lack credibility in the face of secular arguments.

Finally we must make it even more plain that we did at the beginning that the competence of the dogmatic theologian does not extend to the question, however important, whether the various experiences and events which one is considering in speaking of religious enthusiasm can be brought to some degree under a single, common heading. It is presupposed in the dogmatic reflections offered here that this is possible, at least in some measure, even at the cost of neglecting very great differences amongst the particular experiences of religious enthusiasm. If the term 'religious enthusiasm' does not contain any theological common denominator, then our reflections would have to be parcelled out, as it were, to cover the various, disparate experiences of religious enthusiasm. We proceed from the position, admittedly far from certain or free from problems, that in fact all these experiences do have something in common and that this consists in a transcendent experience which touches the centre of the religious subject and in which the subject has an experience of God. Of course the assertion of a common element in such charismatic phenomena is problematic in itself because it is questionable whether this radical, transcendent experience does occur in all such phenomena, even if they are judged to be genuine in themselves from a phenomenological point of view; one might feel on the contrary that some phenomena of this type may precisely inhibit or distort transcendent experience. It is furthermore obvious that to assert a common element is not to define the specific peculiarities and distinguishing characteristics of the various charismatic phenomena. Finally the proposal of a common factor in the different expressions of religious enthusiasm does not imply that a similar transcendent experience of God may not be present in religious phenomena which we would not normally call 'enthusiastic' or charismatic, phenomena such as intense meditation, contemplation, mysticism, as well as moral decisions which lay claim on human freedom in its most ultimate as well as its most superficial aspects. However the assertion of a common element does seem to us to make sense for various reasons. First it makes it possible for theology as such to have something to say about such phenomena; secondly if these phenomena do not possess some generic essence in common, they could be of no religious significance at all but would merely count as strange, psychic occurrences which might attract the interest of a para-psychologist or perhaps a psychiatrist. The obvious criticism might of course be made that if some common factor is attributed to these expressions of religious enthusiasm which covers them all without exception, then the specific character of these expressions is not in any way affected. So appeal to the common element does not enable one to say anything at all about religious enthusiasm as such. But in our view this criticism is in the last resort not valid, since all these expressions of religious enthusiasm, if and when they are genuine (which is by no means always the case), bring more clearly to a person's consciousness the experience of transcendence, an experience which may of course be found elsewhere and in other ways; they make it easier for a person to objectify this experience and mediate it to human freedom in a more intense form than would mostly, though not always, be possible for the majority of mankind in the normal unfolding of the history of individual and collective piety, if this is seen as the history of grace-filled experience of transcendence. To put the matter in summary form: a clear dose, as it were, of grace-filled, transcendent experience is a rare and sporadic occurrence; it is usually found, if at all, in homoeopathic states and in unreflective mysticism[9] (by mysticism is meant here a transcendent experience through grace which is not categorial). It follows that there is and must be transcendent experience in the form of religious enthusiasm. This is true even if the categorial element plays a much greater role in the objectification of the experience from the point of view of the subject than is the case in genuine mysticism. This means that there is much greater likelihood of distortion and corruption in the former than in the latter. Religious enthusiasm is, as it were, mysticism in ordinary dress. It may be noted here, in order to forestall possible objections, that mysticism can be interpreted as an entirely Christian phenomenon, as an expression of faith; properly understood it is the realisation, whether consciously grasped or not, of that 'kenosis' which took place in the death of Christ and was borne, accepted and answered by God through his own self-communication, in which alone ultimate freedom can be achieved. But with these remarks we find ourselves at the end of our preliminary reflections and already embarked upon the thesis which is to be proposed in this essay.

THE MEANING OF RELIGIOUS ENTHUSIASM

Our thesis concerning the theological interpretation of the phenomena of religious enthusiasm amounts to this: it may be admitted first of all that expressions of enthusiasm, in so far as they differ in their particular characteristics from other religious occurrences, are not of necessity specifically religious or experiences of grace. However, through

---

[9] To supplement these remarks cf. K. Rahner, 'Mystische Erfahrung und mystische Theologie', *Schriften zur Theologie* XII (Zurich, 1975), pp. 428–438.

these phenomena a man comes face to face in a particular way with his own transcendence and through it with his freedom and so with his inner reference to God. This goes beyond his day-to-day experience of transcendence and makes him confront in a free and conscious manner the fact that his transcendence is raised up by grace and ordered to the direct and immediate presence of God, in so far as it is accepted with the free consent of faith. Thus in the *totality* of the phenomenon of religious enthusiasm there occurs an experience of grace. This thesis must be spelt out in greater detail but two basic reasons may be given to justify it. First it provides a meaningful framework in which to locate the theological data and enables one, at least in a general way, to interpret the experience of religious enthusiasm as a genuine experience of *divine* grace, a point already made clear in Scripture. Secondly it leaves one room to include all the psychological phenomena, all the oddities and problems of a religious kind which an honest observer can neither ignore nor interpret in their brute reality as manifestations of the divine Spirit, whose operation is essential for their occurrence.

What is the situation, then, of ordinary Christians in their daily piety? They have at their disposal a large store of religious concepts, propositions, motivations and patterns of behaviour which all perform an important function in guiding their daily life and action. But in their day-to-day affairs they do not encounter with any clarity either the heart of their own subjectivity or God himself in his true self-communication. They meet with the conceptual and verbal objectifications of these two principles, which form the poles of tension of Christian and religious life. Of course the genuine realities are 'intended' in the conceptual objectifications of consciousness if the daily piety is itself authentic, a fact which may normally be taken for granted. Moreover it can and should not be disputed that some experience of human transcendence and its radical re-ordering by grace to the direct presence of God is obtained through such everyday piety, even if it is not the object of conscious reflection. But the day-to-day awareness of the pious Christian rests on these conceptual and propositional expressions; it is dissolved and remains fixed in them; it confuses, in the words of Scripture, the letter with the spirit, the word about God with the Word of God and with God himself. It is a secondary matter here whether this resting in the expressions of religion happens quite naïvely and is not felt as the problem of God's distance but rather as consolation, joy, liberation, security and nearness, or whether the pious Christian *suffers* in his daily life from the mediation of true religious reality through conceptual expressions and has the terrible sensation of remaining fixed in a purely human realm without any authentic experience of God himself at all.

How can this imprisonment in the objective and categorial reality of everyday existence, even religious, be broken? When can a man experience his own freedom for what it is in a clearer and more radical fashion and become aware of the ultimate and decisive self-determination of the one, total subject before God, and not merely be faced with this or that object of choice, over which he possesses some control according to certain objective moral norms? How, that is, will we come to a clear and inescapable experience of the real self-communication of God in which he is grasped as the goal of our transcendence and as the underlying ground of our very experience of God? For this is in fact what the Christian doctrine of grace asserts of every religious act, although, as we have pointed out earlier, it then consigns the experience of grace to an objective realm beyond conscious awareness. How will we transcend in our religious acts the endless conceptual objectifications of God which enable us only to relate to him and his word through their mediation, so that God himself remains a remote being, only accessible through conceptual, linguistic and cultic images? When will we grasp this teaching on grace not only in propositional formulae but also in clear and inescapable experience?

If, as I say, we abstract from the phenomenon of the radical 'emptying' characteristic of a mysticism of faith in which a person shares in the descent of Jesus into death, we can say: all expressions of religious enthusiasm, whenever they are to some degree genuine and in earnest, are spiritual events in which the grace filled transcendence of man comes plainly to the fore and in which the subject freely experiences God as both the ultimate goal of this transcendence and the very ground of the experience itself. We do not mean that these phenomena of religious enthusiasm consist *only* in such grace-filled experiences of transcendence and in nothing else besides. This is certainly not true of them as it might be asserted of genuine mysticism. For they possess categorial content of different kinds and are caused by a great variety of factors. But they also contain a genuine, grace-filled experience of transcendence which has an inescapable impact quite different from the grey mask of everyday normality usually superimposed on such experience: In them a man passes 'outside himself'. The true meaning of religion is hidden and made remote by the dominance of its traditional, everyday expressions, even though their real function is to be a sign and pointer towards this meaning. Through religious enthusiasm the objectification of religion is dislodged from its system. The experience of being taken out of oneself makes what is normal and organised in the institutional Church seem provisional and questionable, incommensurate with the meaning it is supposed to signify. A man is thrown back upon his own subjectivity, which no longer appears manageable to him in terms of conceptual expressions and propositional criteria. He then has the courage to entrust himself to something within him which no longer has to be tested and sanctioned by categorial norms but is experienced, at least in a preliminary way, as not being subject to such control, as the realisation of freedom which occurs in the act of self-surrender to the sovereign mastery of God, a mastery which lies beyond our justification. All this at least enables a person to experience in a clear and inescapable manner his own transcendence and inner reference to God, itself sustained by God's self-communication. It is true that these charismatic experiences do not bring about such a grace-filled awareness of God's presence in entirely pure and clear form, for they can distort the real experience of grace in a new way precisely because they break through the imprisoning objectivity of everyday religious awareness. But the experience of religious enthusiasm does make plain the provisional character of all that is, in the broadest sense, 'institutional', i.e. rational language, sacraments and law, and shows clearly that the whole institutional structure, although it can never disappear entirely in this life, is nevertheless in itself a sign which is destined to destroy itself and disappear at the appearance of God. To this extent these experiences render the immediate reality and given-ness of the grace-bearing experience of God more evident and inescapable than is normally the case in everyday, religious existence where the sign all too easily takes the place of the reality which it signifies.

To explain all this more clearly and to establish its truth more firmly, one would have to examine specific experiences of religious enthusiasm, for these vary enormously amongst themselves. Only then would one be in a position to show how each experience mediates in its own way a purer and more radical experience of grace than those which occur in everyday, religious practice, limited as it is to objective categories. But such an exposition is not possible here, if only because I do not regard myself as competent to describe particular expressions of religious enthusiasm from a psychological and phenomenological point of view. One would have to indicate a category in which to locate religious phenomena, in such a way that on the one hand their human reality could be appreciated and, at the same time, critically examined, and on the other hand they could be judged, at least under certain conditions, to be in fact what they claim to be, that is the action of the Spirit of God.

CONSEQUENCES

If we understand mysticism in the sense indicated above, i.e. a radical experience of faith which destroys the conceptual and the categorial in so far as these claim to be ultimate realities, we may regard religious enthusiasm as a sort of mysticism of the masses. Now if this enthusiasm is an experience of the grace of faith, which expresses the grace-filled awareness of transcendence more clearly because the circumstances are psychologically and existentially out of the ordinary, it is evident first of all that, in so far as they are to be distinguished from the experience of grace itself, they are rightly subject to human, critical analysis; their origin and nature, their possible consequences and distortions are to be assessed by human, secular criteria. The one condition for this analysis is the conviction that genuine experiences of grace do exist and that they can in principle occur in experiences of religious enthusiasm, although they are not limited to them. Indeed under certain conditions they may be felt more clearly and with greater impact in these phenomena. A further assumption is that the rational version of man found in the western world, especially amongst intellectuals, is not necessarily the model and paradigm for the whole of humanity. What emerges as the essential character of religious enthusiasm may not in itself be the unsullied manifestation of the 'Holy Spirit', but may possess a particular analogical affinity to him, at least in certain important respects. But given these assumptions, the phenomenon of religious enthusiasm in itself can be assessed by psychology, depth psychology, para-psychology or whatever else, each in its own way, without this being an irreligious and profane attack upon such enthusiasm, an attack which is bound to misunderstand their specific character and importance. We are not faced with the alternatives of being forced either to recognise expressions of religious enthusiasm, at least when they are genuine, as the unadulterated operation of the Holy Spirit, or to discount them from the start, even from the human point of view, as 'rubbish', the result of human religious impulses going off the rails.

It must be granted that with respect to their categorial content and conceptual framework, their particular imagery and distinct prophetic utterances, and the actual impulses which an individual, a community or a society experience in them, they are of human origin and cannot be interpreted simply as divine inspiration which would give their particular categorial content an unambiguous sanction and a heavenly guarantee.[10] But this precisely does not mean that a genuine, grace-filled experience of transcendence cannot be present in those feelings of enthusiasm whose categorial content arouses justified misgivings or even should be rejected altogether on a number of possible counts. Even prophets, for example, who were filled with the Spirit of God, have made mistakes, if one looks at the matter from a purely historical point of view. The language of the charismatically inspired can be psychologically conditioned either individually or socially, even when the experience is genuine, and can be extremely limited and primitive in character. A man who is deeply moved by religious feeling and bewails his sinfulness can be lamenting something which a psychologist of human development may explain as a harmless human weakness, and yet the man's contrition can be quite justified. Someone in a moment of religious enthusiasm may have a 'conversion experience' whose content later proves highly questionable and dated; nevertheless it may have been a genuine experience of conversion in the sense that through a very dubious categorial medium a person can achieve a radically free self-determination and an unconditional acceptance of the sovereignty of God.[11] Critical analysis of the categorial content of religious enthusiasm does not necessarily place in question the basic experience of grace and of the Spirit. Whether this is present, whether the subject has experienced his own freedom and in it grace, this question must be decided so far as possible by other criteria than that of the rightness or wrongness of the content of such experiences taken by itself *alone*. This is especially true in cases where the content of an experience may be quite acceptable and yet the experience itself hardly qualifies as a case of religious enthusiasm, since it is existentially far too shallow and superficial to count as a clear and radical experience of

[10] Cf. K. Rahner, 'Mystische Erfahrung und Mystische Theologie', *Schriften zur Theologie* XII (Zurich, 1975), pp. 428–438.

[11] On the theology of freedom the author has published a collection of his own writings, *Grace in Freedom* (London and Freiburg, 1969).

the transcendent impact of transforming grace. In Catholic theology such criteria are mostly to be found in mystical theology, in as much as this is not only concerned with the transcendent experience of grace in its intrinsic purity (such as in the exclusively mystical images, pictures, appearances, or terms of a John of the Cross)[12], but also takes into consideration mystical phenomena which possess categorial content and in addition treat such content seriously. This means that it is difficult, if not impossible, to distinguish them from those experiences which today would be put under the heading of religious enthusiasm, especially such things as prophecies, proclamations, missions, which may appear less within charismatic communities (because of the mechanics of communication), but which can be aimed at such communities as the audience addressed. But no more will be said here about such criteria. If the correctness of content cannot be made into a clear and decisive criterion for the presence or absence of a genuine religious experience of grace, it cannot function in this way either for the value for a community of such an experience of religious enthusiasm.

The above remarks should not be taken to imply that the categorial content of such experiences is simply irrelevant. Other things being equal, an experience of this type has more chance of being genuine, that is, of being a real transcendent experience of grace which touches the core of personal freedom, if the categorial content is objectively correct, i.e. if it is in some measure an appropriate objectification of the experience of grace. However it should not be overlooked in this case that the objective validity of the categorial content can create the danger of seeming to guarantee the intense and radical character of an experience of grace, simply because the categorial content gives no cause for objections. In order to test the authenticity of the categorial content of such an experience we should use all the normal rules which are valid for the assessment of theological statements and events in general: conformity to the message of the Gospel, to Scripture, to the faith and mind of the Church, etc. Here we will not go further into the matter, except to say that our case raises the question which applies to all Christian statements·and theological texts but in a more acute form than elsewhere, the question, that is, of how the original experience of

---

[12] On St. John of the Cross cf. I. Behn, *Spanische Mystik* (Dusseldorf, 1957), pp. 463–742; A. Winkelhofer, *Die Gnadenlehre in der Mystik des hl. Johannes v. Kreuz* (Freiburg i. Br. 1936); A. Brunner, *Der Schritt über die Grenzen. Wesen und Sinn der Mystik* (Wurzburg, 1972).

grace which took place in the encounter with the historical Christ event is related to the explicit teaching of Christianity in Scripture and tradition. For the latter is after all nothing more than the historical interpretation which has proved valid and authentic for the community of the Church of the original process of the experience of grace mediated through Jesus. But even if this question becomes particularly urgent in the case of religious enthusiasm, nevertheless it is a problem which comes up in all theological discourse and does not require special treatment here.[13]

The dogmatic question should be raised at this point of how the relationship of religious enthusiasm to the Christian community, to the Church, can be assessed and tested. In contrast to the central core of mysticism the expressions of religious enthusiasm make themselves felt precisely within the Christian community as such. This applies both in cases when something like a prophetic message, etc. is directed to a community or to the Church and in cases when an intense experience of individual conversion occurs publicly in the community and seeks recognition through the community. But the relationship of religious enthusiasm to the community and the Church can be referred to that part of ecclesiology which deals with the charismatic element in the Church, with its validity and role vis-à-vis the institutional structure of the Church, and with the obvious tension between the charismatic and institutional elements.[14] One should also call attention to the teaching on 'discernment of spirits', a topic much neglected in contemporary theology, which should enable the authorities in the Church, and others as well, to distinguish between the authentic and the inauthentic expressions of religious enthusiasm. But nothing more will be added on this subject here.[15]

It may be noted that the question we have touched does in fact lie concealed within other departments of dogmatic theology, which cover the topic in an analogous way, although this fact is not immediately evident. At root, for instance, the same problem is involved

[13] On the mediating role of Jesus Christ, cf. the author's theological meditation, *Ich glaube an Jesus Christus* (Zurich, 1968).

[14] The author has dealt fully with this topic in the writings collected in *The Dynamic Element in the Church*, Quaestiones Disputatae 12 (London and Freiburg, 1964).

[15] For the discernment of spirits according to Ignatius Loyola, cf. in this volume, 'Modern Piety and the Experience of Retreats'; bibliog. references will be found there.

when one considers the question, acute in the 19th century and the first half of the 20th, of the relationship between traditional fundamental theology and the apologetic of immanence. The same issue is at stake when the function of the grace of faith is discussed as the reception of the message of the Gospel which comes from without; when the relation of the letter and the spirit in the text of Scripture is considered; when in sacramental theology the exact connection between 'sacrament' and the 'res' of the sacrament is examined; when the Church as the presence of the Spirit and the Church as institution is discussed in ecclesiology. In all these cases it is a question of the relation between two realities which should neither be identified nor completely separated. This relation reappears in phenomenon of religious enthusiasm in that, however spiritual the experience may seem at first, one must distinguish between the real, fundamental experience of grace in the transcendent being of man on the one hand and the categorial content on the other. For this content can both be the cause and medium of a clearer and existentially more radical interiorisation of the transcendent experience of grace and also be its complementary expression, which under certain circumstances may seem in retrospect highly dubious from a historical or individual point of view.

In conclusion we may note that elements are present in a theology of human freedom which involves the historical and corporeal nature of man, as well as in traditional moral theology and in mystical teaching, which could be used for a theological interpretation of an intense experience of conversion, of the reception of the Holy Spirit, and of baptism in the Spirit (leaving aside the question whether baptism admits of different levels) and other such phenomena. The distinction, for example, drawn in moral theology between an act which, though free, is relatively insignificant and one which is of decisive importance for life (a distinction which unfortunately is rarely applied in Catholic theology to any but sinful actions), and the teaching on being 'confirmed in grace' and on the possibility of interiorising this reality, which is found in mystical theology, both contain, despite the as yet unsolved problems they possess, many theological insights which could be of value for the assessment of religious enthusiasm.

4

ANONYMOUS AND EXPLICIT FAITH

T HE topic to be discussed here is the possibility of 'anonymous
faith' and its relationship to 'explicit faith'. By anonymous faith
is meant a faith which on the one hand is necessary and
effective for salvation (under the general conditions which are required
for justification and final salvation, i.e. hope and the love of God and
neighbour) and on the other occurs without an explicit and conscious
relationship (i.e. conceptual and verbal and thus objectively
constituted) to the revelation of Jesus Christ contained in the Old
and/or New Testament and without any explicit reference to God
through an objective idea of God.

We combine in the concept of 'anonymous faith' a lack of an explicit
relationship both to Christian revelation and to God, although it can
of course happen that faith has a clear conceptual and verbal reference
to God and only lacks an explicit relationship to Christian revelation.
We are disregarding for a number of reasons the distinction much
stressed elsewhere in contemporary theology between faith explicitly
addressed to God but without express reference to Christian revelation
in historical form and the 'faith of an atheist'. First the question of the
salvation of those who feel obliged to affirm atheism is an urgent one.
Secondly the Second Vatican Council takes account of such cases.[1]
Thirdly the notion common in the past that a 'natural' revelation or
even a private illumination could provide a relationship to God which
is not a mere metaphysical affirmation of God's existence but involves
a genuine faith in the self-revelation of God, this notion is no longer
tenable because of the contemporary view of the length of human
history and because atheism is a worldwide phenomenon.

[1] Cf. Conc. Vat. II *Lumen Gentium* no. 18; *Gaudium et Spes* no. 22; *Ad
Gentes* No. 7.

We are taking for granted here the theological doctrine that genuine faith is necessary for justification and salvation. This is the general teaching of theologians and was repeated by the Second Vatican Council. We are assuming as well that mere 'good will' based on a purely natural knowledge of God is by itself quite inadequate for salvation and justification, so that the view of Straub, for instance, cannot be sustained that in cases of necessity good will, founded on a formal readiness to believe, without actual faith, i.e. fides virtualis, is enough.[2]

We find ourselves, then, in the following theological situation: genuine faith in revelation is necessary for salvation. But it is not immediately plain what is exactly meant by 'faith universally necessary for salvation'. We are theologically justified in our definition of saving faith if we take into consideration that the teaching of the Church allows a man a chance of being saved as long as he does not grievously offend his conscience by his actions, even if he does not come in the course of his life to an explicit acceptance of the Christian message in faith. But it must nevertheless be affirmed that a purely natural, metaphysical knowledge of God can never replace faith. On the other hand the Church today allows even for non-Christians and atheists who do not act against their conscience a real chance of supernatural salvation and the Second Vatican Council explicitly reckoned on such a possibility.

FAITH NECESSARY FOR SALVATION

The question, then, is: how is it conceivable that these men could possibly achieve the faith which is necessary for salvation? Earlier explanations offered to cover this eventuality simply do not merit serious consideration any longer, e.g. private illumination, possibly at the moment of death; natural revelation which is mediated to a man through tradition; the acceptance of the distant possibility of faith which never reaches a more practical, explicit level of belief because of the personal fault of the individual 'heathen'. These solutions no longer hold water because, since the Second Vatican Council, we must

[2] Cf. the studies, some much older, collected in: A. Straub, *De analysi fidei* (Innsbruck, 1922), with the idea of a 'fides stricte dicta, sed virtualis'; cf. also K. Rahner, 'Membership of the Church according to the teaching of Pius XII's Encyclical "Mystici Corporis Christi" ', *Theological Investigations* II (London and Baltimore, 1963) pp. 1–88.

also reckon with a genuine possibility of salvation, and therefore of faith, being available to those who, without personal guilt, believe quite consciously and explicitly that they are obliged to profess atheism. It is no use saying in this case that a conscious atheist cannot remain free of guilt for long, that either he must in a short time become a convert to explicit theism or his atheism becomes culpable.

We are offering here an optimistic answer with regard to the possibility of salvation. There can exist an 'anonymous faith' which carries with it an intrinsic dynamism and therefore an obligation to find full realisation in explicit faith, but which is nonetheless sufficient for salvation even if a man does not achieve this fulfilment during his lifetime, as long as he is not to blame for this. Naturally such a person would deny, both to himself in his conscious awareness and to others, that he has such anonymous faith and in consequence this doctrine is not directly available for apologetic use. But this does not prevent a Christian from holding that his non-Christian or atheist fellow human being may be an anonymous believer.

The question now follows: what is to be understood by 'anonymous faith', and how is it to be conceived as a real possibility on the basis of valid theological principles? (The question whether such a possibility of salvation, which is universally available and offered to every man, is in fact freely accepted and realised, this question will not be pursued here.) We start from the assumption that the attempt to find an answer is not forbidden by the declaration of the Second Vatican Council that in such cases faith occurs in ways known only to God.[3] For this remark should evidently be taken to mean no more than that the Council itself is neither able nor willing to use its binding authority to lay down anything more precise on the subject. But if the theologian does not venture on his own responsibility and at his own peril to search out these mysterious ways of God, he would be laying the Church's teaching open to the objection that it was simply self-contradictory in that it asserted both that salvation was possible for all men and that faith was necessary.

To answer our question we may proceed from two pieces of data drawn from Christian anthropology, understood in both a theological and a philosophical sense. First there is the doctrine of the unlimited, transcendent nature of the human spirit in knowledge and freedom and secondly there is the dogma of God's universally effective will

---

[3] Cf. Conc. Vat. II *Gaudium et Spes* no. 22; *Ad Gentes* no. 3.

which offers to all men the possibility of reaching their 'supernatural destiny' in the direct possession of God. The heart of our thesis is that, because the universal and supernatural will of God is working for human salvation, the unlimited transcendence of man, itself directed of necessity towards God, is raised up consciously by grace, although possibly without explicit thematic reflection, in such a way that the possibility of faith in revelation is thereby made available. Thus one can speak of genuine faith on condition that a man freely accepts his own unlimited transcendence which is raised up by grace and directed to the immediate presence of God as its final goal. We will now try briefly to expound this thesis.[4]

THE TRANSCENDENT CHARACTER OF THE HUMAN SPIRIT

Man is the being who possesses unlimited transcendence of knowledge and freedom. The inner dynamism of his spirit is directed to absolute being, to absolute hope, to the absolute future, to good in itself, to what is unconditionally right, and thus to God (or whatever one calls the goal of human transcendence which goes beyond all that can be grasped in objective categories). The transcendent reference of man to God is mediated through categorial objects (at least in cases other than genuine mystical experiences). But this object does not necessarily have to be a religious concept. The transcendent reference to God can be found in the mediation of ordinary, secular material, as long as a man by means of this material freely comes to a position of complete responsibility and self-determination. There then exists a conscious reference to God which can be freely accepted, although this is not explicitly reflected upon or treated under the heading of 'God'.

Even if a man does not think of God as part of his conscious vocabulary or even feels that he has to reject such a concept as self-contradictory, he is nevertheless always and inevitably involved with God in his secular awareness. Without reflection he accepts God when he freely accepts himself in his own unlimited transcendence. He does this when he genuinely follows his conscience with free consent, because by such an action he affirms as well the condition of possi-

[4] The author has treated the themes briefly summarised here more fully elsewhere; on the 'transcendent nature of the human spirit' cf. the author's studies in the philosophy of religion; on the 'salvific will of God' cf. the article in *LThK*, V, 165–168; also *Sacr. Mun.* V (London and New York, 1970), pp. 405–409.

bility of such a radical option which is implicitly bound up with this decision, i.e. he affirms God. So an explicit atheist is always involved with God. He cannot avoid this reference to God since it stems from the necessity of transcendence. At the same time he can be an anonymous theist when he recognises in his positive moral decision the unconditional call of conscience, for which the ultimate condition of possibility is the reference to what we call God. Explicit atheism is either culpable or involves an implicitly affirmed theism. This is, however, the precondition for a faith which in a strict sense responds to God's self-revelation; it is the 'potentia obedientalis' for such faith.[5]

THE SAVING WILL OF GOD

The second piece of theological data which is relevant in this context is the universal and supernatural will of God acting for salvation. This is expressed concretely in the communication (at least as an offer) of supernatural grace, whose transforming power is the condition of possibility of genuine saving acts and therefore, most fundamentally, of the act of faith. Two aspects of this supernatural grace should be specially noted here. First the offer of such grace should not be thought of as an occasional event happening periodically in a man's life, at least so long as he is not justified. This grace can in fact exist in the form of a mere offer (as in the case of baptised children), but in the case of adults who have not yet achieved justification grace cannot merely be an intermittent offer. Without prejudice to its gratuitous character, it should be conceived as an abiding possibility of human freedom and can be expressed either in the form of an offer alone, or as an acceptance which brings justification, or as a direct and deliberate rejection.

The second point to be made about such grace is that it transforms human consciousness. Here we can appeal directly to Thomist teaching, according to which supernatural, elevating grace is not a purely ontological reality beyond the scope of consciousness; it also brings a new, a priori, formal object with it which lies beyond the reach of a natural act of the human spirit. This formal object is not to be thought of as a new, distinct item of conscious awareness which is a direct object of reflection, still less as a particular concept or word. It is rather the radical nature of the unlimited transcendence of man itself which is

[5] Cf. K. Rahner, *Hearers of the Word* (London and Sydney, 1969).

consciously known, though not necessarily perceived as an object or fully thought out. This transcendence is ordered by the transforming power of grace to the direct presence of God as its final goal, so that God does not merely remain the distant end point to which human transcendence tends asymptotically through knowledge and freedom, but is constituted as its proper goal. Since God seen as end point of spiritual transcendence and God regarded as immediate possession both form the a priori nature of the human spirit and cannot be simply differentiated by pure reflection, the thesis of the a priori consciousness of grace does not mean that it must be possible to distinguish grace as such from the natural spiritual essence of man by means of reflection upon particular objects of consciousness. This is all the more true given that question whether a person has freely and concretely accepted this grace or not cannot be decisively settled by pure introspection.

The process by which human transcendence is given new depth and purpose and is ordered to the direct presence of God is universal in time and place, because God's saving will is universally operative, even if it cannot be distinguished or given conceptual shape by individual reflection. If God's self-communication is free and if it is consciously grasped by a person, even if this occurs without thematic reflection, then the two conditions for supernatural revelation are realised in the strict sense of the term. Traditional theology also recognises an intrinsically transcendent revelation, even if under another label, in its teaching that historical revelation can only be grasped and understood for what it is through the grace of faith, which is nothing else than the self-communication of God to the human spirit in the depths of its being. If one adds at this point the Thomist doctrine of the new, supernatural, formal object given by grace, then one has already found what we are describing here as transcendent revelation, or, perhaps more accurately, the transcendent factor in revelation.

'ANONYMOUS' FAITH[6]

If a person by a free act in which he accepts himself unconditionally in his radical reference to God raised up by grace, also accepts the basic

[6] The author has frequently considered the question of the 'anonymous Christian' in his writings, although in a slightly different perspective to the one adopted here. The above reflections are meant to supplement these other writings from another point of view.

finality of this movement of his spirit, even if without reflection, then he is making a genuine act of faith, for this finality already means revelation. If this supernatural finality is freely accepted, without explicit reflection, then there exists what we term 'anonymous faith'. Such a transcendence, which is supernaturally raised up and implies revelation, is of course always mediated through some object and therefore is, in the widest sense, mediated historically. This mediating, categorial objectivity, in which a man becomes present to himself and to his own transcendence, does not have to be an explicitly religious act. It can be formed by a particular moral decision in which a man is responsible for himself and accepts (or rejects) himself. To this extent the acceptance of human transcendence in faith, which is supernaturally elevated and so reveals God, can be found in an atheist as well, given that he is absolutely obedient to the dictates of his conscience and so accepts himself and God, at least unreflectively, in so far as he actually realises his own transcendence.

At this point we must state more carefully what is the relationship between this transcendent revelation and the anonymous faith which it makes possible on the one hand, and the historical, Christian revelation on the other. It must also be shown why the transcendent revelation and the faith offered through it to human freedom does not make the historical, verbal revelation superfluous, but rather underlines and reinforces the latter's obligatory character.

If historical, Christian revelation is understood as the process, willed by God in his saving providence and demanded by human nature, by which the transcendent revelation becomes present to itself in history, then there exists no insuperable obstacle to the solution of the problem. Transcendent and historical revelation have a mutual reference: the former acquires historical form and shape in the latter, just as in other cases the transcendent being of man is mediated to itself through history. Historical revelation only realises its proper character through its transcendent counterpart, since it is only effective for salvation if through it the transcendent self-communication of God finds historical expression, the communication, that is, to which we give the name of the grace of faith and justification.

If during his life a person is offered, in a manner which is credible to him, the chance to give objective structure and shape to his being (and therefore an opportunity of supernatural elevation), and if he rejects this possibility, then he is deliberately denying his grace-filled transcendence as well. It is not possible to have 'anonymous faith' when its thematic expression in the Christian belief in revelation is culpably rejected. But as long as a person is not guilty of this and at the same time accepts himself in a moral decision, he assumes at the same time his own radical transcendence, which is ordered to the direct presence of God, and so possesses anonymous faith. This remains true even if the acceptance happens without conscious reflection and the object which mediates this moral decision is not necessarily grasped in a religious or 'theist' manner.

5

FAITH BETWEEN RATIONALITY AND EMOTION

THE above title, which concerns the relationship between faith, rationality and emotion,[1] forces us to feel our way slowly to what I believe to be the heart of the topic. It is perhaps wiser, therefore, not to state at the outset what exactly is meant to the crucial assertion in the following reflections. First of all a few preliminary remarks may be in order, so as to provide a broader survey of the question and thus open the way to the central theme.

THE APPROACH TO FAITH

Faith, rationality and emotion all appear in the title and are set in a certain relationship: it is suggested that faith lies somehow between emotion and rationality. No attempt is to be made here to articulate the notion of faith as it is found in the self-understanding of Christian faith and in Catholic theology. For the central question we are tackling implies that the other two concepts are to be used in order to reach a definition of the idea of Christian faith. Such an attempt to define the essence of Christian faith apparently from without may seem surprising, and indeed hopeless, if one accepts the account of faith normally given in Catholic theology. But the effort should still be made and indeed this is the task, as will gradually become evident, with which these reflections are concerned. Let us, furthermore, leave aside the question of the exact significance of the word 'between' in the title.

[1] The original text served as a basis for a lecture which was one of a series delivered to the Catholic Academy of Bavaria; cf. K. Rahner (ed.), *1st. Gott noch gefragt? Zur Funktionslosigkeit des Gottesglaubens* (Dusseldorf, 1973). The reflections presented here are the result of further revision; cross-references have been added to the author's other writings.

The term is not very clear because it can either be understood as the mere 'between' of a third object lying between two others on the same level, or it can be taken to mean an 'over', so that the middle term in fact contains within it the over-arching and essential principle of unity for the other two terms, *between* which it apparently stands. The words, rationality and emotion, are obscure as well: they do not have an unambiguous clarity which can easily be described, thus making it possible to get to grips with the topic.[2] This does not mean that the subject proposed for discussion is illegitimate. For there are of necessity cases, especially in anthropology, metaphysics and religion, in which it is not possible to proceed in a straight line, as it were, from clear fixed concepts and so reach a new concept, a fresh insight which leaves the starting point undisturbed. Every point of departure of one's limited reflection (and there is always something unavoidably arbitrary about what point one chooses) is to some extent redefined and altered by the feedback which the result of one's investigations produces. It is only at the end of the path that one finds out at exactly what point one stepped on the road.

At first glance rationality seems a perfectly straightforward term. Wherever rationality is present, language and conceptual operations are dominant with ever new conceptual distinctions, logic, discussion, argument and the critical analysis of propositions. Rationality *as such* is not directed in the first instance to the particular content of a proposition; rather it is ordered, in a constantly new way, to the methods and validity of the connection of propositions to one another. It is aimed, therefore, at least approximately and within distinct areas of human consciousness, at the building of systems. It seeks as far as possible, by connecting the propositions in question in a way that is open to systematic control, to analyse their content in the framework of the formal, propositional structure, or at least to trace back in this manner the propositions whose content remains irreducible to as few axioms or basic assumptions as possible.

Rationality poses the question of verification, especially with regard to those propositions which cannot be proved through their clear,

---

[2] For the basic concepts cf. philosophical lexicons, e.g. J. Hoffmeister, *Wörterbuch der Philosophischen Begriffe* (Leipzig, 1944), p. 236 (Emotion) and pp. 576–578 (ratio/rationalismus); M. L. Falorni, *Enciclopedia filosofica I* (Venice and Rome, 1957 ff), 1868–1871 (Emozione) and F. Borgato, *ibid.* III, 1884 (Razionalità). Usually, however, one is referred to 'Affekte', 'Gefühl', etc., as in *LThK*.

formal relationship to each other and through appeal to the rules of valid, propositional logic. Rationality also makes a critical investigation of the pre-suppositions which, though external to the propositions in question, nevertheless have an effect upon them: ones concerning their setting, their place in history, their dependence and effect upon social conditions, their ideological use and abuse, their dependence upon a historically conditioned language, and their general horizon of understanding, both conscious and unconscious. It is also to be noted of course that these 'external' assumptions, which are open to critical and rational scrutiny, mutually condition one another. These characteristics of rationality should suffice for the moment. We will leave aside the question of what ultimate assumptions of transcendental necessity are laid down by rationality, even though this question alone makes clear the fundamental relation between faith and rationality. The position of Catholic theology on this point is that the relationship must be a positive one. For the notion of faith itself forbids one to regard it as an absolutely irrational phenomenon and to locate it altogether outside the sphere of reason. If the totality of such rational questioning is tentatively described as 'philosophy', then there is such a thing as philosophical faith, at least in the broad sense of the involvement of faith with rationality. Propositions of Christian belief cannot be contrary to reason without faith being obliged by its own principles to destroy itself.

Obviously much more could be said about this relationship, but for the following discussion an important, preliminary decision has been taken which will not receive any further justification at this point. At any rate faith and rationality have something to do with each other. Faith is a λογικὴ λατρειά, a 'rationabile obsequium' (Rom 12:1), a reasonable act of worship, as the First Vatican Council explicitly emphasised.[3]

It is more difficult to define the word emotion, even in a provisional fashion. It could simply be asserted that emotion signifies everything in human consciousness, both individual and collective, which escapes the control, in practice even if not in principle, of rationality as we have defined it, in so far as rationality can be carried on in a finite, reasoned process of reflection and work through the contents of human consciousness. This of course only provides a negative

---

[3] Cf. specially Ch. 4, 'De fide et ratione' from the dogmatic constitution, 'Dei Filius' and the corresponding canons, *Denz*. 3009, 3016, 3017, 3033.

definition of emotion and one that is determined by rationality. This negative definition of the term assumes that to some extent emotion is amenable to rational reflection and that ideally emotion and rationality are to be brought into harmony, so that emotion, in so far as it is legitimate, appears reasonable and rationality is accepted as desirable by the emotions. This is true even if the ideal can only be approximately achieved and never totally realised. Our definition does not concern itself in a systematic way with emotions which are rationally determined and verified as legitimate. We are considering emotion in so far as it is not covered by reason. Thus it is crucial for our case that in fact such an element exists in emotion which is not rationally thought through and organised, which cannot be analysed adequately in any conceivable finite process and which is rationally recognised as such. Reason is, therefore, presented with a problem with which it must come to terms in advance of its natural striving to subject everything to rational analysis. On this definition, however, the emotional element includes feelings of the greatest variety and diversity.

If we leave aside those phenomena which lie outside the realm of clear awareness, we would still have to enumerate a great variety of things, both individual and collective: particular moods and individual dispositions, patterns of behaviour biologically determined and conditioned by historical development, impulses and repressions, aggression and fears, both individual and collective, unthought out ideals, opinions, realms of understanding which are biologically, racially or socially conditioned and have an effect prior to any rational justification or analysis. At this point there is no need to give a more detailed account of this emotional element, nor to try to fit it into a conceptual framework which provides clear means of discrimination. What is meant, however, should be relatively comprehensible.

A completely different category of emotion, however, must also be mentioned: the reality of freedom and its objective expressions in history. These phenomena come under the concept of emotion as we have defined it here for a number of reasons. First free decisions and objective expressions inevitably are based on something and a condition of their possibility lies in all the emotional states which we described above. If these are not subjected to sufficient rational analysis, then the free choices which flow from them are subject to the same limitation. No motivation, however rational it may and should be, can be sufficiently thought through (in the sense defined earlier) and justified, so that all emotional factors are excluded. Any reflection upon such motivation is always affected by particular forces which themselves cannot be adequately examined because this would lead to an endless process of reflection.

Another point is that freedom of its essence cannot be subjected to adequate rational investigation. For freedom as such, i.e. the choice amongst a number of possibilities, is independent of its biological, psychological, social, etc. presuppositions. It is creative, which means that it does not, in its own self-realisation, merely put into effect what is sanctioned by reason, but sets goals in a creative manner which cannot be justified by a purely functional rationality. The latter indeed can only present hypothetical models of behaviour of which not even a selection can be justified by reason which operates in terms of function and hypothesis. Rationality is primarily concerned with the effectiveness of means and not with the creative establishment of ends and their justification.

It is not possible here to develop a philosophy and theology of freedom[4] and thus to demonstrate the irreducible originality of freedom with respect to rationality. A mere mention must here suffice. But even if freedom does possess its own peculiar character, nevertheless it is a reality which, in its individuality, can be counted as belonging to the emotional element in man. If one were able to develop a theology and a philosophy of freedom, it would become clear that freedom constitutes the very essence of emotion in comparison with which all other emotional factors would appear derivative, being mere conditions of possibility, a sign of the finite and passive character of created freedom and in the end analysable in terms of freedom.

FAITH AND FREEDOM

From the position now reached we may express the topic, faith between rationality and emotion, more precisely in the form, faith between rationality and freedom. This more exact formulation does not mean that the relation between faith and the emotions of the first type mentioned does not pose difficult questions in human life. Faith is indeed in part determined by such emotions and is continually placed in question by the rational process of critical analysis made of these emotions. This process faith must both permit and sustain. But it

---

[4] The author's most important writings on the theology of freedom are to be found in 'Grace in Freedom' (London and Freiburg, 1969), esp. pp. 203–264.

must always be remembered with regard to faith that just because psychological, social and historical conditions cannot be sufficiently analysed, it does not mean that any possibility of an absolute commitment of faith is thereby destroyed, any more than is the case for other absolute decisions in human life. For these are not rendered impossible and illegitimate in being conditioned by emotions not open to adequate rational reflection. But here we would prefer to restrict our attention to the relationship between faith and the particular emotional factor which is caused human freedom and the decisions which result from it.

I would state as a thesis, without offering any further argument to support it, that the essential nature of freedom is not in itself a neutral possibility either to act or not to act with regard to this or that particular categorial object of choice experienced in an a posteriori manner. Although freedom is always mediated through a particular categorial act, it consists much more in the capacity of the spiritual subject to exercise definitive control over himself, even if this self-determination occurs in space and time, in the length and breadth of an individual's history and therefore cannot be tied down by personal reflection to a particular moment of a man's life. The subject and object of freedom is constituted by the whole man acting with ultimate decision. Freedom means the capacity to act once and for all for oneself without being a mere point of intersection of influences which come from without and lose themselves in the impersonal web of objective causes which we call the world.

If we take this concept of freedom for granted, then our thesis runs that according to Christian understanding the realisation of freedom is identical with faith. This means that faith is not a free activity of a distinct categorial kind which is concerned either with a particular object reaching us from without in an a posteriori experience or with a specific item of knowledge; it is the united and fundamental totality of freedom itself. Wherever freedom as decisive self-determination is positively realised and the object of freedom, namely the human person, is unconditionally accepted for what he is by the subject of freedom which is that very same person, wherever, that is, a person does not reject himself in a final denial, and does not utter an ultimate protest in total scepticism or despair, even though this acceptance is mediated and obscured by categorial objects of choice, then there is present what Christians call 'faith'. This is true even though this identity can be mediated in different ways and ideally should be mediated through the explicitly affirmed content of Christian faith (as 'fides quae').

The thesis of the identity of freedom in its fundamental realisation and faith may sound surprising, and even scandalous, to the religious sensibilities of the average, practising Christian. But at root this position rests only upon assumptions which are indisputable in Christian theology. I will attempt to enumerate the most important of these in the belief that, if they are accepted, a little further reflection will certainly throw light upon the thesis we are proposing.

THE REFERENCE TO GOD

Faith is a *free* act. Even if this assertion, which is expressly stated in the First Vatican Council, is understood to mean merely a particular free action alongside which there exist acts of freedom involving other objects of choice, nevertheless one must ask how the fulfilment of this individual free act is related to that primordial freedom which is whole and undivided and enables a man to achieve ultimate self-determination.

One should add that a genuine and radical philosophy of freedom can and must demonstrate that the essential nature of freedom is only conceivable in and through the transcendent reference of the human spirit in knowledge and freedom to that being, or rather person, whom we call God. Thus the realisation of freedom understood in this fundamental sense inevitably implies the affirmation or denial of God, irrespective of whether the reference to God is the object of conscious verbal reflection or not.[5] Freedom is freedom for or against God; to become aware of this goal of freedom, whether reflectively or not, is to experience for the first time what is really meant by God and is to affirm or deny implicitly or explicitly his reality. To this insight it must be added that human transcendence, ordered to God in freedom and knowledge, is always and inescapably deepened, whether this is accepted or rejected, by what in Christian terms is called grace. In other words this transcendence is raised up by the self-communication of God and brought into direct contact with his presence in what we

---

[5] The background of these ideas is to be found in the author's two older works: *Spirit in the World*, (London and Sydney, 1968) and *Hearers of the Word* (London and Sydney, 1969). The position outlined there should however be supplemented by the works listed in note 4 dealing with a theology of freedom.

call the vision and possession of God.[6] If a man freely accepts himself as he is, even with regard to his own inner being whose basic constitution he inevitably has not fully grasped, then it is God he is accepting. As long as it is a matter of the conscious, though unreflective, acceptance of God in his authentic self-communication, the acceptance is of the self-revelation of God and is therefore faith.

The justification for such an assertion lies ultimately in the teaching of the Second Vatican Council, that genuine faith, whose object is revelation and whose consequence is salvation, is possible for *all* men. It can be found in people who consciously believe they are and must be atheists, as long as they are completely obedient to the absolute demands of conscience, that is, to use our terminology, they accept themselves unconditionally, without self-rejection, fulfilling that primordial capacity of freedom which involves the subject as a whole.[7] If this teaching of the Second Vatican Council is accepted, one can in my opinion only answer the question of how, from a theological point of view, to justify a faith which is universally available and can be realised even by atheists, by accepting the position outlined here of a fundamental identity of faith, taken in a Christian sense, and freedom, of emotion as freedom.

We must return to the question of human rationality as this is currently understood, and, without undermining its value, try to deepen it with regard to its basic presuppositions, even if once again we cannot give detailed arguments to support our account. We may express our thesis thus: the ultimate condition of possibility of rationality is the transcendent reference of man to the unfathomable mystery we call God.

The objective, functional connection of particular phenomena established by empirical reason is grounded as a single whole in the dynamic structure of the human spirit. The reference of the latter transcends the mastery of particular items of information and their systematic arrangement into the totality of possible categories of knowledge and is focused upon the ultimate goal of the whole move-

---

[6] Cf. 'Self-communication of God', *Sacr. Mun.* III (London and New York, 1968) pp. 114–118; *ibid.* IV, pp. 297–305; *ibid.* V, pp. 348–355. This idea is central to the author's position as B. van der Heijden (*Karl Rahner, Darstellung und Kritik seiner Grundpositionen*) has correctly seen, although his broader interpretation does not always do justice to the author's views.

[7] Cf. Conc. Vat. II, *Gaudium et Spes*, Pt. I, ch. 7, Arts. 12, 16, 17, 19, 20, 21.

ment of the human spirit, which we call absolute mystery[8] or God. This reference, which goes beyond all particular, intelligible objects to the incomprehensible mystery, is not just an inescapable fact, an additional possibility set beside rationality; it is precisely the condition of its possibility. If this dynamic reference to the incomprehensible mystery is called 'irrational', in a sense not yet discussed in these reflections, then the inevitable conclusion follows that this irrationality permanently remains the innermost core and condition of possibility of all rationality. Because we possess a primordial reference to the incomprehensible mystery, *therefore* we are able to set ourselves at a critical distance from every individual object and item of knowledge; we can distinguish and arrange particular objects of experience; we are capable of recognizing each individual piece of knowledge as provisional, ideologically suspect or open to improvement.

RADICAL TRANSFORMATION THROUGH GRACE

The reference to the unfathomable mystery of God, which is above reason and yet belongs to the inner being of rationality, is radically transformed, at least in the form of a universally available offer, and directed to the immediate presence of God by what in Christian language is called grace. This radical process no longer leaves God at a distance, approached but never attained, the far off mover of the impulses of the human spirit acting through knowledge and freedom; it makes God in himself an attainable goal, though he still remains an abiding mystery, even in the beatific vision. Thus the process can and should be described as revelation because it touches on the gratuitous self-communication of God to the human spirit. But this is not a reference merely to a particular piece of the history of revelation and salvation through God's self-communication, but forms its essential heart. The whole of the history of revelation and salvation of mankind can and should be understood as the *history in which* the radical refer-

---

[8] On the concept 'Mystery' cf. esp. the author's article in *Handbuch der Theologischer Grundbegriffe* I (Munich, 1962), pp. 447–452 (bibliog). Since the notion is easily taken to mean the unknown or what is as yet unknown (i.e. a question), a thorough account of the exact sense in which the term is being used is reasonable and necessary. In the ultimate analysis a Christian can only accept the existence of genuine mystery, if it embraces human rationality in its proper sense and does not endanger the real responsibility (freedom) which rationality brings.

ence of human rationality and freedom to the direct presence of God as abiding mystery comes to ever clearer expression under the guidance of God's saving providence.[9] The history of revelation is the history of human rationality, in as much as through the Holy Spirit, through God's self-communication in the Holy Spirit, rationality is laid open in its innermost being to the immediate reality of the incomprehensible mystery and comes to full self-realisation in and through history. The history of revelation is the history of rationality under the influence of grace in which reason grasps ever more plainly this mystery as its foundation and master and freely accepts it.

The history of revelation, then, fundamentally coincides with that of human rationality, understood in this radical sense. This intrinsically universal history of revelation becomes the revelation history contained in the Old and New Testaments to the extent that it is recognised as permanently made valid by Jesus Christ and not as corrupted by the free rejection of man. The revelation history which occurs in *Jesus* and is grasped by us in faith should not in the first instance be treated as a particular occurrence, however unique in character, within the totality of salvation history, but rather as that event in which the universal gift of God, bestowed upon the whole of mankind in the Holy Spirit and radically transforming human rationality, achieves clear and definitive historical expression in an irreversible, eschatological form. Christian faith is explicitly present whenever human rationality, transformed by grace and ordered to the direct reality of God, is freely accepted, given that in this acceptance it is understood and recognised that the self-gift of the absolute mystery finds decisive, historical realisation in Jesus Christ and is definitively accepted through the death of the man Jesus on the part of mankind.

Christian faith is not, therefore, a particular event among others, which occurs in the history of human rationality (history taken in a collective and individual sense), but is the primordial act of human rationality as such, which at the same time achieves through faith historical and eschatological self-realisation. The only assumption to be made is that rationality grasps its own disclosure and basis in the mystery, that it recognises its own liberation through God's grace and

---

[9] On the problem of salvation history cf. K. Rahner, 'History of the World and Salvation History', *Theological Investigations* V (London and Baltimore, 1966), pp. 97–114; *Theological Investigations* XI (London and New York, 1974), pp. 99–101; more fully, A. Darlap, 'Fundamentale Theologie der Heilsgeschichte', *MySal* I, pp. 3–156.

its ordering to the immediate presence of this mystery, and accepts the historical mediation of Jesus for its own self-realisation. Christian faith always achieves its full development through the medium of history and ultimately through Jesus, in so far as he has freely accepted the unfathomable mystery in his death and is himself saved and accepted once and for all in what we term his resurrection. But the historicity of Christian faith is not of an arbitrary sort, but rather the one in which human rationality, set free in its very roots for the direct presence of God, is mediated to itself.[10]

Thus Christian faith is not some particular event which could be limited and located anywhere in the area of rationality and emotion, and which must struggle hard to find a place somewhere 'between' these two realities. It is rather the ultimate event of rationality and emotion as a single whole, given only that rationality is grasped as rooted in the mystery of God and emotion is seen as the freedom by which a person comes to definitive self-acceptance and in which rationality, rightly understood, first discovers its genuine fulfilment in the acceptance of the mystery. Since Christian faith forms the totality of rationality and emotion and binds them together, it cannot be determined by any other reality outside itself, or by the experience of such reality, as long as we grasp the basic meaning of faith. It is rather the self-realisation of rationality and emotion coming to free and eschatological fulfilment in history.

This totality, which cannot be determined from without, is at once the simplest thing and the hardest, and the same is true of Christian faith, which consists in the fulfilment of the single human whole. It is the simplest thing in the world, the acceptance, that is, of the unfathomable mystery bestowed upon us,[11] and of the experience of this merciful self-communication as it is victoriously and irrevocably established in human history by the faith and death of Jesus. Christian faith possesses, then, of its essence no particular categorial content which is exempt from the doubts and threats attached to such facts, nor is it immune to the process and experience of ideological criticism.

---

[10] The thesis of a transcendental Christology is summarised in : K. Rahner and W. Thüsing, *Christologie, systematisch und exegetisch*, Quaestiones Disputatae 55 (Freiburg L. Br., 1972), pp. 15–78.

[11] It is essential for this encounter that the incomprehensible mystery is communicated to man as a force of forgiveness i.e. as demanding and effecting a conversion. Cf. K. H. Neufeld, ('Fortschritt durch Umkehr',) *Std Z* 192 (1974), pp. 274–281.

For the ungraspable mystery which, in the strictest sense of the term 'name', is nameless, is not a particular datum of fact. Jesus is only understood as the Christ, that is, as the definitive and victorious self-communication of mystery to the world, if his cross, his *death*, are accepted as the salvation and surrender of a man to this mystery, through which a human being transcends the complexity and the ambiguity of particular facts and experiences and enters the silent mystery of God.

All the remaining content of the Christian faith, and especially the social expression of this faith, namely the Church, does indeed consist in categorial data and particular formulations of these data, but it does not form an independent and additional element to this faith which can only be taught from without; it is rather deduced from the primordial fact of revelation and faith, which is the acceptance of the absolute mystery, first in Jesus and then derivatively in us. The inevitable, categorial expansion of this basic reality into many distinct propositions is a matter of history; it is a process carried on by the collective bearer of the history of revelation through reflection upon it and comes after Jesus and stems from him. It is not primarily undertaken by the individual. But this does not alter the fact that the freely accepted experience of this simple and basic reality must take place in every individual; only then is it an experience of the grace of faith and therefore genuine Christian faith. This process is very different from the indoctrination of propositions which, supported by formal authority, are brought to a person from without and must be accepted as the doctrine of experts not open to verification.

A faith which operates from the most simple and basic datum has the simplicity of the whole but also presents great difficulties. For it must find the verbal expression necessary for its articulation in concepts and realities which are not external and prior to it but rather subsequent, specific and derivative. Faith cannot be defined as a point in a larger frame of reference of human rationality and freedom, but forms the free acceptance of this frame of reference itself, the internal harmony of subject with himself. This is the reason why it is so hard to formulate in human conceptual thought what Christian faith is.

In considering these difficulties one should never forget that the essence of faith as the free acceptance of the single totality of rationality and emotion is never simply identical with any completely successful formulation of it in terms of conceptual reflection. Faith itself does not stem originally *from* the verbal communication of conceptual thought about it but occurs in a great variety of historical forms. These come about whenever a man accepts human existence composed of rationality and freedom in unconditional fidelity to his conscience. This means that the conceptual formulation of faith in the Christian message is in a sense secondary, although not superfluous, in comparison with the primary embodiment of faith.

The Christian message as it develops in revelation and faith may be secondary but this does not mean that the explicit, moral obligation of faith becomes unnecessary. For this message is the legitimate objective form of the primary reality which necessarily seeks historical expression and formulation. Furthermore to refuse to accept such an objective expression would be to deny the primary reality of faith and would therefore be unbelief in the most fundamental sense. Conversely a Christian can only be satisfied with his conformity to the articles of faith handed on to him through the teaching of the Church and often originating in an earlier historical period, when he has as intense an awareness as possible of the interior revelation which is given with the self-communication of God and is usually called grace. He must experience in every part of his life the inner direction of his being in knowledge and freedom to the unfathomable mystery of God. Spiritual instruction in this area, which embodies real vitality and energy, is rarely to be found in the Church today, so that it is hardly surprising if many people try to obtain the experience through mental techniques which either avoid the practices and scrutiny of the official Church or are found outside Christianity. In this respect the Church must have the courage to return afresh to its own experience of spirituality and mysticism which was much more alive in earlier times.[12]

TENSIONS

In proposing the fundamental thesis that at root faith, emotion and rationality form a unity, we should not overlook the tensions and opposition of a derivative but nevertheless essential kind that exist between them. A distinction has been drawn between the basic reality

[12] The different essays in this volume of the Investigations are intended to show how religious experiences of a spiritual or mystical kind can overflow and be transposed into the idiom of theological reflection. In this way the rift, all too common even today, between lived piety and abstract theology may be bridged.

of revelation and faith as the fulfilment of rationality and freedom on the one hand, and the conceptual reflection and verbal formulation of this primary fact on the other. If one considers this verbal expression and the scientific and systematic reflection upon it which is known as theology, then problems naturally arise between faith understood in this sense and human rationality and emotion. On this topic a few comments should be made which touch on the contemporary understanding of these three realities. We are dealing here with the objectified content of faith existing in human consciousness, that is, 'fides quae' (faith as object); we are not speaking of the primary realisation of 'fides qua' (faith as personal act) with which we have been mainly occupied up to this point.[13]

First of all it must be freely and honestly recognised that for an educated person to-day the mass of knowledge arising from the discoveries of the modern sciences, with their attendant problems and diversity, is too great to be mastered by a single individual and therefore generally prevents a person achieving an adequate positive integration and synthesis of the content of his mental world and the formulations of faith. This inevitably creates a state of tension between faith and rationality. It is true that a synthesis between 'fides quae' and modern 'scientia quae' (the objective content of science), if such an expression may be allowed, remains a desirable ideal, a goal to be aimed at even if never attained both for the individual and for the ecclesial community of faith. But in earlier periods knowledge and thought were of comparatively small dimensions and at least an alleged synthesis between the object of belief and the objects of secular knowledge was attainable. What distinguishes us from the past is that today such a synthesis is empirically beyond our reach. This does not mean that a man can allow, with an easy descent into irrationality, assertions of faith and propositions of secular science to exist side by side in a state of evident contradiction. What is to be done in the individual consciousness when someone is totally convinced that he perceives such a contradiction is not under discussion here, since as a Christian a man can and should be assured that such an opposition cannot objectively exist.[14]

[13] The author has said something about the distinction between 'fides qua' and 'fides quae' in his study, 'What is a Dogmatic Statement?' *Theological Investigations* V (London and Baltimore, 1966), pp. 42–66.

[14] On the subject of conscience, cf. K. Rahner, 'On the Encyclical 'Humanae vitae', *Theological Investigations* XI (London and New York, 1974)

This conclusion does not, however, settle the matter, for between straight contradiction of known propositions on the one hand and a positive synthesis of diverse items of knowledge drawn from various sources of experience and knowledge on the other, there lies a third possibility which is the fate of people today, believers included. This third state is one of plurality of propositions of faith and secular knowledge which an individual cannot work through or integrate into an adequate positive synthesis. This plurality is a burden for us and involves our emotions in the widest sense of the term in pain and suffering. We know too much today to be able as believers to integrate all our knowledge with our faith ('fides quae') and create out of them both a harmonious view of the world. We can, however, see from the theological point of view that this situation is not in fact to be wondered at. Christian theology has always recognised that a variety of good and evil impulses exist in man which can never be properly brought together in a person's fundamental stance vis-à-vis God, and has called this state concupiscence or inordinate desire. Today we have become more clearly aware than in earlier times that, in addition to the state of moral concupiscence, that is, plurality on the emotional level, there exists also a state of gnoseological or mental concupiscence, the plurality[15] of diverse secular and theological branches of knowledge. These all condition the human situation despite, and in virtue, of their mutual disparity and lack of harmony, and so maintain human consciousness in a state of basic inner conflict. But given that Christian faith has always taken cognisance of this, at least in the field of moral decisions, such mental concupiscence is hardly surprising. A man may freely take account of it and to be a Christian he does not need to behave as though this situation did not obtain. There are guidelines about how one can face the matter in patience and hope without

---

pp. 263–287; 'Heresies in the Church Today?', *Theological Investigations* XII (London, 1974), pp. 116–141; 'Perspectives for the Future of the Church', *ibid.*, pp. 202–217; 'Kirche im Wandel', *Schriften zur Theologie* VI (Zurich, 1968), pp. 445–478.

[15] On the question of intellectual pluralism today and the 'mental concupiscence' of human knowledge, cf. K. Rahner, 'Pluralism in Theology and the Unity of the Creed in the Church,' *Theological Investigations* XI (London and New York, 1974), pp. 3–23; 'The Future of Theology', *ibid.*, pp. 137–146; 'The Current Relationship of Philosophy and Theology', *Theological Investigations* XII (London, 1975), pp. 61–79; 'The Faith of the Christian and the Doctrine of the Church', *Theological Investigations* XIV (London, 1976), pp. 24–46.

having to deny its existence or sweep it under the carpet. A man can be a Christian and deal honestly with the situation; he is not allowed to use his faith to deny it. Complete success in creating a world view which integrates faith and secular knowledge in a positive and harmonious synthesis is not an ideal which it is open to a Christian to believe attainable during his earthly life.

CHARACTERISTICS OF THE RELATIONSHIP

There is a history involved in the relationship between rationality and the content of faith ('fides quae') in which we must live as believers. If one were to list the special characteristics which determine the relation between 'fides quae' and 'scientia quae' *today*, one might put it as follows.[16]

The relationship between Christian faith and the natural sciences was from the origin of these sciences very tense but has now become more harmonious and relaxed. For no proven discoveries of the natural sciences can be formulated against which Christian faith is obliged to protest. The results of biology, palaeontology, etc no longer meet with opposition from theology. Christian philosophy and theology can maintain an entirely positive stance towards a secret ideal of the natural sciences which foresees as a methodological and heuristic principle the development of as close a unity as possible of all known material phenomena. This ideal theology can applaud, provided only that the natural sciences do not go beyond their methodological assumptions and become blind to the internal structure of the one world which is essentially varied and diverse.

On the other hand the relationship between faith and science is not simply settled in this way. It is a matter much less of a minimal, negative reconciliation between particular theological and scientific statements than of the tension still existing today between a scientific and a religious or metaphysical *mentality*. Here we can merely observe that the enduring burden of this tension belongs to the mental plurality or concupiscence which we have already considered. The coexistence of both outlooks in the same mind is entirely possible if one looks at the evidence offered by the lives of scientists of the highest rank.

[16] Cf. K. Rahner, 'Theology as engaged in an Interdisciplinary Dialogue with the Sciences', *Theological Investigations* XIII (London, 1975), pp. 80–93, esp. pp. 90–93.

With regard to the historical sciences, it is to be noted that here many particular problems have been resolved, in so far as theology has grasped the lesson that in the case of theological statements as well as others a more exact distinction can and must be drawn than before between the meaning of a theological statement and the propositional model and its horizon of understanding, which is conditioned by historical factors. It has been shown that the independence of past and present theological statements and their proper meaning can be maintained despite the fundamental and legitimate process of demythologisation occasioned by the distinction drawn above. Human history understood aright is open to God and contains in itself what must be called divine revelation, without thereby implying miraculous interventions in an otherwise secular world. Nevertheless there persists here too a state of concupiscence in the relationship between secular history with its limited methods and theology as the ultimate interpretation of history which goes beyond history to the mystery of God.

From modern psychology and especially from depth psychology theology has learnt more clearly concerning its own material that man is bodily and not just an abstract subject of spirit and transcendence, a fact which was always known in theology but never filled out with sufficient content. Man is thus a psychic being with an inner shape which can be exactly ascertained and exists prior to the free spiritual activity of the personal subject; he exhibits a structure and mechanisms which cannot be adequately controlled by the spiritual subject. Furthermore techniques exist for the individual and collective direction of the pre-personal psyche which cannot be displaced by a rational and moral appeal to a person as a free spiritual subject.[17] If for this reason theology has had to take a more modest stance concerning man and can no longer claim to the sole representative of anthropology, but is in a position of open dialogue with other sciences, that is all to the good and in fact corresponds to the basic meaning of faith and theology.

Over and above the earlier philosophy of law and the state, there are today a whole range of social sciences, whose existence and rationality faith and theology must be prepared to face. This is of the greatest importance for theology, even though these partners in dialogue did not exist in the past. Such an interchange gives rise to new and difficult

---

[17] Cf. K. Rahner and A. Görres, 'Der Leib in der Heilsordnung', *Schriften zur Theologie* XII (Zurich 1975), pp. 407–427.

questions. One need only consider the philosophy and sociology of language to see its significance for the theology of the word; one might note also the critical analysis of ideology, the research into the secular and social pre-conditions of religion and its institutions, the whole question of the relationship between truth and institution, the critiques by sociology of the traditional ethical models and the traditional understanding of natural law. Of course the critical rationality of the social sciences raises a question mark for theology. But at the same time it must be said that these sciences do not succeed in reducing religion to a historically conditioned phenomenon which is now out of date, if only because of the particular starting point of their methods of analysis nd the questionable nature of their philosophical roots.

We must now break off our reflections. In a situation of insuperable pluralism of knowledge and endeavour characteristic of the present age, faith will always be the object of dispute and opposition, and it cannot in practice reckon on being universally recognised.[18] But it is not the case today that the conceptual and verbal formulation of faith need be in deadly opposition to the rationality of modern science and the general intellectual climate. The presupposition for this hope, which must constantly be re-assessed, is twofold, first that these sciences no longer assert that from their particular categorial starting point everything legitimately falls within their province, and secondly that faith is not essentially understood as a limited body of propositions within the whole social, psychological and historical range of consciousness, but rather the realisation of the single totality of rationality and freedom. The single totality of the reality of man does not exist in a state of hostile competition with the partial dimensions and expressions of human existence, as long as we assume that a man has a task to perform which concerns him as a unified whole and that he has the capacity and duty to give objective expression to this whole, even though the form of expression is limited, historically conditioned and open to the absolute future of the divine mystery.[19]

[18] These remarks should sound a note of necessary realism but should not be taken to imply resignation or defeatism. The author's views on responsible thought and action may be seen, for example, in *Strukturwandel der Kirche als Aufgabe und Chance* (Freiburg i. Br., 1972).

[19] The author's studies on the 'Theology of the Future', taken from *Theological Investigations* Vols. IV, V, VI, VIII, IX, have been collected in the Wissenschaftlichen Reihe des Deutschen Taschenbuch Verlags (dtv 4076; Munich, 1971).

If the essential nature of faith is understood as the single totality of rationality and freedom, it does not follow that possible conflicts and tensions between the *conceptual expressions* of faith on the one hand by which faith comes to have a place, even if in a derivative sense, within the field of conceptual rationality and science, and categorial rationality of a secular kind on the other, that such tensions are ruled out from the start or are already positively resolved. But the believer need not see a fundamental and irreconcilable clash between the conceptual expressions of faith and secular rationality. He will accept the mental concupiscence of plurality in his mind with patience and tranquillity and try to master it as far as possible. And he will go forward in the hope of the promised reconciliation of this plurality which he will obtain on entering the eternal mystery, no longer looking forward to unity in diversity as a mere promise but being able to experience the diversity through the possession of the single mystery. Anselm of Canterbury once coined the phrase: 'irrationalia rationabiliter cogitare',[20] to think out the irrational in a rational manner. If one treats the term 'irrationalia' not in the sense of a primitive irrationality in the face of which basic rational efforts are abandoned as hopeless from the start, but rather as implying the unfathomable mystery which is experienced at the root of our rationality and freedom, then the phrase says exactly what is meant here. Faith is not of its nature something which has to struggle laboriously for a place between rationality and emotion; it is rather the single fundamental whole composed of rationality and freedom. It is, therefore, possible to reflect further on this in a rational way ('rationabiliter cogitare'), to meditate upon faith and its objective expression in freedom and tranquillity, because this meditation itself belongs to faith.

---

[20] This term is meant to cover the famous principle of Anselm, 'Fides quaerens intellectum'. The actual word, however, has not been found as yet in Anselm's writing.

PART TWO

Spiritual Theology in Christian Tradition

6

THE 'SPIRITUAL SENSES' ACCORDING TO
ORIGEN

IF religious, and especially mystical, experience seeks to express the inexpressible despite all the obstacles that lie in the way, then inevitably it must go back to images which come from the realm of sense knowledge.[1] Mystics are happy, therefore, to speak of sight, hearing and taste of a spiritual kind in order to describe their experience of the realities of which they were conscious. Modern mystical theology retains this imaginative language and tries to interpret it.[2] It would seem, therefore, a worthwhile undertaking to sketch the history of the idea of the spiritual senses. One might discover that perhaps not every epoch or school compares mystical experience with the working of the same sense faculty and that their analogies are borrowed primarily from one or other sense perception. This diversity of modes of expression might then be traced back either to a variety of mystical experiences or to the human way of understanding in which the mystical experience was interpreted in different schools and historical periods.[3]

[1] This text, published for the first time in German, goes back to the first major theological study written by the author, which appeared in French in *RAM* 13 (1932), pp. 113–145. Here it has been simplified and abridged, and is included because the theme it deals with is closely connected to the other writings which form this collection. It is also of decisive importance for the author's ideas, and points to a line of thought which remained operative, albeit in a concealed way, in his later work.

[2] Cf. A. Poulain, *The Graces of Interior Prayer* (London, 1950), pp. 88 sq. In the first decades of this century this book played a considerable role in Europe in the discussion of the spiritual senses.

[3] P. Bainvel, editor of the 10th edition of Poulain's work, says in the introduction, p. 19: 'On the lower levels mystics refer particularly to the

THE POINTS OF DEPARTURE IN ORIGEN

We have a modest goal in view here. Our concern is to investigate more closely the points of departure in Origen of the concept of spiritual senses and their influence on the later spiritual literature which arose from them. This essay is thus limited in two ways: first, only a short period is being considered and secondly, numerous religious texts will remain unexamined in which only a single faculty is employed for the metaphorical portrayal of spiritual experience.[4] For one can only speak properly of an idea or doctrine of spiritual faculties when these partly imaginative, partly literal expressions such as to touch God, to open the eyes of the heart, etc. are found in a complete system in which five instruments are involved in the spiritual perception of immaterial realities.[5] If an author then clearly speaks of five spiritual faculties, we are justified in taking into account texts which only refer to a single faculty.[6]

Origen seems to be the first to have formulated such a doctrine of five spiritual senses[7] and he frequently comes back to this topic. We have to wait until St Bonaventure in the Middle Ages to find similarly extensive treatment of this notion.[8] We see the teaching of Origen continued in the literature of the Greek world, and this later stimulated speculation among the Scholastics, but the theme very obviously is the result of tradition and loses its vitality. We may obtain a first impression of Origen's idea from the following piece of his writing:

---

touch, taste, feel or breath of God which are present in them. Understanding and especially sight are only spoken of the higher levels.' Bonaventure, on the contrary, places 'touch' on a higher level than 'sight' in mystical experience. These variations of expressions contain more than a terminological difference; rather they clearly point to a basic divergence of speculative understanding of mystical experience.

[4] Cf. e.g. PS 33:9; 8:9; Ac 17:27; 2 Cor 2:18; Eph 1:18.

[5] This definition is not meant to prejudge the question of the form which the doctrine takes in the individual writers.

[6] The goal of A. Poulain is different from ours, and so he appeals to different texts.

[7] The most important texts in Origen are: *De principiis* 1. I c. 1 n. 7. 9. 11; 1. II c n. 3; c. 9 n. 4. *Contra Celsum* 1. I n. 48; 1. VII n. 34. *In Levit* hom. 31 n. 7. *In Ezech.* hom. 11 n. *In Cant. Cant.* 1. I and 1. II. *In Matth. comm. ser.* n. 63–64. *In Luc.* fragm. 53 and 57. *In Joan.* t. X n. 40; t. XIII n. 24.

[8] Cf. K. Rahner, 'The Doctrine of the "Spiritual Senses" in the Middle Ages: the contribution of St. Bonaventure', in this volume.

'After thorough investigation one can say that there exists, according to the word of Scripture, a general sense or faculty for the divine. Only the blessed know how to find it, as we read in the Wisdom of Solomon, "You discover the divine faculty of perception." (Prov. 2:5). This sense, however, unfolds in various individual faculties: sight for the contemplation of immaterial forms, as is evidently granted to the Cherubim and Seraphim, hearing for the discrimination of voices, which do not echo in the empty air, taste in order to savour the living bread which came down from heaven to bring life to the world (John 6:33), and even a sense of smell, with which Paul perceived those realities which caused him to describe himself as a sweet odour of Christ (2 Cor. 2:15), and finally touch, which possessed John when he states that he has touched with his own hands the Word of life. (1 John 1:1). This sense for the divine was discovered by the prophets . . .'[9]
'Solomon already realised that there are two modes of sense perception, one mortal, transient and human, and the other immortal, spiritual and divine.'[10]

How did Origen arrive at this doctrine? As far as can be discovered, he must have drawn it from no other source than Scripture.[11] Those passages in particular come into question in which religious understanding is expressed in terms which manifest the operations of sense powers.[12] Nothing need be said here about the exegesis of these passages, which in fact simply contain well chosen metaphors and do not involve any doctrine of five spiritual sense faculties.

As mentioned above, Origen bases his conceptions upon the text of Prov 2:5, but he also refers to Heb 5:14. He reads the Old Testament text after his own fashion and does not follow the Septuagint and other translations in interpreting the passage to mean the knowledge

[9] *Contra Celsum* 1. I n. 48 (GCS 2) 98, 9sqq.
[10] *De Principiis* 1. I c. 1 n. 9 (GCS 22) 27,8 sqq.
[11] Philo is not familiar with this doctrine as it is found in Origen. Yet many of his expressions point to it in a preliminary way. References are to be found in the French edition of this study. Clement of Alexandria uses the two scriptural references (Prov 2:5 and Heb 5:4) which served as a starting point for Origen. Apart from 'bodily senses', Tertullian is familiar with 'intellectual senses', whose object is the 'immaterial powers' of the soul (such as good, evil, etc.); he also speaks of the eyes and ears of the inner man, with which Paul saw and heard the Lord.
[12] The scriptural passages used by Origen are: Eyes: Ps 18:9; Eph 1:18. Ears: Mt 13:9; 2 Cor 12:2sq. Taste: Ps 33:9; Jn 6:32sq. Smell: 2 Cor 12:15. Touch: 1 Jn 1:1.

of God as the fruit and reward for labours endured; rather he extracts and exphasises the sense character of the knowledge, from which he deduces that man possesses, over and above his bodily faculties, 'a sense for the divine, which is completely different from the senses as normally described' or simply 'divine faculties of sense'.

In the New Testament passage the early Christians are blamed for not digesting the solid nourishment of the higher knowledge proper for adults and for still needing the milk of the basic elements of Christian teaching. Here it is added that this 'solid food' is the nourishment of 'the perfect', whose faculties are trained to distinguish between good and evil. The commentators interpret this to mean the capacity for moral discrimination[13] but Origen understands the passage in the same way as the Old Testament quotation from Proverbs. The New Testament statement fits even better into his system in that only the perfect (the exact significance of the term requires closer examination) are endowed with these spiritual faculties, which they have brought to a higher level of operation through constant practice.

Origen appeals also to Jer 4:19.[14] His allegorical and systematic method of exegesis tends naturally to read into these texts a theory of five spiritual senses.

THE DEVELOPMENT OF THE IDEA

In his polemic against Celsus, Origen took his teaching a stage further. Celsus had concluded from the Christian dogma of the resurrection from the dead that Christians believed in a material, sense knowledge of God.[15] This notion Origen rejects. When Scripture speaks of eyes, ears, etc., with which God is perceived, then what is clearly meant are eyes, ears and hands which only have the name in common with the bodily organs. And Scripture also refers, which is more remarkable, to a sense faculty for the divine which is radically different from everything which men call sense faculties at all.

At this point the personal tendency of Origen to interpret all genuine religious experience in psychological terms come into play; he

---

[13] It is interesting to note that the exegetes saw in this expression from the Letter to the Hebrews a correspondence with the language of Philo which must have been known to the Alexandrian Origen.

[14] In Matth. comm. ser. 66 (GCS 38).

[15] Contra Celsum 1.VII n.33 (GCS 3) 183,24. Origen rejects this conclusion, cf. ibid. 1 VII n.34.

does this even in the case of mystical experience. It is no accident that the most beautiful and searching exposition of this teaching is to be found in the commentary of the Song of Songs, which since Origen is *the* book for mystics and in which, in his own words, 'Solomon uses the image of bride and bridegroom to awaken in the soul love of heaven and longing for divine blessings and instructs the soul how to climb the path of love of neighbour right up to union with God.[16]

Looked at more closely this view means that beside our five bodily senses we possess five more, the sense faculty of the soul,[17] the divine faculties,[18] the faculties of the interior man,[19] the faculties of the heart,[20] spiritual senses,[21] a 'kind of sense faculty which is immortal, spiritual and divine',[22] 'a sensuality that has nothing sensual in it',[23] 'a higher sense faculty which is not bodily'[24] or 'a divine sensuality, completely different from this reality as normally defined by men'.[25] Frequently he simply speaks of five senses.[26]

Origen derives the existence of these faculties from the scriptural references already quoted and other passages, where seeing, hearing God, etc. is mentioned and where it cannot be a question of the bodily senses. Celsus already knew of the 'eyes of the soul', of which he had heard from the Greeks.[27] But this notion was common among Christians even earlier.[28] The 'animal man' and the unbeliever make a great joke of this doctrine and from their point of view this is hardly surprising, but the believer must allow himself to be instructed by the word of God.[29] Unbelief is shown precisely in the lack of the spiritual senses in certain people, who are then naturally incapable of perceiving spiritual realities.[30]

---

[16] *In Cant.* prol. (GCS 33) 76, 14 sqq.
[17] *Ibid.* (GCS 33) 105,31 and 167,25 sqq.
[18] *In Luc.* fragm. 57 (GCS 35) 260 sq.
[19] *In Cant.* I (GCS 33) 105, 5:16; *In Lev.* hom. 3 n. 7 (GCS 29) 312,15 sqq.
[20] *De Principiis* 1 II c. 4 n. 3 (GCS 22) 131,5.
[21] Cf. *De Or.* 13,4 (GCS 3) 329,14.
[22] *De Principiis* 1 I c. 1 n. 9 (GCS 22) 27,8 sqq.
[23] *Contra Celsum* 1. I n. 48 (GCS 2) 98,22.
[24] *Ibid.* 1 VII n.34 (GCS 3) 185,13 sq.
[25] *Ibid.* 1 VII n.34 (GCS 3) 184,26.
[26] *Ibid.* 1 I. n. 48 (GCS 2) and 1. VII n.34 (GCS 3).
[27] *Ibid.* 1. VII n. 39 (GCS 3) 189,22.
[28] *Ibid.*
[29] *In Cant.* I (GCS 33) 106 sq. and *In Luc.* fragm. 57 (GCS 35) 260 sq.
[30] *In Cant.* I (GCS 33) 107, 7 sqq.

The character of the spiritual senses becomes clearer if one investigates more closely what sort of men possess them, what reality they grasp and how they operate and develop. There are people, as we have seen, whose spiritual sense of sight is blind, of hearing dumb, of smell dull. Origen says explicitly that not every man possesses these spiritual faculties.[31] Thus, for example, the eyes of Adam were closed after his sin.[32] Certain people may develop a particular sense but never come to the full use of all five. So the 'virgins' in the Song of Songs only possessed the sense of smell from following the bride,[33] because they had not yet reached the 'summa perfectionis'.[34] Only the 'perfect', the 'blessed' and the 'just'[35] have control over the use of all the faculties, and here these terms must be given their full breadth of meaning proper to Origen. Such figures as, for instance, Isaac, Moses, the prophets, John and Paul belong to the number of the perfect, as well as the blessed in heaven.[36]

To the possession of the spiritual faculties is allied the knowledge of the 'intellectualia',[37] the 'blessings from above and those which are beyond man',[38] 'of the spiritual',[39] and 'of that which is better than the body'.[40] In basing himself upon Scripture, Origen is able to define the object of each particular sense, as in the following text:

'Christ is grasped by every faculty of the soul. He is characterised as the true light which illuminates the eyes of the soul. He calls himself the word so as to be heard, the bread of life to be tasted. He is called the oil of anointing and nard, so that the soul rejoices in the sweet aroma of the Logos. He became the Word made flesh which can be expressed and comprehended, so that the inner man may lay hold of

---

[31] *In Luc.* fragm. 53 (GCS 35) 259,47. *Contra Celsum* 1. II n. 72 (GCS 2) 194, 18; *ibid.* 1. VIII n. 19 (GCS 3) 236,30.

[32] *Contra Celsum* 1. VII n. 39 (GCS 3) 190, 2 sqq.

[33] *In Cant.* I (GCS 33) 103,19.27.

[34] *In Cant.* I (GCS 33) 110,32.

[35] *In Joan.* t. XIII n.24 (GCS 10) 248,25 sqq. *In Luc.* frgm. 53 (GCS 35) 258, 9 sqq. *In Cant.* I (GCS 33) 105, 1 sqq. *De Principiis* 1. I. C. 1 n. 9 (GCS 22) 27,8 sq. *In Luc.* fragm. 57 (GCS 35) 260,3.

[36] *Contra Celsum* 1. I n. 48 (GCS 2) 98. *De Principiis* 1. II c. 4 n.3 (GCS 131), 4 sqq. *In Cant.* I (GCS 33) 104, 17 sqq.

[37] *De Principiis* 1. IV c. 4 n. 10 (GCS 22) 364, 10.

[38] *In Luc.* fragm. 57 (GCS 35) 261,4.

[39] *In Joan.* t. x n.40 (GCS 10) 218,8; *ibid.* t.XIII n.24 (GCS 10) 248,6.

[40] *Contra Celsum* 1. I n.48 (GCS 2) 98,13. *In Luc.* hom 3 (GCS 35) 20,18: 'superna et divina'.

the Word of life. This same Word of God is all this (Light, Word, etc); it comes to be through the fire of intense prayer and leaves none of the spiritual faculties empty of grace.'[41]

Origen expressly states that only a single reality can affect two faculties simultaneously and each sense grasps the reality in a different manner according to its own specific perfection.[42]

THE EXERCISE OF THE FIVE SENSES

How are the spiritual faculties to be developed? A person does not possess them in the measure which enables him really to grasp 'superna et divina'. The ear may be spiritually deaf.[43] The cause of such insensitivity is to be sought in sin. So Origen alludes to 'contentio' and 'iactantia'.[44] The sinful obstacles he calls 'ignorantia et imperitia' as well as 'malitia' in his system of asceticism.[45]

In order to vitalise the spiritual faculties, both grace and practice are indispensable. For their correct use the Logos itself is the foundation, who bestows light to the eyes of the soul and grace to the spiritual senses, in that through grace he makes room for himself in our faculties.[46] The angels can also influence them and in any event the reality must permit itself to be grasped by the faculties,[47] without the human agent being able thereby to abandon his efforts.

The physical faculties are strengthened by constant practice; it is just the same with the spiritual senses.[48] The efforts of the bodily senses must be followed by the mastery of spiritual faculties,[49] where indeed a great deal of training is required.[50]

[41] *In Cant.* II (GCS 33) 167,25 sqq.
[42] *Ibid.* III (GCS 33) 180,25 sqq; *ibid.* II (GCS 33) 172,8sqq.
[43] *Contra Celsum.* 1. II n. 72 (GCS 2) 194,18.
[44] *In Cant.* I (GCS 33) 107,10 sq.
[45] *Ibid.* 1 (GCS 33) 105,22 sqq.
[46] *Contra Celsum* 1. VI n. 151 (GCS 3) 202, 17; *ibid.* 1. VII n.39 (GCS 3) 190,2 sqq. *In Matth.* comm. ser. n. 63 (GCS 38); *In Matth.* t. XVI n. 11 (GCS 40). *In Cant.* III (GCS 33) 203,28: 'sensibus mihi animae videtur lumen praebere'; *ibid.* II (GCS 33) 168,4 sq. *De Principiis* 1. II c. 9 n.4 (GCS 22) 167 sq.
[47] *In Matth. comm.* ser. n.64 (GCS 38); according to the general principle that angels can cause contemplation. cf. *De Principiis* 1. III c. 2n. 4 (GCS 22) 250,20 sqq. *In Luc.* hom. 3 (GCS 35) 20-23: this idea runs through the whole homily. *Contra Celsum* 1. II. n. 72 (GCS 2) 194, 11 sqq.
[48] *In Ezech.* hom 11 n. 1 (GCS 33) 423 sq. *In Cant.* I (GCS 33) 105, 14 sqq.
[49] *In Levit.* hom 3 n. 7 (GCS 29) 312,15 sqq.
[50] *In Luc.* fragm. 53 (GCS 35) 258,10 sq.

The first and most important condition for this is faith. In addition Origen speaks of 'eruditio' and 'industria' as well as attentiveness to the mystical sense of Scripture.[51] At the same time a man must free himself from domination by the physical faculties, so that the eye of the soul has clarity of vision to the extent to which we close the eye of the body.[52] Above all it is prayer which exercises the spiritual faculties.[53] Everyone who trains himself in this way becomes one of the 'perfect'. No one who has really grasped Christ with his senses can be turned aside by anything else. Christ is everything for him; what he sought he has found in Christ. The divine senses first achieve total fulfilment at the moment when we enter into direct communion with Christ. Then we are finally set over great things having been faithful in small things.[54]

To connect this notion to the rest of Origen's psychological ideas, one should first of all point to the well known distinction between soul and spirit. The exact relationship between the two in his mind is not easy to work out, but the basic idea is that the spirit becomes soul as it voluntarily sets itself apart from God and the soul is transformed into spirit by being cleansed in the material world, its place of purification, and by return to God.[55] But the terminology of Origen is not entirely clear. Often spirit and soul mean the same thing,[56] so that they appear, especially in his ascetical writings, to be two aspects of man set over against each other.[57] This obscure mode of expression explains why Origen often speaks of the 'faculties of the soul', although knowledge of the divine is restricted according to his teaching to the 'spirit'.[58] But

[51] *In Cant.* II (GCS 33) 166,19 sqq. *In Matth. comm.* ser. n.63 (GCS 38). *In Cant.* I (GCS 33) 105,23.

[52] *Contra Celsum* 1. VII n.39 (GCS 3) 190, 6 sqq. *In Joan.* t. x̄ n.40 (GCS 10) 218,4 sqq.

[53] *In Cant.* II (GCS 33) 168,3-5. *Contra Celsum*. 1. VII n.44 (GCS 3) 195 sq. *De orat.* 9,2 (GCS 3) 318,26 sqq.

[54] *In Cant.* I (GCS 33) 103,27 sqq. and 104,17 sq.

[55] *In Principiis* 1. II c. 8 n.3 and *ibid.* 1. 1c. 8 n.4 (GCS 22); cf. *DThC* X1/2 (Paris 1931) 1532–1534 (G. Bardy).

[56] Cf. *De Orat.* 27,2 (GCS 3) 364,23 sqq, where several ideas are used in the same sentence with the same meaning. Similarly *Cantra Celsum* 1.VII n.4 (GCS 3), 156,4 sq.

[57] Cf. *De orat.* 24,2 (GCS 3) 353,24 sq. *In Joan* fragm. 3 (GCS 10), 486,32 sq. *Contra Celsum* 1. VIII n.52 (GCS 3) 267,24. cf. also *DThC* t1/2 (Paris, 1931) 1534.

[58] *In Cant.* 1 (GCS 33) 105,31; *ibid.* II (GCS 33) 167,25 sq. *In Ezech.* hom. II. n. 1 (GCS 33) 424, 1 etc. It also comes before the 'taste of the soul', the

the expression 'faculties of the spirit' is also to be found.[59] This implies that the spiritual faculties should be treated as organs of the spirit directed to the understanding of spiritual realities. Their specific functions are attributed by Origen to the 'spirit', which recognises the 'incorporea' and 'intellectualia' and discovers the divine sense, while the intellect only reaches a certain higher level of insight.[60] The 'spirit' alone grasps invisible and spiritual blessings.

When reference is made to the five spiritual faculties as organs of the 'spirit' by which spiritual realities are perceived, one must not overlook the analogy which rests behind the employment of the names of bodily organs for the capacities of the spirit. These concepts are to a greater or lesser extent to be taken in an imaginative sense.[61]

Did Origen really conceive of five distinct organs operating in religious knowledge? Or were spiritual sight, hearing, etc. not rather for him different imaginative expressions for the 'spirit', the real organ of perception? The first alternative seems the more probable, since Origen can also characterise the spiritual senses as powers of the soul,[62] which are, as it were, different species of the general divine sense, as appears in the works of Solomon.[63] In his view the power of the soul is to be distinguished in the spiritual faculties from the power of taste[64] in the same way as the bodily senses differ among themselves. According to Origen not every man possesses all the spiritual senses, but often only one or other of them. When he stresses the imaginative significance of these expressions, he means to point out that these scriptural terms are to be understood in an imaginative sense in that they can be ascribed to spiritual sense faculties and not to physical ones.[65]

'smell of the soul', etc.

[59] *De Principiis* 1. Ic. 1 n.7 (GCS 22) 24,8.9

[60] *De Principiis* 1. IIc. 8 n.2 (GCS 22) 154,27 sqq. and *ibid.* 1. IV c. 4 n. 10 (GCS 22) 364. The close relation between the 'spirit' and the sense of the divine is particularly evident here.

[61] *Contra Celsum* 1. VII n.34 (GCS 3) 185, 11 and *ibid.* n. 38 (GCS 3) 188,21 and *ibid.* 1. VI n.61 (GCS 3) 132, 3. *In Luc.* fragm 53 (GCS 35) 259,30. *De Principiis* 1. IC 1 n. 9 (GCS 22) 26, 15 sqq. *In Exod* hom 10 n.3 (GCS 29) 247,22. *In Cant.* prol (GCS 33) 65, 15 sqq; 66,4 sqq.

[62] *De Principiis* 1. I c. 1 n. 9: Powers of the soul; cf. *In Luc.* fragm 53.

[63] *Contra Celsum* 1. I n.48 (GCS 2) 98,12.

[64] *In Joan.* t. xx n.43 (GCS 10) 386,23 sq.

[65] What is said about the relationship of the 'spirit' to the spiritual senses, applies also to the relation of the 'principale cordis' (according to the transla-

THE PLACE OF SPIRITUAL FACULTIES WITHIN THE SYSTEM

How does this doctrine fit into Origen's thinking as a whole? Two basic principles of his spiritual system must first be outlined, although we do not of course have the scope here for a detailed exposition of his ascetical and mystical teaching.

Normally a division within the spiritual life between an active and a contemplative side is deduced from the distinction between 'soul' and 'spirit', a contrast, that is, between 'praxis' and 'theory',[66] between 'men of action' and 'men of theory'.[67] It is easy to see the relation of these two aspects of *Way of the Lord*[68] in Origen's psychological doctrine. According to him the 'soul', in contrast to the 'spirit', possesses two sides, aggression and desire, as he repeatedly remarks.[69] The moral danger for the soul ultimately lies in the passions and errors to which it is prone. So the task of the spiritual life is to combat these passions and errors in order to purify and sanctify the soul. This is the role played by the active, practical life. In Origen's language the obstacle to be tackled is called 'bad' or 'evil', and the goal to be striven for virtue, proper behaviour, righteousness or the observance of the laws of God.[70] At the highest point of the 'active life' a man arrives at

---

tion of Jerome and Rufinus) to these senses, so that the two are synonymous. Jerome also uses the term 'mens', i.e. precisely in the sense of 'spirit'. This is the favourite usage of Origen for the principle of religious knowledge; cf. *In Jer.* hom. 5 n. 9 (GCS 33) 39, 7–8.11; *In Num.* hom. 10 n.3 (GCS 29) 63,19: 'principale ... quod solum recipere potest mysteria veritatis et capax esse arcanorum Dei', also *In Cant.* II (GCS 33) 170,14 sqq. The perceptions of the spiritual senses can also be explained by their effects upon the 'principale'; cf. *Contra Celsum* 1. I n.48 (GCS 2) 97,32 sqq. Thus Origen can see perfection in the possession of the spiritual senses and can call it either 'the kingdom of God' or 'the blessed state of the spirit'; cf. *De orat* 25 (GCS 3) 359,9 sq.

[66] *In Luc.* fragm. 13 (GCS 35) 283,8; *ibid.* hom. 1 (GCS 35) 9,26–10,1, etc.

[67] *Select. in Psalm.* (PG 12, 1652 C ; 1249 D; 1581 D); cf. *In Joan* fragm. 36 (GCS 10) 512,23.

[68] *In Joan.* t..VI n. 19 (GCS 10) 127,29 sq.

[69] *In Luc.* fragm. 54 (GCS 35) 260,10 sq. *In Ezech.* hom. 1 n. 16 (GCS 33) 340,3 sq. 20 sq. *In Gen.* hom. 1 n. 17 (GCS 29) 20,23 sq.; *ibid.* hom. 2 n. 6 (GCS 29) 38,16 sq. etc.

[70] Cf. *Select in Psalm.* (PG12, 1304 B; 1552 D; 1684 D). Surprisingly enough the clearest formulations of Origen's spiritual teaching are to be found in the *Selct. in Psalm.* However, it is not certain that the whole work is authentically that of Origen and should only be used therefore with reservation. But the undoubtedly genuine writings of Origen provide enough evidence of his spiritual teaching to guarantee the accuracy of our account. On the *Select in Psalm* cf. E. de Faye, *Origène* (Paris 1923), t.I. pp. 210–213.

'indifference' or 'apathy'[71] and close to this point, or at least on the same level, there appear love and purity.[72] Such an active life necessarily precedes the contemplative, for, as we saw, purity is the precondition for knowledge of God, which forms the heart of the contemplative life. Only knowledge of God removes the labour of the active life.[73] In this sense praxis comes before theory;[74] practical men have their place in the forecourts of house of the Lord, while men of theory dwell in the house itself.[75] This ordering of the stages of the spiritual life is not reversible.[76]

The realm of the 'spirit' is 'theory'[77] and the essence of the contemplative life is precisely 'spiritual knowledge',[78] a bread, in Origen's words, 'which contains what is hidden and makes clear faith in God and knowledge of the things of God',[79] and stands therefore in direct contrast to the normal bread of the observance of divine commands. The obstacle to be overcome here is the 'spirit's' absence of knowl-

---

[71] *Select. in Psalm.* (PG 12, 1085 B; 1672 C). Apart from the *Select in Psalm*, the expression 'apathy' is rarely found in Origen.

[72] If the whole meaning of the active life consists in meditation, then the significance of love and purity rests on their close connection to theory. Only the pure man is capable of it. cf. *Contra Celsum* 1.III n.60 (GCS 2) 255,7; *ibid.* 1 IV n. 96 (GCS 2); also *ibid.* 1 VI n.69; 1 VII n.33 and 45 (GCS 3) 196,17 sq. etc. It is characteristic of love that the fall of the spirits is presented as the separation from love and contemplation; love is above all the other virtues and above every form of knowledge. Despite this, the intellectual aspect of perfection is over-emphasised.

[73] *Select in Psalm.* (PG 12, 1644 b).

[74] *Ibid.* (PG 12, 1173 B).

[75] *Ibid.* (PG.12, 1652 C).

[76] *Ibid.* (PG 12, 1641 D–1644 A). Knowledge of God and not innocence makes man blessed. (cf. PG 12, 1588 C).

[77] *In Ezech.* hom. 1 n.16 (GCS 33) 340,21.

[78] Cf. footnotes 66 and 67.

[79] *In Levit.* hom. 13 n. 3 (GCS 30) 472,4 sq. Here and at similar places we touch on a problem that can only be mentioned in passing. What connection is there between Origen's spiritual doctrine of the distinction between the active and the contemplative life and his idea, suspect to many, of two classes of Christian? The one class is content with faith, observance of the commandments and the foolishness of the cross, while the other achieves perfection, and possesses divine wisdom through a deeper revelation of the word of God and a secret tradition. The doctrine of the two classes of Christian could paradoxically either be expressed in the two levels of the spiritual life or be an erroneous opinion of gnostic origin, as J. Lebreton believes; cf. *RSR* 12 (1931) pp. 165–196: 'Die Stufen der religiosen Erkenntnis nach Origenes'; G. Bardy, *DThC* X1/2 (Paris, 1931), 1514–1516; E. de Faye, *Origène*, t.I–III (Paris, 1923).

edge.[80] Without hesitation Origen stresses the priority of contemplative over the active life[81] and values the latter merely as a preparation for the former. However in his view one cannot exist without the other.[82] Thus even the ordinary Christian has some understanding of the Trinity, which is precisely the summit of the contemplative life.[83]

'Theory' affects the active life to the extent to which it is set apart from what is of the physical senses. Origen is even able to point out the dangers of higher knowledge.[84] But what does this 'theory' exactly consist in? This will become clearer if we take a closer look at the three stages of the spiritual life, which Origen recognises in addition to the distinction between the two aspects of the soul alluded to above.[85] For he often distinguishes 'praxis', 'physical theory' and 'theology'.[86] A similar triple division is evident in the distinction between 'mystical', 'physical', and 'ethical' dogmas.[87] Numerous examples of this could be adduced.[88]

In any event, according to this triple division, the knowledge of the Trinity, that is 'theology', appears as the 'perfectio scientiae'.[89] More detailed exposition of these three levels is to be found, using other terms, in Origen's commentary on the Song of Songs, where he distinguishes between the 'ethica', the 'physica' and the 'enoptica'.[90]

---

[80] *In Joan.* fragm. 3(GCS 10) 486,32. *In Luc.* fragm. 54 (GCS 35) 260,8. *Select. in Psalm.* (PG 12, 1429 A; 1545 B; 1549 C).

[81] *Select in Psalm.* (PG 12, 1581 D; 1652 C). Martha is regarded as less perfect than Mary: *In Luc.* fragm. 39 (GCS 35) 252,5 sq. 21 sq.

[82] *In Luc.* fragm 39 (GCS 35) 252,4. A life of virtue flows from constant prayer; cf. *De orat.* 12,2 (GCS 3) 324, 25 sq. *Select in Psalm.* (PG 12, 1088 AB).

[83] *In Levit.* hom. 5 n. 3 (GCS 29) 340, 17 sq. *Select. in Ezech.* 6 (PG 13, 785 BC).

[84] *Select in Psalm.* (PG 12, 1644 A). *In Ezech.* hom 9 n. 5 (GCS 33) 414, 27 sq.

[85] This division is found in many passages of Origen which are not mentioned here; thus a distinction is drawn for example between 'agnitio (ratio) fidei (intuitus et inspectio contemplationis)' and 'perfectio operum'; cf. *In Cant.* III (GCS 33) 216,3 sqq.

[86] *Select in Psalm.* (PG 12, 1641 D).

[87] *In Jer.* fragm. 14 (GCS 33) 241, 3 sqq. Origen adds a 'perhaps' and indicates a certain hesitation; cf. *In Cant. prol.* (GCS 33) 75,9 sq., where he still keeps this triple division.

[88] *In Gen.* hom. 14 n.3 (GCS 29) 123,25 sq; 124,17 sq.; hom 6 n. 2 *Ibid.* ·67,28 sq.; 68,19 sq.

[89] *In Num.* hom. 10 n.3 (GCS 29) 74,6 sq.

[90] *In Cant.* prol. (GCS 33) 75,8 sq.

Rufinus calls these 'moralis', 'naturalis' and 'inspectiva' in his transla-tion.[91]

The 'moralis' corresponds to 'praxis', although it signifies a science rather than a rule.[92] Because of his obedience and observance of the commandments Abraham is the model for this type of knowledge,[93] for whoever has reached this level corrects his behaviour and observes the commandments.[94]

The 'physica' is called 'natural where one refers to the nature of the whole of reality, so that nothing happens in life contrary to nature and everything serves the purpose for which it was brought into being by the creator.'[95] Whoever understands this recognises 'by distinguishing between the cause and the nature of things that he must overcome the vanity of vanities and strive for what is eternal and permanent'.[96] So the 'physica' is 'knowledge and discernment of transient beings'.[97] Its goal is the insight that 'all that is visible is corruptible and fragile, so that anyone striving for wisdom grasps it in this way; he disdains it without hesitation and esteems it lightly, renouncing all that is earthly and stretching out for the invisible and eternal'.[98] The model for this is Isaac, 'who dug wells and discovered the depths of reality'.[99] Obvi-ously the 'physica', therefore, presents a religious outlook on the world and has a moral rather than a scientific purpose. But does the 'theory of the immaterial' belong still to the 'physica' or to the 'inspec-tiva'? The answer is not entirely clear[100] but the matter is of no great importance.

'Inspectiva' means the sort of knowledge 'in which we go beyond what is visible and grasp something of the divine and heavenly reality, perceiving through this faculty alone that the latter things surpass bodily appearance'.[101] The object in this case is the same as in the Song

[91] Ibid.
[92] Ibid. (GCS 33) 75,17 sq. Also: 'vitae instituta componens'; ibid. 76,8 sq. and ibid. 77,29 and ibid. 78,15 sq.
[93] Ibid. 78,23.
[94] Ibid. 79,13.
[95] Ibid. 75, 19 sq. and 76,10 sq.
[96] Ibid. 78, 2 sq. and 79, 14 sq.
[97] Ibid. 78, 16 sq.
[98] Ibid. 78, 5 sq.
[99] Ibid. 78,29 sq.
[100] According to Origen the 'scientia incorruptibilium' belongs to the 'naturalis', while knowledge of all immaterial realities is proper to the 'inspec-tiva'.
[101] In Cant. (GCS 33) 75,21 sq.

of Songs: 'the love of the perfect soul for the word of God',[102] which leads to 'the contemplation of the godhead'.[103] The soul strives for the invisible and the eternal; the model for this is Jacob, 'because of the contemplation of divine things'.[104]

Each of these stages corresponds to one of the books of Solomon: the book of Proverbs belongs to the 'ethica'; Ecclesiastes corresponds to the 'physica', and the Song of Songs to the 'enoptica'.[105] The Song of Songs stands in the final place because only someone with the 'ethica' and the 'physica' already behind him can understand it.[106]

We are now in a position to fit Origen's idea of the five spiritual senses into his overall system of thought. As already stated, only the perfect are in possession of all five spiritual faculties. In consequence only they can make use of the five senses since they have gone through the active life and reached a state of 'apathy', of freedom from the passions; they have arrived at perfect purity and love through observance of the commandments. They are persuaded of the vanity and transitoriness of the visible world and thus the way lies open for them to the kingdom of God, to insight and 'theory'.[107] Therefore the 'pure spirit'[108] can ascend to the contemplation of divinity itself, the Trinity and the divine Word. All five spiritual senses come into operation, each one being touched by the grace of the Word.

These conclusions are not mere deductions since Origen himself relates the activity of the spiritual senses to the ascent of the soul to the 'enoptica'. In this sense he explains the passage in the Song of Songs, 'the aroma of your ointments surpasses all other fragrance' (1:3), to mean the state in which the soul has mastered for itself all learning,

---

[102] *Ibid.* 78,14 sq.
[103] *Ibid.* 78,17 sq.
[104] *Ibid.* 78,30 sq.
[105] *Ibid.* 77,30 sq.
[106] *Ibid.* 78, 10 sq. The same triple division is found in other passages, e.g. *De Principiis* 1. III n.3 (GCS 22) 259,18 sq ... 'sanctae et immaculatae animae cum se ommi affectu omnique puritate voverint Deo et alienas se ab omni daemonum contagione servaverint et per multam abstinentiam purificaverint se et piis ac regliosis imbutae fuerint disciplinis participium per hoc divinitatis assumunt, et prophetiae ac ceterorum divinorum donorum gratiam promerentur'. The division of 'theory' or rather the triple division of the spiritual life is found also in: *In Joan.* t. 1 n. 28 (GCS 10) 36,14 sq. *Contra Celsum* 1. VII n. 46 (GCS 3) 198,13 sq. *In Joan.* t. XX n. 34 (GCS 10) 371 sq.
[107] *Select. in Psalm.* (PG 12, 1581 D).
[108] *Ibid.* (PG 12, 1304 C and 1424 C).

whether this is 'ethica' or 'physica'.[109] All this knowledge was aroma for the soul, yet, as he continues, at the moment when the soul comes to awareness of the divine mysteries and truths and is permitted to cross over the threshold and arrive at wisdom itself, which comes neither from the world nor from its masters but is God's own wisdom accessible only to the perfect, at this moment it has reached the stage where it may grasp the unutterable mysteries and can properly say, 'odor unguentorum'. This spiritual and mystical knowledge surpasses all the aromas of moral and natural philosophy.[110] The soul, guided by Christ, follows his scent like 'the soul which is practised in the moral and then also in the natural sphere'.[111] 'And this only happens in so far as his aroma (that of Christ) is taken in. What do they (that is, the companions of the bride in the Song of Songs) do when their hearing and sight, feeling and taste are filled with the Word of God and each is endowed with its proper virtue corresponding to its nature and capacity?'[112] 'And so those who have reached the highest degree of perfection and blessedness rejoice with all their senses in the Word of God.'[113] This agrees exactly with Origen's conception of the 'perfect', when he explains the Word of God and God himself as the object of the spiritual faculties.[114]

THE USE OF THE SPIRITUAL SENSES

One requires a special grace from God in order to be able to make use of the spiritual faculties. This is true both for 'theology' and for 'enoptica'. 'For with this (sc. grace) a man comes to the contemplation of, and longing for, unseen and eternal blessings. But in order to obtain them properly we have need of mercy. The only condition for this is that after realising the beauty of the divine Word, we can allow ourselves to be set on fire with saving love, so that the Word itself deigns to love the soul in which it has encountered longing for it.'[115]

'It is possible for us with the grace of God to recognise the truth but

[109] *In Cant.* 1 (GCS 33) 100,12 sq.
[110] *Ibid.* 100,21 sq.
[111] *Ibid.* 102,28 sq.
[112] *Ibid.* 103,27 sq.
[113] *Ibid.* 105, 1 sq.
[114] *Contra Celsum.* 1. VII n.34 (GCS 3) 184,14 sq.; *ibid.* n.39 (GCS 3) 190,3 sq. *De Principiis* 1. I c 1 n.9 (GCS 22) 26, 15 sq.
[115] *In Cant.* prol. (GCS 33) 79, 17 sq.

it does not rest with us whether we are counted worthy of spiritual knowledge.'[116] Thus the spiritual senses can grasp nothing if God does not bestow his merciful grace upon a man. Origen's doctrine of the five spiritual senses consists in his psychological notion of 'theology', which he treats as the highest degree of the spiritual life.

Did Origen intend to use his doctrine to give a clearer account to the psychology of mystical experience in the proper sense of the term?[117] This point is not easy to settle and a sure answer would require a special investigation. For Origen does not appear to separate clearly popular knowledge of God from mystical experience. All knowledge of God according to his account is more or less mystical, without it being absolutely necessary for someone to have genuine mystical understanding.[118] So one should not immediately try to find a description of mystical experience in such language of Platonic enthusiasm. Also the way in which ecstasy is definitely excluded makes it doubtful whether Origen had really experienced mystical states.[119] He speaks rather of the difficulty of finding charisms.[120] This prevents us, how-

[116] *Select in Psalm.* (PG 12,1424 B).

[117] Cf. the controversy about the mysticism of Origen, which has remained inconclusive: C. A. Kneller, 'Mystisches bei Origenes', *St. M–L* (1904), pp. 238–240 and H. Koch, 'Kennt Origenes Gebetsstufen?', *ThQ* 87 (1905), pp. 592–596.

[118] For Origen, God belongs to every form of knowledge; cf. *Select. in Psalm.* (PG 12, 1164 B); however he allows a natural knowledge of God as well which arises from creation, e.g. *In Rom.* 2, 13 (PG14,892 B); *De Principiis* 1. I c. 1 n. 7 (GCS 22) 24,19 sq.; *Contra Celsum* 1 VIII n.37 (GCS 3) 188,2 sq. Externally it seems heavily influenced by mysticism, although it should not be regarded as genuine mystical experience (Plato's influence). Origen writes: 'We make it clear that man is by nature quite incapable of feeling God and of finding him in a pure form, unless the one sought comes to his aid', *Contra Celsum* 1. VII n.42 (GCS 3) 193, 16 sq. Cf. A. Miura-Stange, *Celsus und Origenes* (Giessen 1926) pp. 64 sq. To this notion corresponds the strong emphasis laid on the moral dispositions which are required for knowledge of God, e.g. purity. It seems difficult to find in Origen 'the outline of a theory of mystical knowledge', (cf. G. Bardy, *DThC* XI/2 (Paris, 1931) 1536).

[119] Cf. *De Principiis* 1.III C. 3 n.4 (GCS 22) 260,27 sq. *In Ezech.* hom. 6 n.1 (GCS 33) 378,6 sq. *Contra Celsum* 1. VIII n.3 and 4 (GCS 3) 154 sqq. Cf. A. Zöllig, *Die Inspirationslehre des Origenes* (Freiburg i.Br. 1903), pp. 69–70. Evidently Origen attracts a 'manic ecstasy'; whoever is filled with the Spirit must be completely free without ecstasy and can reject the inspiration of the Spirit. This does not fit genuine divine ecstasy, which Origen did not consider at all. Similarly with regard to mysticism of a Montanist type; cf. Fr. Leitner, *Die prophetische Inspiration*, (Freiburg i.Br., 1896), pp. 119 sq.

[120] *Fragm in Prov.* (PG 13,25 A).

ever, from seeing a psychology of mystical experience in his doctrine of the five spiritual senses. Nevertheless it must be granted that Origen applies this notion to a type of knowledge which is of a mystical character, although he sets it clearly apart from general religious understanding. The spiritual senses remain active in his view in eternal bliss. They comprehend the angels, the Cherubim, and even God, though it is assumed that these latter allow themselves to be so perceived; otherwise every effort of the spiritual eye would be fruitless.[121] Furthermore Origen uses his teaching of the spiritual senses to explain prophetic inspiration.[122] He proposes a 'deep' interpretation of the story of Isaias and Ezechiel.[123] He mentions, too, in connection with the doctrine of the spiritual senses the two events which counted in tradition as the high points of biblical mysticism, the vision of God by Moses and the rapture of Paul into the third heaven.[124] It is evident, then, in Origen that the spiritual senses can be the organs of mystical knowledge.

THE LATER INFLUENCE OF THE DOCTRINE

A few remarks may be added here to show the later influence of Origen's teaching, although no comprehensive survey will be attempted.

Evagrius of Pontus is a disciple of Origen in this matter as in his whole spiritual teaching.[125] Thus we read: 'The "spirit" possesses five spiritual senses which are its means of perception and with which it fulfils the purpose of creation. Sight reveals to it the essence of things; hearing allows it to grasp their foundations; with the sense of smell and pure and holy aroma is sensed which is pleasing to it and its house; through touch genuine trust develops'. Elsewhere he writes: 'Just as every art demands a living faculty which is suitable for it, so the

[121] In Luc. hom. 3 (GCS 35) 20 sqq.

[122] On this inspiration, cf. Fr. Leitner op. cit. pp. 142 sq. and A. Zöllig, op. cit. pp. 58 sq.

[123] Contra Celsum 1. I n.48 (GCS 2) 98,9 sq.

[124] De Principiis 1 II c.r n.3 (GCS 22) 131,3 sq. Similarly In Joan t. XXXII n.27 (GCS 10) 472,31 sq. Contra Celsum 1. IV n.96 (GCS 2) 369, 14 sq., and 1. I n.48 (GCS 2) 99,15 sq. Cf. also, In Cant. I (GCS 33) 109,11 sq. In Jesu Nave hom.23 n.r (GCS 33) 446,25 sq.

[125] On this dependence cf. W. Bousset, Apophthegmata, (Tubingen, 1923) and M. Viller, 'Aux Sources de la Spiritualité de saint Maxime', RAM 11 (1930) pp. 156–184; 239–268.

"spirit" as well needs a spiritual sense for the discernment of spiritual things'.[126]

Evagrius' manner of expression is more accurate than that of his master; the 'spirit' possesses five spiritual faculties corresponding to its nature. He speaks of the spiritual eye, of the eye of the soul or of spiritual sight, etc.[127] The fact that they are organs of the 'spirit' clearly proves that their operation relates to the 'theoretical' dimension. The 'praxis' and its goal, namely 'apathy' or freedom from passion[128] are pre-supposed here. His use of terminology seems to create a problem for knowledge of the Trinity which he sometimes distinguishes emphatically from any other type of knowledge.[129] But even in this case it is a matter of 'sight' and a 'way of seeing' and a 'perceiving'.[130] Given these expressions, Evagrius must regard even knowledge of the Trinity as dependent on the spiritual senses. Their operations, however, are envisaged in the following manner: the bodily senses perceive sensual things;[131] in comparison with the spiritual organs of perception, they grasp only a part and not the whole of the perceived object.[132] This is surpassed by the 'perception of the spiritual organs', which penetrate more deeply the reality already grasped by the bodily senses and discover much more about it than do the latter.[133] The spiritual faculties, in fact, either comprehend nothing or the whole reality, whose deepest meaning they communicate.[134]

[126] W. Frankenberg, *Evagrius Ponticus* (GAb, NF XXII/2) Berlin, 1912) Syriac with Greek translation; cr. *ibid.* pp. 155 and 79, and also W. Bousset, *op. cit.* p.318.

[127] *Cent.* II, 80; VII, 44; II, 28; VII, 27; II, 62 (Frankenberg, 183; 461; 147; 451; 175).

[128] Cf. M. Viller, *op. cit.* p. 168; this seems also to be the meaning of *Cent* 1,37 (Frankenberg, 81).

[129] Cf. *Cent* II, 16; III, 41; V, 63 and epist. 58 (Frankenberg, 141; 217; 347; 607). Cf. M. Viller, *op. cit.* pp. 244, 246 and 164; *Cent.* II 47; VII 19 and epist. 29 (Frankenberg 161; 429; 587).

[130] *Cent.* V.51.52.57.63; *Gnost.* 151; *Antirr.* (Frankenberg, 339; 341; 343; 347; 553; 547).

[131] *Cent.* V.57 sq., *ibid.* I.34; II,80 (Frankenberg, 343; 79; 80). All these expressions carry the same meaning and describe bodily sense perception.

[132] *Cent.*II, 28 and 80 (Frankenberg, 147 and 183).

[133] *Cent.* II, 80; V,58 (Frankenberg, 183; 343).

[134] *Cent.* II, 28 and 35. (Frankenberg, 147 and 155). What is said here only refers to the perception of immaterial realities, i.e. spiritual phenomena in the strict sense. One does not rightly grasp now the physical sight of bodily realities differs from spiritual perception, unless spiritual perception consists in the knowledge of the foundation of things.

They have, therefore, a more difficult role. For here 'theory' should become evident,[135] in which the individual senses are apportioned, each in a different way. The eye perceives the existence of these immaterial beings, spiritual hearing grasps their inner meaning, the sense of touch lends certainty to these perceptions and finally smell and taste comprehend them in a more affective manner.[136] It is from this point that the human gaze ascends to the light of the Trinity.

Although one of the faculties, the eye, is apparently the organ of 'theology', as has already been pointed out, its operation is quite different here than in 'physical knowledge'. At this level the perception of the spiritual senses is closely linked to the activity of the bodily faculties, so that each is brought into operation by the other.[137] This entirely material point of departure disappears on the higher level. In this 'state beyond the forms', in pure prayer, the spiritual eye perceives more as the light of the Trinity, the light without images.[138] This light is ultimately the highest that exists and yet remains at the same time 'eternal unknowing'.[139] In order to reach this point an ever increasing purity is needed, which can be achieved with angelic assistance.[140] Indirectly Evagrius implies that not everyone possesses all the spiritual senses and may here and there only have control of one or another of them. Many men can in his opinion perceive the smell of demons.[141]

---

[135] *Cent.* V.34 (Frankenberg, 341) has the same meaning: the deepest sense of physical realities from a religious and moral viewpoint. Babai interprets it in this way in his commentary on *Cent.* V,54 and 58 (Frankenberg, 343 and 345). Origen explained the 'physica' in the same way; *Cent.* I,33; II,80; V,57 (Frankenberg, 79; 183; 343).

[136] *Cent.* II 35–36; II 27 and V.54 (Frankenberg, 155, 147, 341).

[137] This is certainly the meaning of *Cent.* II,80. (Frankenberg, 183). Cf. *Cent.* II 80; V,57. 60. 61. (Frankenberg, 183; 343; 345). *Cent.* V,61 must accordingly be interpreted as follows: physical perception arouses the awareness of the deepest spiritual meaning which can be drawn from these sense realities (*Cent.* II,80, 35 sq.) Conversely this awareness awakes the memory of the physical perception of these objects. The relation between physical perception and 'theory' in the 'physica' assumes that 'theory' is dependent on physical perception. On this point *Cent.* IV, 85 (Frankenberg, 315) and V,56 (Frankenberg, 343) agree, as do other passages in Evagrius, cf. M. Viller, *op. cit.* pp. 248–256.

[138] *Cent.* II, 29; IV, 87; V,51 and 61; VI, 26; VII,4 and 30 (Frankenberg, 149; 315; 339; 345; 415; 427; 455).

[139] *Cent.* III,88 (Frankenberg, 257).

[140] *Cent.* V.52; 57; VI,35 (Frankenberg, 341; 343; 383).

[141] *Cent.* V.78 and VII, 44 (Frankenberg, 353; 461).

This, then, forms the main outline of Evagrius' teaching. The many passages which are parallel to Origen's own writing do not require separate mention here.

It is evident, however, that Evagrius does make additions to the theory of mystical experience. This development would become clearer if one were to pursue his spiritual teaching in detail, an investigation which exceeds the scope of this essay.[142] The view of Bousset seems to us mistaken when he says about Evagrius's conception of the five spiritual senses: 'His spirituality is taken to extremes and takes on a new physical and sensual force.'[143] However it is true that the following passage from the 'Mirror of the Nuns' does seem to provide a certain justification for this opinion: 'The eyes of the virgins see the Lord, the ears of the virgins hear his words, the mouth of virgins kisses the bridegroom, their sense of smell is attracted by the aroma of his perfumes, and their hands touch the Lord.'[144]

As is well known Diadocus Photicus is heavily influenced by Evagrius.[145] But he is not familiar with any doctrine of five spiritual faculties, but only of 'one spiritual sense', 'a sense of the spirit', etc. On this topic P. Horn has made a closer investigation.[146] The differences between the two views are easily understood. Diadocus is more or less familiar with an experience of knowledge coming from the indwelling of God in the purified soul. The soul recognises its right relationship to God and experiences divine consolation, which gives a man total fulfilment. On this basis Diadocus can state that the purified person possesses a single perception in contrast to the five bodily senses.[147]

---

[142] For this, parallels can be found in Origen, at least if one restricts one's attention to the actual content of the texts. However, a considerable difference exists between the writers. One finds a concern in Evagrius, but not in Origen, to detach mystical from ordinary knowledge and to highlight its peculiar characteristics.

[143] W. Bousset, *op. cit.* p. 318; cf. F. Cavallera, 'Bespr. zu Bousset', *RAM* 6 (1925) pp. 80–83.

[144] Cf. H. Gressmann (ed.) *Mönchs-und Nonnenspiegel* (Greek) (TU 39,46; Leipzig, 1913), p.151.

[145] Cf. R. Reitzenstein, *Historia monachorum und Historia Lausiaca* (Gottingen 1916), cap. V: 'Egagrius und Diadochus von Photike', pp. 124–142. Cf. M. Viller, *op. cit.* p. 263.

[146] 'Le sens de l'esprit d'après Diadoque de Photice', RAM 8 (1927) pp. 402–419.

[147] *De perfectione spirituali*, cap. 24; 25; 29; ed. Weis-Leibersdorf (Leipzig, 1912); new edition: E. de Places, *Diadoque de Photice. Oevres spirituelles* (SC 56; Paris, 1955), pp. 84-163.

He has no difficulty in referring to the eyes of spirit, to the perception of the divine light and its illumination.[148] It is surprising to discover how often he uses the images of tasting and savouring to describe religious experience.[149] In one passage he even speaks of 'sniffing out the aroma of supernatural good deeds'.[150]

Pseudo-Macarius maintains more accurately than Diadocus the doctrine of the spiritual senses in his spiritual homilies. Bousset has rightly affirmed that he too lies under the influence of Evagrius and, at least indirectly, of Origen.[151] The question of the authorship and authenticity of these homilies does not concern us here; the solutions attempted by Stoffels, Stiglmayr, Marriott, Villecourt and Wilmarts are well known.[152]

In any event Pseudo-Macarius accepts that there are five spiritual senses of the soul which are sanctified by the grace of the Holy Spirit and are then truly 'wise virgins'.[153] This image makes on suspect a direct dependence upon Origen, who had already compared the five spiritual faculties to the wise virgins in the Gospel. These powers are brought into operation by the temptations of evil forces as well as by the graces of the Holy Spirit.[154] Pseudo-Macarius regards these five spiritual senses as natural faculties, since, according to him, their operations can remain on a purely natural plane, i.e. without grace.[155] In prayer God can enter the soul through all the senses[156] and Christ, who sanctifies a man and fill him with his own divine spirit, bestows new eyes, new ears and a new language upon him.[157] Through sin the eyes of the heart are so blinded that they no longer see the glory of God, which Adam could see before the Fall. Satan has darkened the

[148] Cf. J.E. Weis-Liebersdorf, Vorwort 5,2; cap. 9 (10,25); cap. 14(16,17); cap. 40(46,5); cap. 71(88,11); cap. 85(116,17).

[149] Cf. *ibid.*

[150] Cf. *ibid.*

[151] W. Bousset, *op. cit.* p. 319; J. Stiglmayr, 'Makarius der Grosse im Lichte der kirchlichen Tradition', *ThG1* 3 (1911), pp. 274–88. The author refers directly to Origen (*ibid.* p. 280).

[152] Cf. O. Bardenhewer, *Geschichte der altkirchlichen Literatur* III, (Freiburg i. Br., 1912), pp. 87–93; also J. Stiglmayr, Pseudo-Makarius und die Aftermystik der Messalianer', *ZkTh* 49 (1925) pp. 244–260.

[153] *Hom.* 4 n. 7 (PG34, 477).

[154] *Hom.* 50 n.4 (PG 34, 829 A).

[155] *Hom.* 4 n. 7 (PG 34, 477).

[156] *Hom.* 33 n. 1 (PG 34, 741 B).

[157] *Hom.* 44 n. 1 (PG 34, 780 A).

eyes of the inner man and made his ears deaf. But Christ gives back health to the inner man. A divine light illumines the spiritual eyes, which were previously darkened by sin.[158]

A section from the 4th Homily, relevant to our topic, is found in Simeon Logothetes (Metaphrastes) in the second half of the 10th century;[159] he quotes the text practically verbatim, but adds an explanation which completely alters the meaning.[160] Apparently the Greeks of the period had already entirely forgotten the earlier teaching of the five spiritual senses.[161]

Finally we should note traces of Origen's doctrine to be found here and there outside spiritual writings. Basil the Great, for instance, is clearly referring to Origen in the way he tries to prove the doctrine of the five spiritual senses from scriptural passages. He uses the names of the bodily senses for the powers of the soul.[162] Still more obvious is the influence of Origen upon Gregory of Nyssa. In his exposition of the Song of Songs the theory of the five spiritual faculties is explicitly presented as a teaching of the 'philosophy' of the Song of Songs. Further evidence is here unnecessary.[163]

Traces are also to be found of a doctrine of five spiritual senses in the Latin patristic literature, although it would be hard to prove the influence of Origen in this case. But in this connection mention should at least be made of Augustine and Gregory the Great.[164]

---

[158] *Hom.* 45 n. 1 (PG 34, 785 D). *Hom.* 33 n. 4; *Hom.* 28 n. 4 sq., *Hom.* 25 n. 10; *Hom.* 14 n. 1 and 6 (PG 34, 744C; 712 sq; 673CD; 569 D; 573 C). Cf. W., Bousset, *op. cit.* p. 319.

[159] Cf. O. Bardenhewer, *Geschichte der altkirchlichen Literatur* IV (Freiburg i. Br. 1924), p. 89.

[160] *De elevatione mentis* n. 4 (PG 34,893A).

[161] In the 7th Century Maximus the Confessor matched the five spiritual senses with the powers of the soul which were familiar from other sources; cf. *Ambig. liber* (PG 91,1248A).

[162] *In princ. prov.* hom. 12 n. 14 (PG 31, 413–416).

[163] Gregory himself refers to Origen's commentary on the Song of Songs, *In Cant. prooem.* (PG44, 764AB). In addition there are numerous points of contact between the two commentaries; cf. *In Cant.* hom. 1(PG44,780CD) Gregory interprets Prov 2:5 in the same way as Origen.

[164] Origen naturally has a certain influence upon Latin thinking through the translations of Jerome and Rufinus. For Augustine, cf. *Serm.* 159 C. 3 sq. (PL 38,869); the proof of the 'sensus interiores' recalls the use of Scripture in Origen. Cf. also *Tract in Joan.* 18 c. 5 n. 10(PL 35, 1542); *De civ. Dei* XI c. 27 n. 2 (PL41,341), *Solil.* 1 c. 6 n. 12 sq. (PL 32,875 sq.); *Conf.* X c. 6 and 27 (PL

The influence of Origen's ideas clearly makes itself evident in the speculations of the Scholastics. Numerous texts prove the point beyond doubt. A passage from the 3rd homily on Leviticus serves as one of the important patristic sources and is continually quoted in support of the theory of spiritual senses.[165] But the ideas of the Scholastics themselves on the spiritual senses are not here our topic of discussion. The purpose of this investigation was to provide a historical study of Origen's doctrine of the five spiritual senses, without intending to add a great deal about their value and importance.

⁕

32,782 sq., 795). Augustine was familiar with *De Principiis* by Origen (cf. *De.Civ. Dei* XI c. 23 – PL 41,336). The idea of the spiritual senses may come from this source. The comparison of the senses with the five prudent virgins is also common in Augustine. *Epist.* 187 c. 13 n. 4d (PL 33, 847) is important for scholastic speculation about the five spiritual senses. For Gregory cf. *Moral.* VI c.33 (PG 75,973 sq.) among other references, where the 'sensus mentis, sensus animi, sensus interni' are discussed. There is also frequent mention of the 'occuli cordis', e.g. *Hom. in Ezech.* II hom. 1 n. 18 (PL 76,948B).

[165] Cf. *In Levit.* hom. 3 (GCS 29) 31Z. This text was better known that the rest, since it was to be found in the usual glossary (Lev 7:5). It was used by e.g. Alexander of Hales, *Summ. Theol.* II inq. IV tract. I sect. II qu. 3 tit. 1 memb. 3c 1 (Quaracchi, 1928, n. 381 sq.), also by Albert the Great, *In III sent.* dist. 13 A art. 4 (ed. Borgnet t. 28,239); by Bonaventure, *In III Sent.* dist. 13 dub. c litt. magistri (Quaracchi t. III, 291); by Thomas Aquinas, *In III Sent* dist. 13, exp. textus (Parma t. VII, 145 sq.).

7

THE DOCTRINE OF THE 'SPIRITUAL SENSES' IN THE MIDDLE AGES

THE CONTRIBUTION OF ST BONAVENTURE

W̲E have already investigated the origins of the doctrine of the five spiritual senses.[1] In this essay the historical development of this notion will be pursued further. The fullest account is to be found in the mystical theology of St Bonaventure, so that it is obviously advisable to deal primarily with the work of this doctor of the Church. Earlier and later testimony can and should only be introduced to give the main outline of the history of the idea of the five senses without any attempt being made to treat the matter fully.

In the case of Bonaventure also only those texts will be considered which deal explicitly with the five faculties. Wherever only one or other spiritual sense is mentioned, or there is a purely metaphorical reference to religious experience, the testimony is too uncertain to be relevant for our concern.[2]

We have already drawn attention in a summary way to traces of this doctrine in the works of the Latin fathers, especially in those of Augustine.[3] Despite the brief and general character of these texts, they

---

[1] Cf. in this volume: 'The spiritual senses according to Origen' and also the fuller French version of the text in *RAM* 13 (1932), pp. 113–145. The present essay also appeared first in *RAM* 14 (1933), pp. 263–299 in French. A section was published in German in *ZAM* 9 (1934), pp. 1–19. The text has been abridged and slightly revised for publication here.

[2] This means that certain passages are excluded which are quoted by other authors in their treatment of the 'spiritual senses'.

[3] On Augustine cf. the essay referred to in footnote 1. Strangely enough *Sermo* 159, 3–4 (PL38,869) was never used in later periods, although it is a clearer proof of Augustine's knowledge of the doctrine of the true spiritual senses (even if not in a mystical sense) than *Confess.* X 6,27.

are important for their influence and confirmation of later scholastic speculation on the matter. For after Origen Augustine was the real master for medieval theology on the subject of the five spiritual faculties. Certainly one has to move to the classic scholastic writers before one comes across any original conception of the spiritual senses after the patristic period. All that was achieved in the time between Origen and Bonaventure was to prevent the doctrine from passing into complete oblivion. Among the 12th century mystical writers one finds only three who mention the teaching, Bernard of Clairvaux, his friend and biographer William of St Thierry and his disciple Alcher of Clairvaux. But even Bernard's remarks do not go beyond the division, allegories and parallels,[4] which remained common in the Middle Ages. He remarks in a sermon: 'Just as the soul bestows sense powers to the body, so the soul of our soul, that is, God himself, furnishes our soul in his own way with five senses. They are nothing else than the various possibilities of loving each corresponding reality: sight is the love of God.' According to this, Bernard basically recognised only a single spiritual sense, which is fundamentally directed to religious phenomena. William of St Thierry is completely dependent upon Bernard and repeats in his work 'De natura et dignitate amoris'[5] the latter's ideas. In his writing only sight has a religious character, even if he does say: 'Through the five spiritual senses the soul is bound to God with the help of love'. At another point in the same work he relates each spiritual sense to a particular period of the history of salvation.[6] This recalls similar notions in Origen.[7] But on the whole the statements of Bernard and William are too general in character to admit of a definite conclusion whether the sense intended here is really meant. But they should not be ignored since in the high Middle Ages they frequently serve as authoritative testimony on the question of the spiritual senses.

The contribution of Alcher of Clairvaux on this topic is of greater importance. In his small tratise *De spiritu et anima*,[8] which in subsequent centuries was generally ascribed to Augustine, he presents

---

[4] *Sermo* 10 de diversis 2–4 (PL 183,567–569).

[5] Cf. *ibid.* cap. 6 n. 15 (PL 184,390–391); cap. 7 n. 16–20 (PL 184,391–394).

[6] Cf. *ibid.* cap. 10 n. 26 sqq. (PL 184, 397–399).

[7] *Comm. in Matth.* t. XV n.33 (GCS 40). The same idea also appears later in Gerson.

[8] This work is only attributed to Alcher; the text is in PL 40, 779–832.

a good summary of the earlier psychological tradition.[9] He speaks of the spiritual faculties in two places: 'the senses of the outer man, it must be stressed, are to be found in a similar fashion in the inner man, for spiritual realities are accessible, not to the bodily, but to the spiritual senses'. In the same way as Origen and Augustine before him he attempts to find scriptural proof for the existence of these spiritual faculties.[10]

Other writings influenced the speculation of the classic scholastic authors on the subject of the five spiritual senses in addition to the testimony of the 12th century Latin mystical thought. Mention should be made of the *Glossa ordinaria* and the quote from Origen it contains through which, in addition to the work of Augustine, an idea originating in Greek mystical writing penetrated the Middle Ages. There was also another basis for the new development of the doctrine which played a part at the time. Peter Lombard stated in one passage[11] in his *Sentences* that in Christ the head of the mystical body, all the senses are to be found, while the saints only possess the sense of touch. This remark in the manual apparently contradicted the assertion of Origen, which was well known from the *Glossa ordinaria*. The solution to the problems this caused gave the commentators on the Sentences the chance to discuss the spiritual faculties.

Finally reference should be made to the indisputable influence exercised by the meaning of the word 'sensus' in classical Latin and at later periods. Apart from sense knowledge the word also signified the highest spiritual principles and their operation. In the religious terminology of the 12th century we find a 'sensus spiritualis'[12] in contrast to the 'sensus carnalis', and similarly a 'sensus cordis', a 'sensus animae' and a 'sensus intellectualis'. It was not long before the parallel of 'sensus carnalis' and 'sensus spiritualis' influenced the discussion of the five spiritual senses.

Building upon these elements the medieval şcholastics developed the notion of the spiritual senses, showing the greatest respect here, as

---

[9] Cf. Ueberweg-Geyer, *Die patristische und scholastische Philosophie* (Graz, 1951), p. 260.

[10] Cf. *De spiritu et anima* cap. 9 and 49 (PL 40, 785 and 815); Dt 32:39; Ps 33:9; Lk 8:46; 2 Cor 2:15; Rev 2:29.

[11] Cf. the work referred to in footnote 1; III *Sent.* dist. 13 with reference to Augustine's *epist. 187 to Dardanus* cap. 13 n 40 (PL 38,847).

[12] A few examples: Hugh of St. Victor, *Miscellanea* 1. I tit. 24; tit. 162 PL 187,490 and 559); Richard of St. Victor, *Beniamin minor* cap. 5 (PL 196,5), etc.

in other questions, to the tradition of all the ancient concepts, distinctions, etc. But logical thought had already evolved too far for it to be possible to regard everything as acceptable simply on grounds of antiquity. On the other hand such material could not be used without distinctions being drawn. So many ancient notions, which writers did not want just to abandon, came to convey a meaning which could be retained in the period when in themselves they were forgotten; for they no longer expressed something which could not be stated more simply without their use.

The process was similar in the case of the spiritual senses. They were commonly explained in a manner which set their content firmly within the framework of more reliable ideas and rendered them in fact superfluous. Only when direct mystical experience and lively interest in its significance occurred, was any attempt made to find a genuinely meaningful interpretation of mystical theory. This is, however, exactly the case with St Bonaventure.

THE IDEA OF THE HIGH MIDDLE AGES

The doctrine of the five spiritual senses is to be found for the first time in the classical scholastic period in the *Summa aurea*, the commentary of the *Sentences* by William of Auxerre.[13] The question is treated in the section dealing with heavenly beatitude. Essentially, however, he is familiar only with one spiritual sense, the intellect, which reaches perfection through faith. But we are entitled even here to speak of five spiritual senses in as much as the intellect can have various acts which are distinguished 'in their working and their enjoyment' although not at all in their essential principle of operation. Evidently the question, known from other sources, of the relation of spiritual senses and powers is summarily resolved in the sense that every other power apart from the intellect and will is denied. But in this way the spiritual senses are still merely different modes of activity of the intellect, which completely envelops God.

The direction in which future speculation about the spiritual senses was to develop remained true to this assumption. William of Auvergne maintains this position.[14] Yet he does not speak directly of

---

[13] *Summa aurea* 1. IV (Paris, 1500) fol. 300–301. William died in 1231 or 1237, cf. *LThK* X (1965), 1128–1129.

[14] *De virtut* cap. 11 (Orleans, 1664; reprinted, Frankfurt, 1963), 145–147; *De Universo* II pars 2 cap. 13, *ibid.* 856.

these five senses but combines them in a group, 'gustus spiritualis, visus spiritualis, olfactus spiritualis, odoratus spiritualis'. Surprisingly he connects 'gustus spiritualis' with the 'donum sapientiae', and apportions the different senses partly to the intellect and partly to the will:[15] sight and hearing belong to the intellect, while tast and smell are identified with the 'virtutes motivae'.

A little later than these two writers, Alexander of Hales also deals with the five spiritual senses in his *Summa*. What is novel in his treatment is that he clearly inserts the idea into his whole system of psychology. Having discussed the intellectual powers of the soul, he turns to the act of the power of insight.[16] He states that insight is also called the spiritual sense. There is no doubt here that the spiritual sense is understood as an act and not a power. By analogy to the bodily senses, the intellect (sensus spiritualis) is described as the spiritual sense. However there are five spiritual senses, not because so many different powers exist, but because the intellect can grasp the same object in various ways.[17] At any rate it is clear that such a conception fits a disembodied soul or an angel, which are directed to 'intelligibilia', and would only be hindered by the activity of bodily powers.[18] Evidently it is a question for Alexander of Hales of the idea of the five spiritual senses, but his interpretation is so oversimplified that the notion is in fact superfluous.

A more important contribution to the problem is provided by Albert the Great, for he connects the five spiritual senses with mystical knowledge. This idea does not figure in Alexander's thinking at all. In Albert we have to some extent all five spiritual senses,[19] and he also describes them as acts ordered to the intellect and will. Spiritual taste and feeling are expressions of the will, which experiences the blessings

[15] *De Virtut.* op. tit. 146.

[16] *Summa* pars II q. 69 (Venice, 1675), 115–118; Quaracchi, 1928, t. II inq. IV. tract. 1 s. 2 q. 3 tit. 1, membr. 1–2 n. 368 sqq, pp. 446 sqq. *Ibid.* q. 70, Quaracchi 1928, m. 3 n. 381 sqq, pp. 459 sqq.

[17] *Ibid.* pars II q. 70 m. 1 p.118–119 and Quaracchi 1928, m. 3 c. 1 n.381, pp. 459–460; also m. 2 p. 119 and Quaracchi cap. 2 n. 382, 461.

[18] *Ibid.* m. 3–6, p. 119–120 and Quaracchi 1928, c. 3–6. n. 383–386, S.462–464; cf. J. A. Endres, 'Die Seelenlehre des Alexander von Hales,' *PhJ* 1 (1888) pp. 24–55; 203–225; 257–296 (esp. 283–284).

[19] We leave aside here Albert's problem of the extent to which Christ, as head of the mystical body, possesses these senses, i.e. graces, which do not pass to the members of the body. In III *Sent.* dist. 13 art. 4 (edit. Borgnet) t.28, p. 240.

of God. To the objection that a spiritual sense is a form of knowledge and therefore must be related to the intellect, Albert gives the perceptive reply that, in addition to the knowledge received from without, there is also knowledge coming from the experience which enables a man to perceive divine reality. For according to a phrase of Pseudo-Denis, a man suffers the divine reality and experiences this in spiritual taste and feeling.[20] The other senses belong to the perception of the truth, i.e. to the intellect.[21] By analogy to the bodily senses the spiritual senses belong metaphorically to the intellect which knows God. The angels also possess them. As far as we can tell, Albert is noteworthy for his view that feeling and taste are of lesser importance than the other senses. This is also the form in which the doctrine appears in the works of Anthony of Padua and Thomas Aquinas.[22]

ST BONAVENTURE

There is a notable literature written on Bonaventure's doctrine of the five spiritual senses.[23] Before embarking on a closer analysis of his

[20] Cf. *De caelest. hier.* cap. 15/5 5 (edit. Borgnet) t. 14, p. 414; all the spiritual senses seem to be described as acts of the intellect, but even here the object of taste and touch is the *good*.

[21] In III *Sent.* loc. cit.

[22] *De caelest. hier.* cap. 15/5 5; cf. edit. of Borgnet, p. 417; it is not easy to see how this fits with the identification of 'cognitio experimentalis' and the senses of touch and taste, for Albert regards the sense of smell as the highest and thus explicitly disregards the order of value among the physical senses. The remarks about angelic faculties are not taken into account here, *op. cit./5* 5–6 (p. 415–422). Cf. J. Heerinckx, 'Les sources de la théologie mystique de S. Antoine de Padoue', *RAM* 13 (1932), p. 239 and idem, 'S. Antonius Pataviensis auctor mysticus,' *Antonianum* 7 (1932), p. 69 sqq. On Thomas Aquinas, in III *Sent* dist. 13 expos. (ed. Parma) t. VII p. 145–146; *In Philipp.* cap. 2 1. 2 *ibid.* p. 513; *In Psalm.* 33 n. 9 *ibid.* t. XIV p. 266.

[23] Cf. E. Longpré, 'la théologie mystique de S. Bonaventure', *AFrH* 14 (1921) esp. 51–53; idem, 'Bonaventure', *DSAM* I, 1768–1843; Fr. Andres, *Die Stufen der Contemplatio in Bonaventure Itinerarium* (Munster 1921); R. Carton, *L'expérience mystique de l'illumination interieure chez Roger Bacon* (Paris, 1924), esp. pp. 242–245; B. Rosenmoeller, *Religiöse Erkenntnis nach Bonaventura* (Munster, 1925), passim; D. Dobbins, *Franciscan Mysticism* (New York, 1926), esp. pp. 51 sq; J. M. Bissen, *Les degrés de la contemplation* (Paris, 1928/30); J. Bonnefoy, *Le Saint-Esprit et ses dons selon S. Bonaventure* (Paris, 1929); Et. Gilson, *The Philosophy of St. Bonaventure* (London, 1938); St. Grünewald, *Franziskanische Mystik* (Munich, 1932); J. Bonnefoy, *Une somme bonaventurienne de théologie mystique* (Paris, 1934); H. Koenig, *De inhabitatione Spiritus*

ideas, a problem raised by P. Bonnefoy must be resolved. In his view Bonaventure does not always mean the same thing when he speaks of the spiritual senses in different parts of his writings. On the contrary, the same words express different realities which are quite disparate: spiritual perceptions, the principle behind such perceptions, gifts of grace in the order of knowledge and the affections, habits of knowledge, and natural powers. In treating the investigations of other scholars he merely remarks: 'The basic error of these attempts to bring together the various statements on the subject lies in the view that all the passages in which Bonaventure speaks of "sensus spiritualis" deal with one and the same phenomenon'.[24] The search for 'a synthesis' is for him anachronistic. But in our opinion P. Bonnefoy is wrong. One must start with the clear statements of Bonaventure that the spiritual senses are acts and not new powers.[25] Here he is saying nothing new and is not contradicting, *pace* Bonnefoy, any earlier mystical tradition.[26] These acts touch on the intellect and will, which are perfected by three operations: by means of the virtues, the gifts of grace and the blessings of beatitude. If one sticks to this line of thought, which presents no internal contradiction, then there is no reason to interpret the different texts on the spiritual senses as though they referred to quite disparate phenomena.[27] Otherwise one must allow with P.

Sancti (Mundelein 1934); St. Grünewald, 'Zur Mystik des hl. Bonaventura', *ZAM* 9 (1934), 124–142; 219–232 (a discussion of our study); F. Beauchemin, *Le savoir au service de l'amour*. (Paris, 1935); F. Imle, *Das geistliche Leben nach der Lehre des hl. Bonaventura* (Werl, 1939); J. Friederichs, *Die Theologie als spekulative und praktische Wissenschaft nach Bonaventura und Thomas von Aquin* (Bonn 1940); R. Guardini, *Systembildende Elemente in der Theologie Bonaventuras* (Leiden, 1964); A. Elsässer, *Christus der Lehrer des Sittlichen* (Munich, 1968). The works of Bonaventure are quoted from the 10 volume critical edition of Quaracchi (1882–1902).

[24] J. Bonnefoy, *Le Saint-Esprit et ses dons Selon J. Bonaventure* (Paris, 1929), p. 214.

[25] *Ibid.* p. 212. Cf. *In III Sent* dist. 34 pars 1 art. 1 (T. III 7376).

[26] *Ibid.* p. 214. The long prevalent error that Poulain regards the spiritual senses as new powers of the soul seems ineradicable, although he himself expressly affirms the opposite; cf. *Katholik* 92 (1912), p. 291.

[27] Here it is a question purely of 'sensus stricte acceptus' (*III Sent* dist. 13 dub. T. III 291 b). In this sense the spiritual sense in Bonaventure is one-sided. The word 'sensus' can in itself mean a new power, so that the expressions of Bonaventure in the context of the 'sensus spiritualis' can often suggest the idea of a power. But these ideas lose nothing of their force if one sees in them the perception of the sense rather than the sense itself; the corresponding statements are quite intelligible if they are given this meaning. The acts can have

Bonnefoy that in a single text the same word can be used with completely different meanings, with the result that no coherent thought can be obtained from it.[28]

What is the nature of Bonaventure's doctrine? Surprisingly he does not include it in his treatment of psychology but refers to in in connection with grace. This already clarifies to some extent the mystical character of the spiritual senses.

For Bonaventure the soul in a state of grace has three modes of operation: through the virtues, the gifts of the Holy Spirit and the blessings of beatitude.[29] By these means the powers of the soul are corrected (habitus virtutum, potentiae rectificantur); their activity is made easier, they develop and become stronger (habitus donorum, potentiae expediuntur); finally they are brought to the perfection which a man can achieve on earth (habitus beatitudinum, potentiae perficiuntur). Although these three modes of operation are already present in the soul in a state of grace, they do not have their full effect at the same moment;[30] rather each of them corresponds to one of the three stages of the spiritual life: beginning (purification), development (enlightenment) and perfection.[31] The perfect man enjoys the sevenfold gifts of the blessings of beatitude and reaches the state of profound peace. But through the gift of wisdom love is also made easier, which is a preparation for the blessings of peace and finds its fulfilment in it.[32] When the soul has acquired such peace, then it experiences of necessity spiritual joy, the fruits of the Holy Spirit. At this point a man is on the threshold of contemplation, which is exercised precisely in the acts of the spiritual senses. Consequently it is a question here not of new modifications or powers but rather of acts, that is, applications of

---

their principle either in the intellect or in the will. The soul in possession of the three theological virtues regains the acts of experiential perception, since it has gained the theological virtues which form the principle of their operation. Bonaventure treats the senses as perceptions and so as acts. In summary we maintain that a 'comprehensive viewpoint' can be found in the texts of Bonaventure, in the sense that he is always dealing with acts of the soul which is perfected by the threefold modification of the virtues. This remains valid even in cases when the actual form of words points rather to powers.

[28] J. Bonnefoy, *Le Saint-Esprit et ses dons* ... (Paris, 1929) pp. 210 and 212.

[29] Cf. *Breviloquium* V 6 and III *Sent* dist. 34 art. 1 q. 1 (edit. Quaracchi t. V 285 sq. and III 735 sq.)

[30] III *Sent* dist. 34 art. 1 q. 2 (III 739 sq.)

[31] *Ibid.* 1. 3 (III 7426); *Brevil.* V 6 (V 256 ab).

[32] *Brevil.* V 5–6 (V 2576–2596).

the modifications which already have names to describe them in contemplation.[33]

A closer examination of the principles of these acts, that is, of the spiritual senses, leads to the same conclusion as that drawn by P. Bonnefoy, namely that the operation of the highest principles, the blessings of beatitude, is involved.[34] But the result for contemplation is that, for Bonaventure in contrast to modern mystical theology, the gifts of the Holy Spirit are of secondary importance. This is clearly stated in Bonaventure and in the Breviloquium comes first in the arrangement of the contents. But Bonaventure's doctrine of the blessings of beatitude is too little known to allow one to gain from it a deeper understanding of his thinking on *all* the spiritual senses.[35]

The two other modifications of the soul, the virtues and the gifts of grace, are so closely connected to contemplation that they also provide a real deepening of the spiritual senses. One should take note of the operation of the blessings of beatitude in the case of some of the senses, and so be able to work out what is the specific character of the sense in question. The two ultimate principles in the treatment of these senses are intellect and will; given Bonaventure's view of the relationship of these two powers of the soul,[36] it is hardly surprising that he can refer the same operation to two faculties. It is natural for him to regard the five spiritual senses as acts both of the intellect and of the will.[37] But just as the various operations relate in a different way to the intellect and the will according to their own particular character, so do the spiritual senses.

Spiritual sight and hearing are closely associated to the intellect;

---

[33] *Brevil.* V 6 (259–260) and III *Sent* dist. 34 art. 1 q. 1 (III 7376); Rosenmoeller does not bring out clearly the act quality of the senses in Bonaventure. It was Bonaventure, and not post-Tridentine Scholasticism, who was the first to overcome the oversimplified schema of Aristotle, here intelligence, there will, in the case of the spiritual senses.

[34] J. Bonnefoy, *op. cit.* pp. 97–98. The exact nature of the contemplation whose acts are constituted by the spiritual senses requires further study.

[35] It is well known that in Bonaventure the theological virtue of hope is connected with the gift of counsel, as it is in another aspect with strength and fear. In addition, hope has to do with the spiritual sense of smell.

[36] Cf. I *Sent.* dist. 3 pars 2 art. 1 q. 2 (I 84–87); II *Sent* dist. 24 pars 1 art. 2 q. 1 (II 560); III *Sent* dist. 27 art. 1 q. 1 (III 591), where Rosenmoeller speaks of a 'mutua circumincessio' of the powers of the soul; cf. Rosenmoeller, *op. cit.* (bibl.)

[37] III *Sent* dist. 13 dub. 1 (III 292a).

taste smell and touch relate rather to the will. This also determines the way they are connected to the theological virtues. Thus faith is first of all rooted in the intellect; from faith proceed spiritual sight and hearing[38] as soon as the corresponding operation of gifts and blessings have their effect. Hope, and especially love, are rooted in the will, from which the spiritual sense of smell and the higher senses, the taste and touch of love, proceed.[39] It is to be remarked at this point that the gift of understanding and the blessing of purity of heart correspond to the virtue of faith, while the gift of wisdom and the blessing of peace[40] are ordered to the virtue of love. As acts, the spiritual senses arise from three determinations of the soul; spiritual sight from faith, the gift of understanding and the blessing of purity of heart; taste and touch from the virtue of love, the gift of wisdom and the blessing of peace. Thus the principles of the spiritual acts of contemplation, i.e. the spiritual senses, are worked out as far as possible.

THE OBJECT OF KNOWLEDGE OF THE 'SPIRITUAL SENSES'

In a general way Bonaventure describes the object of the spiritual senses when he speaks of the 'perceptiones mentales circa veritatem contemplandam' or the 'usus gratiae interior respectu ipsius Dei', or even of the 'usus spiritualium speculationum'.[41] But to avoid misinterpreting Bonaventure's view point, we must be careful about these descriptions for two reasons. First it cannot be deduced from these accounts that the 'contemplatio' and 'speculatio' which are proper to a man on his long journey from sense perception to ecstasy are realised by the spiritual senses, or, in other words, that these acts are simply spiritual senses in Bonaventure's use of the term.[42] Such a conclusion

---

[38] Cf. III *Sent* dist. 23 and 27 (III 475 sq. and III 604b); also *Itin.* cap. 4 n.3 (V 306b). The presence and effectiveness of the other two series of operations are implicitly assumed here. The spiritual senses are not identical here with the 'habitus', as Bonnefoy, *op. cit.* p. 313, believes. The account in the *Itinerarium* corresponds closely to that of the *Breviloquium* where these senses are explicitly described as acts (V 258b).

[39] III *Sent* dist. 26 art. 2 q. 5 (III 579 sq.) and *Itin.* cap. 4 n. 3 (V3066).

[40] III *Sent* dist. 34 pars 1 art. 2 q. 1 (III 744b); *Brevil.* V 5 (V 257b); *ibid.* V 6 (V 259b); *de Donis Sp. S.* coll. 2 n. 3 (V 463a).

[41] *Brevil.* V 6 (V 260d); III *Sent* dist. 13 dub. 1 (III 291b); *Brevil.* V 6 (V 258b).

[42] This is the view of R. Carton, *op. cit.* pp. 245–246; 249–250. In Brevil V 6 (V260a) the sentence 'quae quidem contemplatio ... Sed consummatur in

runs counter to the fact that the doctor of the Church regards the spiritual senses as acts which are concerned with the stages of perfection and with the acquisition of the highest 'habitus' of the blessings of beatitude.[43] Secondly one should not assume from this description that these gifts possess a definite intellectual stamp, for some of them belong primarily to the realm of the affections. In summary we may say that the account describes the general manner of their operation rather than a series of exact distinctions. It implies that as acts of contemplation the spiritual senses simply have God as their primary object grasped as a present reality, without providing a more precise analysis.[44]

Some of the texts in Bonaventure give a clearer picture of the object of the spiritual senses, particularly when the perception of a particular phenomenon is attributed to a given sense.[45] These passages will be referred to frequently in what follows. A comparison between the two main passages from the *Breviloquium* and *Itinerarium* points to Christ as the reality grasped by the spiritual senses, the 'verbum increatum, inspiratum, incarnatum'.[46] Spiritual hearing grasps the 'verbum increatum', so that the soul hears its voice and highest harmony. Spiritual sight perceives the Word, because the soul is dazzled by its light and brilliant beauty. The spiritual sense of smell perceives the 'verbum inspiratum' when the soul experiences the lofty aroma of the Word. Spiritual taste savours the 'verbum increatum' when it enjoys

gloria sempiterna' must be understood as an additional comment to the foregoing 'circa veritatem contemplandam'. But this does not allow one to say that the spiritual senses can be referred as intellectual acts of perception to every possible object of the 'speculation' which is then described.

[43] *Brevil.* V 6 (V 258b). Here contemplation must be taken in the strict sense. That this operation signifies the highest level of perfection is clear from II *Sent* dist. 34 pars 1 art. 1 q. 1 (III 737a); *ibid.* dist. 36 q. 2 (III 795b); IV *Sent* dist. 1 pars 1 q. 6 (IV 28b); *Brevit.* V 4 (V 256a-b). Of course, the senses can be perfect in different ways and so correspondingly can the acts of contemplation.

[44] Cf. R. Carton, *op. cit.* p. 246; the assertion that God is the principal object of the senses must be brought into harmony with another idea of the senses whereby they are the perception of 'spiritualis refectio', i.e. of created grace. Cf. *III Sent* (III 738a).

[45] *Brevil.* V 6 (V 259b); *Itin.* cap. 4 n. 3 (V 306b); cf. *Coll. in Hexaem.* III n. 22 (V 347a); *Sermo 9 in Epiphan.* (IX 166b–167a). These texts were used by the *Centiloquium*, Hugh of Strasburg, Rudolf of Biberach, Peter of Ailly, Nadal, Polanco; vide infra.

[46] In Bonaventure e.g. *Coll. in Hexaem.* IX n. 1–4 (V 372–373).

the sublime delight of its sweetness. The spiritual sense of touch grasps the 'verbum incarnatum' and its powerful grace.[47] This description of the object of the spiritual senses undeniably possesses both depth and beauty, but it must also be admitted that the attempt to discover a special object for every sense, a 'ratio' through which it perceives the Word, is rather forced. Even though Bonaventure's dialectical skill and his ingenuity in drawing distinctions can cope with this difficulty, the impression remains that, despite the parallels with the physical senses and their object (splendor, harmonia, fragrantia, dulcedo, suavitas), a genuinely penetrating analysis of the specific character of the spiritual gifts as acts of contemplation has not been achieved. From another point of view, however, one can go further, but only for sight, touch and spiritual taste.[48]

Putting the various texts together one can see that spiritual sight is indebted to the act of faith, the gift of understanding and the blessing of purity of heart, in so far as we can refer to a spiritual sight which belongs in a general way to the five senses, although this only applies when the highest mode of operation, purity of heart, is at work. To these three modes of operation there correspond according to Bonaventure three stages of the supernatural knowledge of God[49] and he connects them explicitly with the acts of these three modes of operation. Thus it follows that the act of the third and highest stage of divine knowledge is nothing other than the spiritual sense of sight, the act of purity of heart.[50] The three stages are characterised as follows: the first consists in the simple acceptance of revealed truth in virtue of faith and understanding, in the measure that such truth allows itself to be discovered in the 'traces' of the mysterious divine life found in material things. The second stage bestows a deeper understanding of these mysteries according to their internal principles, in as much as they can be reached by the gift of understanding through consideration of the 'likenesses' and 'images' of God existing in spiritual creation.[51] But it is the third stage which alone is of particular interest

[47] For the order of the senses we follow the *Itinerarium* which assesses them according to the principles from which they originate (will higher than intellect); cf. *III Sent* dist. 13 dub. 1 (III 292 a). In the *Brevil* the sense of taste includes 'sapientia ... comprehendens ... verbum et splendorem.'
[48] Cf. *De reduct. artium ad Theol.* n. 10 (V 322b); another division in, *Sermo 14 in Epiphan.* (IX 168b–169a).
[49] For the following, Cf. J. Bonnefoy, *op. cit.* pp. 180 sq.
[50] Ibid. p. 191.
[51] III *Sent* dist. 34 and 35 (III 737a and 778f); *Brevil.* V 4 (V 256b).

here; this consists in the simple vision (simplex contuitus) which is reserved to purity of heart, which 'alone is permitted to gaze upon God'.[52] For an account of the 'simplex contuitus' we need only follow P. Bonnefoy.[53] It involves a vision of the first truth which is immutable, and of its eternal ideas which form the ultimate principles of all creation. This 'contuitus' finds its internal unity in our becoming aware of the direct operation of eternal truth upon our own spirit. Of course this simple vision of God is not a direct perception of the divine essence free of any intermediary. Such a thing would be an impossible occurrence in the mystical realm in this life, if one leaves aside the extraordinarily rare case of 'raptus'. 'Non videtur in sua essentia sed in aliquo effectu interiori cognoscitur.'[54] Thus the 'contuitus simplex' is 'an infallible fore-knowledge of the eternal foundations which comes through particular images bestowed upon our spirit.'[55]

With regard to the highest act of the will, the sense of taste corresponds to that of sight. Although it is far from easy to determine exactly where Bonaventure locates spiritual taste in the overall framework of his mystical theology, one can obtain a perfectly correct idea of its character by saying that it is an appreciation by the affections of the influence of created divine grace with regard to the direct experience of God. Taste is for the will what sight is for the understanding. Spiritual taste consists in 'suscipere ab ipso (Deo) delectationes'.[56] Certainly Bonaventure states quite categorically that taste is less perfect than feeling or touch which, as will be shown shortly, signify the direct union of love with God through ecstasy. Consequently taste can only be the direct, affective experience of created salvation, a created 'dulcedo', which allows God to be grasped as the principle of this 'dulcedo'. Bonaventure explains this experience as the essence of taste,[57] yet it also seems to be the stage of mystical development which proceeds the ecstatic union of love.[58] In summary we may conclude from all these remarks that spiritual taste appears to

[52] III *Sent.* dist. 35 q. 3 (III 778a).
[53] Cf. J. Bonnefoy, *op. cit.* pp. 182–183.
[54] II *Sent.* dist. 23 art. 2 q. 3 (II 544).
[55] J. Bonnefoy, *op. cit.* p. 183; For the philosophical angle, cf. B. A. Luyckx, *Die Erkenntnislehre Bonaventuras* (Munster, 1923) pp. 205 sq.
[56] *Itin.* cap. 4 n. 3 (V 306b).
[57] *Brevil.* V 6 (V 259b).
[58] *Serm 1 in Sab. sancto* n. 3 (IX 269a). Ecstasy proper here corresponds to 'amplexus'.

be the act of the will which can be directly felt with complete fulfilment.[59]

The 'simplex contuitus', vision, is the final goal of human understanding on earth, and yet it is not the last step of mystical progress or the highest form of contemplation in this world. For 'contuitus' only offers, according to Bonaventure, a 'contemplatio mediocris' in contrast to 'contemplatio perfecta', the 'excessus ecstatici'.[60] The most fundamental reason for this distinction is that spiritual sight, the act of the blessing of purity of heart, is not direct union with God but rather knowledge 'in interiori effectu'. The 'excessus ecstaticus' is, by contrast, the experience of the will, the union with God of a more direct love. Its act is 'spiritual touch', the highest spiritual sense. Ecstasy and spiritual touch are one and the same.

ECSTASY[61]

How is the nature of ecstasy to be understood in contrast to mystical knowledge 'in effectu interiori', and how is the relationship of spiritual touch to ecstasy to be interpreted?

In the first place ecstasy is to be distinguished from 'raptus',[62] which is an extraordinary occurrence. The latter is a direct, clear vision of God through the intellect, and is a foretaste of the beatific vision as an 'actus gloriae'.[63] This is a privileged and exceptional state which Bonaventure thinks, for instance, St Paul enjoyed, but not Moses.[64] Thus 'raptus' and ecstasy should be clearly distinguished, as in fact Bonaventure explicitly does. For him ecstasy is not extraordinary and he attributes qualities to it which 'raptus' cannot possess.[65]

[59] Cf. III *Sent.* dist. 34 pars 1 art. 1 q. 1 (III 738a).

[60] *Coll. 20 in Hexaem.* n. 9 and 10 (V 427a); cf. J. Bonnefoy, *op. cit.* p. 195.

[61] The basis of what follows is to be found in the section of this study already published in an expanded form under the title, 'Der Begriff der ecstasis bei Bonaventura' in *ZAM* 9 (1934), pp. 1–19. Since the original version was too long, it has been shortened for publication here.

[62] In addition to the concept 'ecstasy', the expressions 'excessus mentalis', 'amplexus', 'excessus anogogici', 'amor ecstaticus' and 'anagogica unitio' are also used in Bonaventure to refer to mystical experience.

[63] Cf. *Coll. 3 in Hexaem.* n. 30 (V 347b–348a) and II *Sent.* dist. 23 art. 2 q. 3 (II 544b).

[64] II *Sent* dist. 23 art. 2 q. 3 (II 544b); III *Sent* dist. 35 q. 1 (III 774b).

[65] For Bonaventure ecstasy is 'docta ignorantia', 'caligo', 'ignote ascendere', etc. This does not correspond to 'raptus', which is 'actus gloriae'; cf. II *Sent* dist. 23 art. 2 q. 3 (II 546a).

As was indicated above, ecstasy is set apart not only from 'raptus' but also from a knowledge of God which is mediated by the created effects of grace. In this regard we are essentially at variance with the interpretation of Longprés and Grünewald[66] and in basic agreement with Gilson and Rosenmoeller.[67] It is, however, impossible here to investigate more closely the essence of 'cognoscere Deum in effectu interiori', since this would demand clarification of the question whether this stage of knowledge of God in Bonaventure is a mystical phenomenon as this is currently understood.[68] Here it is sufficient to stand by the assertion; 'Non videtur (Deus) in sua essentia sed in aliquo effectu interiori cognoscitur'.[69] Ecstasy, on the contrary, is to be sharply distinguished from intellectual experience of the created effects of grace, even of a mystical kind, since it is the direct experience of God, direct in the proper ontological sense, and not only in the sense that the experience of the created effects of grace (which are, therefore, recognised) allows a practically direct knowledge of God as their underlying cause (in the form of a 'medium in quo'). Bonaventure makes the distinction quite clear: 'Cognitio viae[70] multos habet gradus; cognoscitur enim Deus in vestigio, cognoscitur in imagine, cognoscitur et in effectu gratiae, cognoscitur etiam per intimam unionem iuxta quod dicit Apostolus: Qui adhaeret Deo unus spiritus est. Et haec cognitio est excellentissima, quam docet Dionysuis quae est in ecstatico amore et elevat supra cognitionem fidei secundum statum communem.'[71] Here a clear separation is made between 'congoscere in effectu gratiae' and 'cognitio per intimam unionem', which represent different degrees of knowledge of God. The higher of the two, which is not achieved through the medium of the operations of grace, is described as a knowledge through 'intima unio', which con-

[66] Cf. E. Longpré, *La théologie mystique de S. Bonaventure* (Florence, 1921) and St. Grünewald, *Franziskanische Mystik* (Munich, 1932).

[67] Et. Gilson, *The Philosophy of St. Bonaventure* (London, 1938) and B. Rosenmoeller, *Religiöse Erkenntnis nach Bonaventura* (Munster, 1925).

[68] Grünewald assumes a mystical quality for 'cognoscere in effectu gratiae'; i.e. ecstasy is 'cognoscere in effectu gratiae' and yet mystical. He makes use of the texts accordingly.

[69] II *Sent* dist. 23 art. 2 q. 3 (III 544b). This text is rightly quoted to exclude a direct intellectual vision of God. But this does not necessarily mean the exclusion of all direct union of love with God.

[70] 'Viae' is stressed in contrast to 'patriae' according to the context. 'Raptus' cannot be meant here.

[71] III *Sent* dist. 24 (III 531b).

sists in ecstatic love and is the one taught by Denis. It is not hard from this text to understand the connection between knowledge of God, 'unio' and ecstatic love: ecstatic love (an act of the will) effects union with God, which permits an experience of God that surpasses any in which God is perceived in the created operations of grace. The experience of God contained in 'intima unio' is not 'raptus'.[72] For the latter is, according to Bonaventure, not a 'cognitio viae'. Furthermore it would be hard to understand why 'raptus' should be characterised as ecstatic love, whereas in other places ecstasy is described as 'amor ecstaticus' and as 'intima unio'.[73] Moreover the background reference to the teaching of Denis is elsewhere not given for 'raptus' but for 'ecstasis', and in exactly those passages where the latter is plainly distinguished from 'raptus'.[74] In consequence it is ecstasy which in III Sent. dist. 24 dub. IV is clearly distinguished from 'cognoscere in effectu gratiae' as the higher stage.[75]

Another text makes it clear that, far from treating ecstasy as a form of knowledge of God which is mediated by the created operation of grace, we should rather regard it as the direct experience of God in the proper sense of the term, that is, without any intermediate perception: 'Est cognoscere Deum in se et in suo effectu. Est cognoscere Deum in effectu, hoc est videre per speculum et hoc dupliciter: aut per speculum lucidum et oculum et sic videbat primus homo ante lapsum; aut per speculum obscuratum et sic videmus nos modo ... Alio modo cognoscitur Deus in se; et hoc dupliciter: aut clare et hic modo a solo Filio et a beatis; alio modo in caligine, sicut Beatus Dionysius de Mystica theologia. Et sic vidit Moyses et sublimiter contemplantes, in quorum aspectu nulla figitur imago creaturae. Et tunc revera magis sentiunt quam cognoscant.'[76]

According to Bonaventure, therefore, we should assume a 'cognoscere' or better a 'sentire' of God which is a direct process ('in se') without any intermediary means of perception (not 'in effectu'). This

---

[72] According to Bonaventure 'raptus' is not a 'cognitio viae'. Consequently, he does not need to mention it in this list.

[73] Coll. 2 in Hexaem. n. 29 (V 341a).

[74] II Sent dist. 23 art. 2 q. 3 (II 544b).

[75] Longpré wrongly appeals to this passage to prove that even ecstasy is a 'cognoscere in effectu gratiae'. But all that is stated is that ecstasy is not 'conspicere Deum in claritate suae essentiae'.

[76] Coll. in Jona. I n. 43 (IV 255b–256a).

experience is to be distinguished both from the knowledge of Adam[77] in paradise and from the 'visio beatifica'. It is naturally true that this 'sentire Deum in se' is contrasted with 'cognoscere in effectu', and appears beside 'visio' as a direct experience of God. It is not a matter of a psychological impression of something which in fact is a mediated knowledge of God. Rather we are dealing here with a directness which is also characteristic of the beatific vision. And yet in Bonaventure's view there must also be an essential (that is, qualitative and not merely quantitative) difference between ecstasy and the beatific vision. This is the reason why he speaks of 'sentire' rather than 'cognoscere', that is, of experience rather than knowledge. This remark of Bonaventure should make us wary of putting too much weight on expressions such as 'knowledge', etc. used in his account of 'ecstasy'. It is a question of a mysterious experience, not of intellectual knowledge.[78]

This 'feeling God himself' is not 'raptus' but ecstasy, that is, the highest (normal) mystical experience, which Bonaventure describes in II *Sent.* dist. 23 a.2 q.3. The text runs as follows: 'Concedo tamen nihilominus quod oculi aspectus in Deum figi potest ita quod ad nihil aliud adspiciat, attamen non perspiciet vel videbit ipsius lucis claritatem, immo potius elevabitur in caliginem, et ad hanc cognitionem elevabitur per omnium ablactionem, sicut dicit Dionysius in libro de Mystica theologia, et vocat istam cognitionem doctam ignorantiam. Haec est, in qua mirabiliter inflammatur affectio, sicut eis patet qui aliquoties consueverunt ad anagogicos elevari excessus.' It is generally agreed that this description refers to ecstasy and this is clear from the account itself. For 'raptus' is plainly distinguished from this mystical experience by the following phrase: 'Quod si Deus aliquid ultra faciet, hoc privilegium est speciale, non legis communis'. 'In caligine sentire Deum in se' is identical with ecstasy, as we can see from a comparison with *In Joan.* I n.43:

[77] The knowledge of Adam in the garden of Eden is for Bonaventure the standard of mystical experience, in so far as it is an intellectual experience of God. Thus, II *Sent* dist. 23 art. 2 q. 3 speaks without distinction of Adam's knowledge and of the mystical knowledge of the intellect.

[78] This distinction between 'sentire' and 'cognoscere' shows where the solution to the problem lies of how there can be a direct experience of God which is not the 'visio beatifica'. On this level of knowledge in the broadest sense, Bonaventure characterises the experience of ecstasy as 'sentire'. In consequence, he ascribes it to the 'affectus' alone. At the same time, he distinguishes it from 'videre', the term he uses to describe 'visio' and 'raptus' (II *Sent* dist. 23 art. 2 q. 3).

II *Sent.*	*In Joan.* I n.43
a) oculi adspectus in Deum figi potest ita quod ad nihil aliud adspiciat	a) in quorum adspectu nulla figitur imago creaturae
b) in caliginem	b) in caligine
c) sicut Dionysius dicit in libro de Mystica theologia	c) sicut Dionysius dicit de Mystica theologia
d) mirabiliter inflammatur affectio	d) magis sentiunt quam cognoscant

If one recalls that in II *Sent.* ecstasy 'in caliginem' is to be distinguished from 'raptus' and from 'visio', and that it also appears in *In Joan.* I n.43 where 'in quorum adspectu nulla figitur imago creaturae' is only a variant upon 'sentire Deum in se', then there can be no doubt of the identity of the experience described in these two passages. Similarly it is clear that this experience is different both from 'raptus' and from the mediated knowledge of God. Consequently the reference must be here to ecstasy, regarded as an ontologically direct experience of God.

The attempt has been made to explain the crucial text from *In Joan.* I n.43 by means of 'raptus'[79] but this attempt cannot be regarded as successful. For if one wanted to reconcile 'raptus' at this point with the remark in John's Gospel (1:18) that no man has seen God, it would not be necessary falsely to assert that 'raptus' was 'in caligine' (how is that possible, since it is 'actus gloriae'?) Instead one would merely have had to repeat that 'raptus' is an experience of those who enjoy what is a special privilege for 'men on the way', to whom the assertion of John 1:18 applies. For these and other reasons the text must be dealing with ecstasy, an immediate experience of God.

This is not contradicted by the text from the commentary on the Sentences, although this passage is normally regarded as the classic proof for the view that even in ecstasy God is only grasped by means of the recognition of the created operations of grace. To interpret this text correctly, one need only hold that Bonaventure wished to exclude direct, *intellectual*[80] vision of God on this earth, for such vision would, at most, be quantitatively different from the beatific vision. If one is looking for a direct or indirect understanding of God, then there is no need to speak of ecstasy, since it is not relevant to the question of what

[79] Cf. St. Grünewald, *op. cit.* p. 88, note 199; also p. 43, note 57.
[80] A 'visio intellectualis' (II 546a), in which God is directly 'intellectui praesens', means a more or less clear vision of God'.

kind of intellectual vision of God was possessed by Adam. A more precise understanding of ecstasy reveals a qualitative difference from the beatific vision, since it consists essentially and exclusively in an experience of God in the 'apex affectus'.[81] Ecstasy does not figure in the question posed in this text, and is only mentioned by Bonaventure in a couple of asides.

Bonaventure shows why even a weaker form of the beatific vision is not to be attributed to Adam: the highest level of normal perception on earth is 'ignote ascendere' according to Denis. Vision itself, even of a weaker type, would be something more perfect in comparison with this. Therefore Adam's intellectual knowledge of God can only be a 'cognoscere in effectu interiori', which is definitely to be distinguished from 'ignote ascendere'.[82] Bonaventure summarises his point of view by saying that it is only glory, 'in qua non solum asperceret divinum effectum, sed etiam ipsum vultum desideratum ... Concedo tamen nihilominus quod oculi adspectus in Deum figi potest ita quod ad nihil aliud adspiciat, attamen ...'.[83] The qualification makes the contrast mentioned above unmistakably clear: Bonaventure evidently presumes that 'docta ignorantia' is a direct experience of God, while denying that it is a 'vision of the brightness of the light itself'. On the other hand, this knowledge is not mediated by the created effects of grace; that is to say, ecstasy has a quite specific quality. This is confirmed with still greater clarity by a more precise investigation of the nature of ecstasy. One merely has to show that ecstasy is an act of the 'apex affectus', while 'visio' is primarily an act of the intellect. Thus Bonaventure does not fall back into the previously rejected notion that only a quantitative difference of clarity obtains between earthly mysticism and the vision of the blessed.[84] Attempts to weaken the directness of the ecstatic experience of God as taught by Bonaventure would only involve one in contradictions.[85] Ecstasy, however, also forms a contrast to the knowledge of God bestowed by the operations of grace.[86]

[81] As 'sentire Deum in se', Bonaventure can set it together which the 'visio beatifica' over against 'cognoscere in effectu' (cf. Coll. in Jona. I n. 43).

[82] II Sent dist. 23 art. 2 q. 3 (II 544b and 546a).

[83] Ibid.

[84] Ibid. (II 544a).

[85] Cf. St. Grünewald, op. cit. pp. 87–110.

[86] Our interpretation agrees with that of Gilson; similarly Rosenmoeller, op. cit. pp. 185 sqq. 'Unmittelbarkeit der Gotteserfassung der Ekstase.'

How can this direct experience of God be made comprehensible? As we said above, ecstasy is the direct union of the soul with God, and this contact is realised essentially and exclusively in the 'apex affectus', that is, in an affectivity which is higher and more interior than the intellect.[87] In the experience of the direct spiritual union with God in the highest point of the soul every activity of the intellect as such is excluded. The reason for this is that the innermost part of man lies beyond the intellect.[88] Here God dwells exclusively, which means that no one else can touch this highest point of the spirit,[89] the innermost depths of a man. A man may, however, enter the innermost part of his spirit through ecstatic union and here he reaches the highest point of his soul. The whole mystical enterprise up to this point was nothing other than the gradual return of a man to the interior domain, as ascent to the highest point of the soul. Because this can only be reached in 'affectivity', a man must leave behind him all intellectual activity at a certain point on his mystical path on this earth.[90] This assertion should not be qualified in the sense that what is proposed is in fact an imperfect act of knowledge, such as is always required by a finite intellect in relation to the infinite. The truth is rather that ecstasy does not involve the intellect at all. This explains why mystical union is an entry into darkness, into a divine obscurity. This 'night' and the exclusion of the intellect are essential to ecstasy, since it is not a weaker form of direct intellectual vision of God, for this only realises its fulfilment (excessus), that is direct contact with the essence of God,[91] in the beatific vision (and in 'raptus'). Ecstasy, by contrast, is the obscure experience of the direct union of love with God. Thus the difference from 'visio' is qualitative and not merely quantitative.

How are we to conceive the direct experience of a union of love? The principle that nothing can be willed which is not first known raises a notable difficulty here. According to Bonaventure this union

[87] *Itin.* cap. 7 n. 4 (V 3126); *Coll. 2 in Hexaem.* n. 30 (V 341b); *Serm. 4 in Epiph.* (IX 162b); cf. also *Brevil.* V 6 (V 260a); III *Sent* dist. 24 dub IV (III 531b).

[88] Cf. *Coll. 2 in Hexaem.* n. 29–31 (V 341a/b).

[89] *De myst. Trinit.* q. 1 art. 1 fund. 10 (V 46a); II *sent* dist. 8 pars 2 q. 2 (II 226/7; I *sent* dist. 1 art. 3 q. 2 (I 41a), and *de scientia Christi* q. 4 fund. 31 (V 20b).

[90] III *Sent* dist. 35 1. 3 (III 779b); cf. *ibid.* dist. 31 art. 1 q. 1 (III 689a); *coll. 2 in Hexaem* n. 32 (V 342a); *ibid. 20 in Hexaem* n. 11 (V 427a).

[91] *Itin.* cap. 7 n.4 (V 312b); *coll. 2 in Hexaem* n. 30 (V 341b); *de scientia Christi* q.7 (V 40 sqq.)

can and must be experienced in some real way. Admittedly it is of a peculiar kind[92] compared with other forms of knowledge, but what is particularly obscure is how to interpret it except as intellectual knowledge. This is precisely what Bonaventure seeks to do. He did not explicitly address himself to this problem, but he could have offered the following reflections which would fit in with his basic line of argument. In every act of will and of love the object is not already grasped by the will in virtue of its intentional presence to the intellect; rather it must enter the will on its own account.[93] The direct ecstatic union of love is realised without the assistance of the intellect; therefore the reality of God's own essence must be the 'informing object' of the will (more precisely of the 'affections') in its innermost being. For in ecstasy the 'apex affectus' is 'transformed'[94] completely into God. In Bonaventure's view an object can under certain conditions be perceived without the creation of a rational representation to make perception possible, because the object is itself present as a principle of perception. Thus in our case it happens that the 'apex affectus', in which God is present, is not merely a capacity of the same order as the intellect. As the highest and most interior element in the soul it belongs to a deeper level of reality than the intellect and all that is related to it in the same order of being and can be characterised as will or normal 'affection'. Now this highest point of the soul (according to the genuine Franciscan model) bears a closer resemblance to the will than to the intellect.[95] Nevertheless this 'apex' lies deeper than the will and is the ground of the soul which supports the capacities of both understanding and will. If, according to a general scholastic notion of

[92] Bonaventure says 'sentire' and not 'cognoscere' in order to describe the experience before 'theory' which he then develops from this experience.

[93] One should note the scholastic doctrine of 'pondus amoris' which was coming to play a role in speculation on the Trinity. It does not seem to be found in Bonaventure, but he does explicitly affirm an 'information' of the 'apex affectus' by God in 'ecstasy'.

[94] *Itin.* cap. 7 n. 4 (V 312b); cf. also *ibid.* n. 3 and 6. Because every other created 'information' of the apex of the soul is excluded (and on the other hand this 'information' by God far surpasses the creative power of the apex), Bonaventure also calls ecstasy 'sapientia nulliformis'. Cf. *Coll. 2 in Hexaem* n. 8 (V 337b) and *ibid.* n. 28 (V 340b).

[95] Bonaventure states this principle in respect of the intellect. Cf. B. A. Luyckx, *Die Erkenntnis Bonaventuras* (Munster, 1923), pp. 175 sqq; 182–183. It is then extended to the experience of God by the 'apex affectus'. The 'virtutes interiores' are 'quasi circulus intra circulum' according to Bonaventure; cf. *Serm. 4 in Epiph.* (IX 162b). Cf. also St. Grünewald, *op. cit* p. 83, note 182d.

the metaphysic of the soul, the capacities of intellect and will spring somehow from the deepest and innermost ground of the soul, then the soul must possess these capacities as a unity in the depths of its being, capacities which develop 'outwards' into two separate faculties. Now if God touches this deepest point from within, giving form to it, as it were, then the 'apex affectus' will become conscious of this direct union of love without the intellect taking any active part.[96] Naturally the soul experiences God directly in the ground of its being only as the motive power of ecstatic love which leaves all knowledge behind it, and in consequence the experience remains obscure until the intellect as well is flooded, without being blinded, by the dazzling brilliance of God in the beatific vision. But at any rate God is here the dark fire of love.[97]

After this description of the main outline of Bonaventure's theory of ecstasy, a number of questions remain open which cannot be pursued in detail here. In summary we might say that in itself the account given by Bonaventure should be regarded as a remarkable attempt to resolve the problem of reconciling the specific character of the mystical life of grace, which cannot be reduced to the experiences of the normal life of grace, with the fact that direct vision of God face to face is the reward of heaven and not the lot of pilgrims. It is not the only conceivable solution to this problem but it is the one which falls least into the error of reducing the specific character and the sublime heights of mystical experience. It is also significant how strongly in this theory the darkness, the 'night character' of the highest mystical experience is stressed. Certainly the influence of the Areopagite makes itself felt at this point. But the way this idea is taken up, and the way the darkness of mystical experience is clarified by means of a metaphysical system quite foreign to Denis shows that the theme of the night in the mysticism of Bonaventure is not just a piece of tradition. In his theory the darkness, the night (if we may use the terminology of John of the Cross) is not so much a preparatory state of testing

[96] In ecstasy the powers of the soul flow back in some measure into the ground of the soul and remain suspended in the higher state (*Serm. 4 in Epiph.*). If this is the explanation of how the 'apex affectus' can really experience the union of love without the aid of the intellect, then Bonaventure is not a forerunner of the mystical theory (e.g. of Vincent of Aggsbach) that the mystical union of love occurs without any knowledge; for in Bonaventure the apex *experiences* it in ecstasy. Cf. E. Vansteenberghe, *Autour de la docte Ignorance* (Munster, 1915).

[97] *Itin.* cap. 7. n. 6 (V 313b) and *Coll. 20 in Hexaem* n. 11 (V 427a).

prior to the highest mystical experience, but the experience itself. Recent investigations into the mysticism of John of the Cross[98] show that in this point also Bonaventure anticipated the deepest ideas of the mystical doctor of the Church.

ECSTASY AND SPIRITUAL TOUCH

In brief one may say that spiritual touch is nothing else than the act by which the soul grasps the substance of God in ecstasy. Thus the examination of the nature of ecstasy was in no way a diversion from the main topic; it was rather an attempt to determine more precisely what Bonaventure understood by spiritual touch. Ecstasy and spiritual touch belong together and this identification can be shown in a number of ways. First of all it is noteworthy that, when Bonaventure treats of the spiritual senses in a general way, ecstasy is mentioned.[99] Further in his view feeling and touch form the highest and most spiritual sense since it unites a person most fully with God, the highest spirit, and signifies the experience of union with God.[100] The highest blessing, that of peace, is to be found in spiritual touch. Ecstasy, however, arises from peace and this is expressly referred to spiritual touch: 'ut *transiens* in illud (Verbum) per *ecstaticum* amorem recuperat . . . tactum'.[101] In the Breviloquium he writes about spiritual touch: 'Adstringitur summa suavitas sub ratione Verbi incarnati inter nos habitantis corporaliter et reddentis se nobis palpabile, osculabile, amplexabile per ardentissimam caritatem quae mentem nostram per *ecstasim* et raptum *transire* facit ex hoc mundo ad Patrem.'[102] Here it is made quite clear that touch is the act of love in ecstasy. When we review the character of ecstasy in Bonaventure's account, it strikes us at once that this experience is best rendered by the term 'contact'. The

---

[98] Cf. J. Baruzi, *Saint Jean de la croix et le problème de l'expérience mystique* (Paris, 1931).

[99] *Brevil.* V. 6 (V 259b–260a); *Itin.* cap. 4 n. 3 (V306b).

[100] III *Sent* dist. 28 art. 2 q. 1 (III 604b); cf. *ibid.* dist. 13 (III 292a).

[101] *Itin.* cap. 4 n. 3 (V 306b). On the spiritual senses, cf. also the fact that not all acts of a lower sort are here like those of cap. 7. It is already a question of the soul which 'purificatur, illuminatur et perficitur' through the three theological virtues. That is, the soul is 'perfect', and so these acts should not be regarded merely as preparation for mystical experience (cf. E. Longpré).

[102] *Brevil* V 6 (V 259b). Gilson and Rosenmoeller both believe that the spiritual senses play an active part in ecstasy. But they do not connect ecstasy so closely to touch as we do.

mystic experiences of the direct presence of God in 'a totally obscure encounter', as Meister Eckhart expresses it.[103] The two characteristics of directness and darkness in the experience of God are best expressed by the word 'contact'. Bonaventure offers the term in the spirit of his philosophy and theology and discovers the principle of this 'night' in the essentially *affective* nature of the direct grasp of God.[104]

The speculative power and the mystical depths are indeed remarkable which Bonaventure has applied to the traditional teaching of the five spiritual senses in order to clarify the nature of mystical experience. Bonaventure has also managed to integrate the traditional material into his own system of mystical theology.[105] The number five remains perhaps a trifle arbitrary and as a result Bonaventure was not entirely successful in assigning to each sense distinct mystical experience as the specific object of perception. Thus the sense of smell and hearing remain more or less superfluous for the account of spiritual contemplation and its various levels. In this there lies a certain weakness in the rigid doctrine of the five spiritual senses. However this proves how successful were Bonaventure's efforts to give content to the rather a priori and schematic teaching and bring it a little closer to reality. His partial success makes one able to assert that the doctrine of the five spiritual senses is not merely a period piece, a speculative a priori game which has no contact with the real world. If his success was not complete, the fault lies not in Bonaventure but in an inescapable flaw inherent in the doctrine of the spiritual senses. Within the scope of this essay it is not possible to make a critical assessment of the content of Bonaventure's teaching and come to a conclusion about the extent to which his views on contemplation and ecstasy correspond to reality. Rosenmoeller has raised a question about the sources of Bonaventure's teaching of the spiritual senses.[106] We are conscious

[103] Cf. Traktat 11 (Ausg. Fr. Pfeiffer, *Deutsche Mystiker des 14 Jahrhunderts* II, Stuttgart 1857/Reprint 1924, 507, 29). This edition is poor, but a more recent one is not available.

[104] Understandably, this ecstatic union is linked to the experience of the highest beatitude (at least in general terms). Bonaventure uses images and expressions of the sense of taste to describe it. However, subjective feeling should not be regarded as the mark of ecstasy. Taste is less perfect than touch in Bonaventure. Yet it can occur in ecstasy since it is rooted in the 'affectus' and is not affected by the exclusion of the intellect.

[105] Cf. *De plant. parad.* n. 16 (V 579a); *Soliloq.* cap. 1 n. 44 (VIII 43); *Serm. 2 in dom 12 post Pent.* (IX 401b–402a); *De S. Agnete serm.* 2 (IX 510b).

[106] *Op. cit.* p. 201

that in this study we have drawn attention only to a few of Bonaventure's predecessors; however the few examples we noted indicate that Bonaventure added nothing new to the substance or the many particular details of this teaching. At any rate even the discovery of new sources could not rob him of the achievement of being the first of the Scholastics to have given to this doctrine real content which expresses the direct experience of mysticism.

Finally we must complete this account of the spiritual senses by adding a few remarks about the later development of the doctrine. In the same century as Bonaventure mention should be made of Roger Bacon.[107] Although his brief comments do not suffice to show whether he was directly dependent on Bonaventure, nevertheless the fact that he allotted the spiritual senses to the fifth stage of the 'scientia interior' between the blessings and the fruits, indicates at least kinship, if not dependence, with the teaching of Bonaventure. To the 13th century there also belongs the *Compendium theologicae veritatis* of Hugh Ripelin of Strasbourg. In the section on the spiritual senses he takes over, with no great understanding, the exposition found in the *Breviloquium* of Bonaventure.[108] Here there is also a connection in his teaching between the blessings and the fruits; the fact that this is found in the 'most well known and complete manual of the Middle Ages'[109] provides clear evidence for the spread of the doctrine in this period. The *Centiloquium* also takes over the ideas of Bonaventure with almost as close a verbal similarity; it is the work of an unknown 14th century writer. If one remembers the extraordinary dissemination of these two manuals, then an echo of the teaching is almost certainly to be expected in the German mystics. Meister Eckhart offers eloquent witness of this.[110] Precisely because he lacks any clear theoretical doctrine, his expressions provide a notable example of the use of the idea of the five spiritual senses for the description of higher mysticism. A clear witness of the growing influence of Bonaventure is found in the middle of the 14th century in another German, Rudolf of Biberach. In his *On the seven gifts of the Holy Spirit*[111] he scarcely makes any use of

[107] *Opus maius* II, edit. S Jebb (Venice, 1750), p. 338. On Bacon's doctrine of the five spiritual senses, see R. Carton, *op. cit.* pp. 242 sqq.

[108] Cf. *Comp. theological veritatis* V cap. 56 (Edit. Borgnet XXXIV 191 Alberts d. Grossen). He forgets sight and says 'sub ratione splendoris audit.'

[109] Cf. *DThC* VI 902.

[110] Cf. footnote 103.

[111] Pars 1 cap. 3 (edit. Vives VII 590) and pars 2 sect. 7 cap. 2 (ibid 637).

Bonaventure's ideas, but in his *On the seven ways of eternity*[112] greater originality is evident. Here the operation of the five senses is a sign of the influence of love in the life of the soul. However in their activity they meet with the corruption of our nature and with their own omissions. Only the grace of Christ and concentration on the interior life can overcome these obstacles. In particular Jesus offers in the eucharist the nourishment necessary to enable the soul not to lose these faculties. The bread 'strengthens all the interior senses; it arouses them so that each can lay hold of its proper object. All the senses recognise God made man, who is hidden in the sacrament. This reference to the eucharist is the most original element of Rudolf's teaching on the spiritual senses.

In the 15th century five authors deserve mention, Bernadine of Siena, Peter of Ailly, his disciple Gerson, Denis the Carthusian and Harphius. Bernadine describes how in heaven the souls savour their bliss with every spiritual sense and how these senses are tortured in the sufferings of hell.[113] The *Compendium Contemplationis* of Peter of Ailly devotes the whole third tractate of 13 short chapters to the spiritual senses.[114] They are different from the bodily senses but their nature is hard to determine. He holds to the view of a 'quidam' which is the same as that of Bonaventure. The senses communicate to us a 'experimentalis notitia' of spiritual realities. In the fourth chapter these senses are divided according to three faculties: 'memoria, potentia intellectiva, potentia affectiva seu volitiva'. The subsequent chapters describe the nature of the act of the senses and its object. Finally individual senses are considered, the obstacles to them and, in conclusion, the means of salvation. Gerson is also familiar with this teaching but does not add anything new.[115] Denis the Carthusian writes in his commentary on the *Heavenly hierarchy* of Denis the Areopagite as follows: 'Denique hi quoque quinque sensus interiores in nostris sunt animabus'.[116] In fact they refer here only to intellectual joy which is

---

[112] Dist. 4 art. 2 (edit. Vives VIII 443 and 464–472). This forms the fullest medieval account of the spiritual senses.

[113] *Op. omn.* (edit. de la Haye; Venice 1745) I 301B *serm. 57 de gloria corporum beatorum* art. 2 cap. 2; II 72A, *serm. 11 de indicio generali* art. 3 cap. 3.

[114] Cf. *Tractatus et sermones compilati* ... Petro de Ailliaco (Argentinae, 1490) fol. 23–25.

[115] Gerson, *Op. omn. serm. 2 de omnibus sanctis* (Antwerp, 1706), III 1523 sq.

[116] Cf. Art. 77, *op. omn.* (Tournai, 1902), XV 254; *Enarrat. in Boetii de cons. philos.* II prosa 1 art. 1 (Tournai 1906), XXVI 159; cf. cap. 15 3 (PG 3) 332 A–B, where the bodily senses are used in an allegorical way for the intellectual

treated in its various forms. Finally Harphius gives a complete account of the spiritual senses[117] without going further than Bonaventure. Because of the success of his *Theologia mystica* it is not without importance that in this area he transmits the tradition of Bonaventure.

In the 16th century Blosius witnesses to this teaching.[118] Like Peter of Ailly he relates the senses to the three powers of the soul: memory, intellect and will. At this period what is particularly interesting is the attempt to connect the doctrine of the five spiritual senses with the 'Use of the Senses' in the *Spiritual Exercises* of St Ignatius Loyola. Various outlines and preparatory drafts from this period, which appeared before the official 'Directory' of 1599, make use of Bonaventure's teaching or that of Rudolf of Biberach in order to clarify the 'Use of the Senses'. Thus Polanco and a 'Directorium Granatense' wish to leave the possibility open of employing Bonaventure's doctrine for the explanation of the 'Use of the Senses'.[119] Gilles Gonzales, however, declares himself against this method.[120] In the official Directorium the 20th chapter entirely omits any reference to this teaching.[121] This is not the place to treat the question of the correct interpretation of the Ignatian use of the senses. The connection between it and the ancient doctrine of the five spiritual faculties is only one of the many of the indications which favour such an interpretation of the use of the senses. The latter was very widespread before the official Directory and it was not seen as an easy exercise, nor was meditation regarded as 'more intellectual' and 'generally higher' in comparison. On the contrary the use of the senses was regarded as 'more intellectual' and as 'a certain participation in vision', as a 'higher form ... more difficult' than meditation.[122] In this view the use of

---

powers of angels.

[117] *Theologia mystica* 1 cap. 15; cap. 38; II pars 5 cap. 35 (edit. Rome 1587), 153; 221 sq; 833.

[118] *Institutio spiritualis*, praef. (Opera, Antwerp, 1632), 297.

[119] *Monum. hist. SJ, Monum. Ignat.* ser II, 812–813 (Polanco) and 961 (Granatense).

[120] *Ibid.* 901; 918–919; 1047–1048.

[121] *Ibid.* 1150–1151.

[122] For this interpretation of the senses cf. *Monum, hist. SJ Monum Ignat.* ser II 1096–1097 n. 15; A. Gagliardi, *Commentarii seu Explanationes in Exercitia spiritualia S.P. Ignatii de Loyola* (Bruge, 1862) 22–24; L. Palmensis, *Via Spiritualis* V. 1 1. 3 cap. 7 (edit. Nonell; Barcelona, 1897), 397–400. Here we are not dealing with those who later held this view, since we merely wish to explain how it was that before the appearance of the Directorium in 1599, Bonaventure's doctrine was connected with the use of the senses. The writers

the senses was placed next to the prayer of the heart and of simplicity. Taken as an allusion to Bonaventure this is less remarkable and unreasonable than may at first sight appear. The justification of seeing a relationship between Bonaventure and Ignatius will not be discussed here. It should merely be stated that the idea of the five spiritual senses was well known to the Jesuits of the first generation; Nadal and Peter Faber provide evidence of this.[123]

The two great classical figures of Spanish mysticism, Teresa of Avila and John of the Cross, are not familiar with the doctrine in the form which has been investigated here. In their main writings which expound the psychology of mysticism, only the empirical foundations of the doctrine are present; the direct character of mystical experience can more easily be expressed through images taken from immediate sense perception and the peculiarities of a particular mystical experience have their analogue in the expression of one or other of these senses. Thus Teresa writes: 'The first stage of supernatural prayer, as I have experienced it, is an interior concentration which is felt by the soul. It seems to possess new senses in itself which roughly correspond to the external senses.'[124] John of the Cross speaks of the feeling of the soul, of spiritual hearing and spiritual eyes, of the 'sense of soul', 'spiritual sense', 'rational and higher sense' and of 'spiritual taste'.[125] He also compares the four ways of pure spiritual perception (vision, revelation, hearing, spiritual sensations) with the different sense perceptions.[126] It can be presumed that he has in mind a similar division to that of Bonaventure when he distinguishes between 'knowing him (God) through his effects and works' and the essential communication of his divinity; the latter is characterised as 'the touch of naked substances, the knowledge of the soul and divinity'.[127] Evidently John of the Cross is inevitably as Bonaventure drawn to 'touch and feel' when

---

quoted above all received their spiritual formation before 1599.

[123] *Monum. hist. SJ, Monum. Nadal* IV 677 sq; cf. K. Rahner, 'Über die Gnade des Gebetes in der Gesellschaft Jesu', *Mitteil. aus d. deutschen Provinzen SJ* 13 (1935) 399–411 (Transl. of the relevant text); *Monum. hist. SJ, Monum Fabri Memoriale* n. 69, 527; n. 343,656; n. 345,657 and n. 436,693.

[124] Letter to Rodrigo Alvarez, cf. Bouix, *Lettres*, t. 1 (Paris 1861), 379 = Letter 78.

[125] Cf. the references in J. Baruzi, *Saint Jean de la croix et le problème de l'expérience mystique* (Paris, 1931) p. 361.

[126] *Subida* II 21 (E.C. I 223).

[127] *Cantico str.* XXXII V. 2 (E.C. II 589). Similar expressions are often found in John of the Cross.

it is a question of portraying the highest mystical experiences. Naturally he employs images derived from all the physical senses in order to describe mystical states.[128]

Is the absence of a specific doctrine of the five senses in classical modern mysticism a real reason for the disappearance of this notion, which previously received such emphasis and importance? In fact E. Lamballe was even capable at the beginning of this century of imagining that the whole idea originated from A. Poulain. Or have perhaps the flaws inherent in the doctrine itself been the cause of its demise? In any event it plays scarcely any part in the exposition of mystical occurrences, even in cases when it receives mention. It suffices to refer to Luis of Granada, du Pont, Sandaeus, Surin, Nouet, Angelus Silesius, Honoré de Sainte-Marie or Scaramelli to illustrate this point.[129]

In the more modern period the doctrine of the five spiritual senses attracted fresh attention. This is due to the influence of A. Poulain, who gave greater importance to it than is usually the case in the definition of mystical prayer. Among the other writings which deserve specific mention is an article in *Katholik*, as well as the work of Saudreau, Lamballe, Tanquerey, Grabmann, Richstaetter, Maumigny, Hamon, Juan de Guernica, Arintero, Seisdedos, Bainvel and Dorsch. In addition reference should be made to works on the Exercises of Ignatius published by Sinthern, Maumigny, Maréchal and Brou, as well as the studies of Bonaventure's teaching mentioned above.[130] A

---

[128] Cf. J. Baruzi, *op. cit.* 362 and 719, where mention is made of M. Carré–Chataignier, *Essai sur les images dans l'oeuvre de Saint Jean de la Croix.*

[129] *Guia de los pecadores* I 1. 1 cap. 5, 1; *Meditationes* t. I, Praef. 11; *Clavis pro theol. mystica* (Cologne, 1610); on this cf. *Katholik* 92 (1912), p. 107; *Traité de l'amour de Dieu* 1. 3 cap. 6 (Paris, 1879), pp. 142–143; *Conduite de l'homme d'oraison dans les voies de Dieu* 1.6 entret. 14 (Paris, 1856), t. II pp. 269 sqq; *Cherub. Wandersmann* V, 351 (Munich, 1924) p. 351 (Silesius is dependent upon Sandaeus); *Tradition des Pères et des auteurs ecclesiastiques sur la contemplation* t. I pars 2 dist. 10; on this cf. *Katholik* op. cit., *Dirett. mist.* III cap. 5 and 13.

[130] Cf. *Katholik* 92 (1912), pp. 97–112, 171–182: 'Zur Theorie von den fünf geistlichen Sinnen;' cf. *ibid.* pp. 291–298, 372–375 and 446–447. Saudreau often mentions the spiritual senses in his discussions with A. Poulain; cf. *Les degrés de la vie spirituelle* II (Paris, 1912), p. 69; *L'état mystique* (Angers, 1921), pp. 310 sq. 320 sq., 341; *La contemplation, principes de théologie mystique* (Paris, 1913), p. 28; *Precis de théologie ascétique et mystique* (Paris, 1924), p. 848; *Wesen und Grundlagen der Kath. Mystik* (Munich, 1923), pp. 50–51; *Mystische Gebetsgnaden und ignatianische mystik* (Innsbruck, 1924), pp. 208 sq.; K. Richstaetter,

direct mystical experience which makes use of the 'spiritual senses' is to be found in the accounts of an Ursuline nun, Mother Salesia Schulten.[131]

This brings us to the end of our outline of the history of the doctrine of the five spiritual senses. B. Rosenmoeller has expressed the hope that a history of this idea could provide solid information about the psychological and epistemological foundations of modern mysticism. We fear, however, that it has not been possible in this first attempt to realise this hope. The direct character of mystical experience is always described in images which are derived from the world of sense perception. Even the finest shade of difference between various mystical experiences can best be clarified for the layman with the assistance of comparisons which stem from the realm of physical sensations; of course this also touches on the limits of analogy. If one assumes five different faculties which correspond analogically to the bodily powers of sensation, then one is going quite a long way beyond the empirical data. If one wants to avoid this difficulty – and attempts to do so have nearly always been made – and one describes the senses as acts of intellect and will, then it is no longer obvious why there should be exactly five types of such intellectual activity. This move in fact undermines the raison d'être of the whole notion, for it does not provide any fresh knowledge and says nothing more than could be said without it. This remains true even if in the meanwhile well-chosen metaphors are selected from the realm of sense perception. If one tries, like Bonaventure, to fill out the a priori vacuum with empirical content, then one reaches the conclusion that analogies drawn from direct sense experience are indeed necessary and valuable but that a doctrine of *five* spiritual senses, taken as exactly parallel to physical

---

P. Maumigny, *Katholische Mystik* (Freiburg, 1928), pp. 171–176; *Pratique de l'oraison mentale* II (Paris, 1909), pp. 29–38, 338–339; *DThC* V (1891); *Introducción a la Mística Franciscana* (Buenos Aires, 1925); on this, *RAM* 8 (1927), p. 421; *Evolución mística* III (Salamanca, 1930), pp. 575–581; *Cuestiones místicas* (Salamanca, 1927), pp. 70 sq., *Principios fundamentales de la Mística* III (Madrid, 1914), p. 355; A. Poulain, *The Graces of Interior Prayer* (London, 1950); *Präsideskorrespondenz* 20 (1926), p. 96; G. Harrasser, *Studien zu den Exerzitien des hl. Ignatius* I (Innsbruck, 1925), pp. 78–70; *Saint Ignace, maître d'oraison*, (Paris, 1925), pp. 181 sq.

[131] Cf. K. Richstaetter, *Mater Salesia Schulten und ihre Psychologie der Mystik* (Freiburg i. Br. 1932), pp. 105, 160–163, 166–167, 169, 173, 175, 177, 179 sq., 190, 200, 203, 211.

senses, is superfluous.[132] Only the conservatism of the medieval mode
of thinking provides a reason for the long continuance of the teaching,
which had become unnecessary in its ancient form. Furthermore its
interpretation as exemplified by Bonaventure's exposition shows that
it is not without significance whether the metaphors used to portray
mystical experience are derived from the sense of touch or sight. For a
difference of metaphor can clarify a difference of mystical experience.
The problem we were considering was a limited one; the only conclusion it leaves us is that progress in this question demands an examination of the common linguistic usage of mysticism prior to an idea of
five senses, i.e. an investigation of the whole use of the images which
come from sense experience.[133] In this broader context some of the
partial results of this study could acquire greater significance. Research
into the language of mystics and their use of metaphors and images
could then perhaps open up the area in which the mystic depicts his
experience in the most original fashion, and where, consciously or
unconsciously, he is least influenced in his expression by the categories
of his philosophy. This might lead to a more independent presentation
of secondary, reflective descriptions of mysticism. These secondary
accounts always mirror the outlook existing outside the world of
mysticism. The partial answer contained in this study leads, therefore,
to a more important problem which cannot be discussed here.

[132] One would be tempted to register an objection based on this assertion.
If the medievals merely saw metaphorical expressions of the mystical acts of
intellect and will in the doctrine of the five senses, then the doctrine should not
be treated by itself without something being said about the use of these
metaphors. But such a study would require a series of preliminary enquiries
which far exceed the limits of a single essay. Moreover, the history of the five
spiritual senses does form a clearly defined chapter in the history of metaphors
which are drawn from the realm of sense perception and used to portray
mystical realities.

[133] Of course special attention should be paid to the accounts of mystics
who have had genuine mystical experience and have an original, personal style
of describing it. One should exclude everything which is not based on experience or stems second hand from mystical accounts for which images, concepts, etc., are followed without discrimination.

8

MODERN PIETY AND THE EXPERIENCE OF RETREATS

THE topic proposed here doubtless opens up a number of perspectives and this unavoidable range of options could easily lead to disappointed expectations. It should, therefore, be clearly stated at the outset that here the subject to be discussed is the place occupied today in the history of spirituality by the Ignatian Exercises. The exact meaning of this provisional description of our topic will become plainer in the course of the following reflections, but the stress lies as much on the term, 'history of spirituality' as on the word 'today'.[1]

Our task is to bring together the historical and spiritual background of the Exercises and the contemporary situation of today and tomorrow, a situation whose main characteristics are likely to increase in intensity. Put somewhat differently, it is a question of seeing how the Exercises are affected when they are taken from the world in which they originated at the beginning of the so-called modern period, which both gave them their characteristic stamp and which in turn they decisively marked, both in religious and secular terms. For today they must enter a new historical and spiritual context at the 'end of the modern period',[2] one in which they are not so naturally at home. These thoughts may seem at first glance abstract, laboured and far-fetched to those who are looking for modern retreat models or

[1] This essay is based on a talk addressed to retreat givers in Vienna in the autumn of 1974. The text has been considerably revised and a shorter version was published in *Gul* 47 (1974), pp. 430–449.

[2] This expression goes back to the title of a well-known work of Guardini, *The End of the Modern World* (London, 1957), which appeared in Basle in 1950 and later in Wurzburg (1959).

want to test their practical effectiveness in the modern world. And yet such reflections may contribute to a clearer understanding of all the doubts and questions which surround the modern retreat. What in fact is going on when one tries to give a retreat today without simply slipping unthinkingly into the old formulae? What should a retreat look like which fits into our spiritual and historical landscape? The presuppositions and character of these questions involve much that is uncertain and hypothetical; they also perhaps neglect a great deal and do not permit a comprehensive survey or an obvious arrangement of the material. Still the search must be pursued in good heart.

PRESUPPOSITIONS

In order to locate the problem of retreats today, we should at least remind ourselves briefly what is the context of our search, namely that the Church possesses a genuine history in which its reality can develop. This means that the Church remains itself in all its aspects and yet at the same time lives a true and authentic history, which does not merely involve external accidents, clearly recognised as such, but implies an actual historicity of its substance, dogma, worship, the composition of 'iuris divini' (and not only 'iuris humani'), spiritual life and the relation to the world. Of course the dialectic thus proposed of the enduring and essential identity of the Church and its authentic historicity raises a host of difficult problems, particularly because permanence cannot be regarded as a static characteristic nor historicity as a set of changing externals separate from the substance of the Church. The one cannot be so clearly divided off from the other. Without being able here to go into the matter more closely, we may assume here that the relation of change and identity in the Church cannot simply be expressed in terms of the model of substance and accidents (dogma – theology, divine law – human law, etc.). This would lead at best either to a purely verbal harmony or to a trivialising of the Church's historicity. The causes of change need not occupy us here, how far that is, the control of the Spirit as the innermost realisation of the Church is to be grasped as something over and above the secular influences which are unquestionably at work. In any event we can be sure that the Church of Jesus Christ does experience something genuinely 'new' in its life, which is neither 'the way things have always been' nor something reduceable to superficial triviality. Historically new phenomena can occur in the Church even if they cannot be completely grasped as such by the historical subject. This is particularly true when what is new first appears and forms the immediate destiny of the subject who reflects upon it for whom the new future emerges slowly amidst doubt and pain. Traditional Church history tends to remain too tied to directly comprehensible facts and to be unclear in its reflection and designation of the newness of an epoch. It often characterises periods of history as divisions which are defined in relation to world history external to the Church and to its influence upon the history of Christianity. However the newness of an epoch is always prepared for in advance in the abiding essence of the Church and thus it can be interpreted in retrospect, when its true character becomes clearly apparent, as what in fact has always been there; it can be discovered as a lived, conscious reality which was already present in an earlier form. Yet at the same time the novelty of an epoch is genuinely something fresh. This is shown by the fact that it only emerges for what it is against the opposition of those who, being of a conservative caste of mind, act in defence of the permanent substance of the Church and only discover new elements to be what has always been known and lived when the novelty has proved itself and is already taken for granted by a later generation.

Newness as a mark of a whole period of Church history does not of course simply dissolve and disappear because of later developments, even if it is also true that in a subsequent era it does not retain the same form it once possessed as the characteristic stamp of a particular period of history. Once new, it underlies the changes of later history and remains embedded in subsequent phenomena. In this it no longer plays the part of simple novelty but retains an irrepressible vitality and a future effectiveness. This is in fact already given in the reality of history if it is to remain faithful to itself.

In detail it is hard to determine in the face of the continual ebb and flow of history what is transitory in a new development and what is permanent, when the form of novelty, though not the actual content, is overtaken by a later period. This truth applies even to the reality and knowledge which the Church has grasped in a historical process of development as dogma which is permanently valid even in future ages. Even in this case the distinction between abiding essence and specific form cannot be made without ambiguity and possible misunderstanding. Even a new dogmatic expression comes to light and finds clear definition under transitory historical and social conditions.

These remarks should make it plain that, although something new which has appeared at a particular period can be permanently maintained, we do not regard Church history simply as a process of evolution which always produces higher levels of perfection. This is true even if we leave aside the fact that human history, in contrast to non-human evolution, always involves freedom and this applies also to the Church, so that there is a history of refusal, guilt and infidelity to what perhaps should be maintained. The point of mentioning these presuppositions of change and continuity was to render the following observations more intelligible.

THE SPIRITUAL EXERCISES AS A CHARACTERISTIC DOCUMENT OF THE MODERN PERIOD

The first thesis may be formulated as follows: the Exercises of St Ignatius[3] are a fundamental document of the post-Reformation Church, which had a decisive influence upon its history; the Church of this period corresponded to the general western culture of the modern era, even if it also possessed its own specific character; the Exercises brought something genuinely new into the Church which in the present situation of 'the end of the modern period' is both passing away and being maintained in a remarkable fashion. It is worth illustrating and verifying this thesis and spelling out the consequences for the Exercises.

A) THE MODERN FOUNDATION

However bold the venture may seem, we must first take a look at the modern period in the secular meaning of the term. The question here is not when exactly it began, whether as early as St Thomas Aquinas and the anthropocentric shift[4] embodied in his thinking or with the rise of Nominalism in the late Middle Ages, with its attack on universals in favour of the individual being, or with Luther's Reformation,

---

[3] Ignatius Loyola, *Spiritual Exercises* (London, 1963, trans. by Thomas Corbishley S. J.); cf. J. Leclercq, A. Rayez, P. Debongnie, Ch. Schmerber, 'Exercises spirituels', *DDSp.* IV (Paris, 1961), 1902–1949; also I. Iparraguirre, G. Dumeige, G. Cusson, 'Ignace de Loyola', *DDSp* VII (Paris, 1971), 1226–1318; for the background cf. H. Rahner, *Ignatius von Loyola und das geschichtliche Werden seiner Frömmigkeit* (Graz and Salzburg, 1949).

[4] This is the thesis proposed by J. B. Metz, *Christhiche Anthropozentrik* Munich, 1962).

or Descartes's philosophy of the transcendental subject, or with the rise of modern science with its exact method of quantification, whose start is itself hard to date.[5] Naturally it cannot be denied that in many ways the modern period was shaped in advance by the history of Greek and western culture and that the spirit and history of Christianity were of essential and irreplaceable importance for the formation and the background of the modern period.

Medieval man thought and lived on God and the world, on universals and order formulated in appropriate norms. His personal reflection upon himself, his spirit and his freedom was conducted, if it occurred at all, in relation to these objective realities in which he knew from the start he was included as a part in the whole. Naturally the groundwork existed for a philosophy and theology of the free personal subject; indeed this was inevitable given the background of the Christian doctrine of grace, redemption, predestination and individual salvation history. However they formed only a partial beginning and did not provide a point of departure and a foundation for the trust and commitment to the objective reality of God, the world, nature and order.

The modern period radically altered this picture. In this context it is not of great significance that the modern period of the individual subject finds self-expression in an enormous variety of ways, which are often self-contradictory. The central fact is that of the individual subject itself, which applies even when the person freely and deliberately accepts and appropriates the traditional realities of a 'philosophiae perennis' and of Christian faith, i.e. when the subject belongs to the Church and maintains this connection, regarding himself not merely as a member of a profane world but as a person directed to God. In the transcendent, a priori structure of his being the crucial starting point is this initial subjectivity, which is revealed as the primary certainty. The state of creative freedom can no longer be understood as an instance and application of a general norm. It is set over against the surrounding world and is no longer experienced as part of an already given order of reality. The other characteristics of the modern period need not be discussed here. It will be enough to recall the type of rationality by means of which the world is not only confronted and reflected upon, but which also seeks to control the

---

[5] Cf. on this question from the point of view of the natural sciences, P. E. Hodgson, 'Zweifel und Gewissheit in den Naturwissenschaften', *StdZ* 193 (1975), pp. 187–198.

world as the object of creative and free planning, and thereby shapes it as a living environment. Modern man uses his technical intelligence to transform the natural world and create society and is thus driven to question inherited tradition. He seeks to unite different areas which have been separated by a historical no-man's land into a single world civilisation. He possesses the basic tendency towards critical analysis, excluding nothing a priori from the range of his enquiry.

b) SELF–DISCOVERY BEFORE GOD

The Ignatian Exercises were both an influential factor and a significant document of the modern age, or so our thesis ran. This claim must be studied more closely. It cannot of course be disputed that Ignatius and his work are, and will always be, bound up in many ways with earlier epochs of the Christian faith and the Christian Church, precisely because of the enduring effects of the modern era. But it is not surprising that Ignatius, both at the beginning and later, was suspected of being an 'Alumbrado'.[6] We cannot dismiss it as a matter of course, nor regard it as a biographical triviality, that the religious path of Ignatius starts with a subjective experience of consolation and desolation[7] which cannot properly be the object of 'objective' control. If we take the words in his autobiographical account seriously and do not treat them as a pious exaggeration, thus rendering them ineffective, then we cannot but be aroused and deeply disturbed when we read, for instance, that mystical experiences provide the whole content of faith, the totality of our understanding of God and the world, even supposing the Scriptures were to be lost.[8]

Let us turn at once to the basic conception of the Exercises. Through their use the creator and creature should be placed in solitary contact with each other. In this situation the retreat master can quite happily be regarded as the Church's representative, but in Ignatius's view the less he enters the solitude of creature and creator the better.[9]

---

[6] On this concept cf. the corresponding article by J. Vincke, *LThk* I (1957), 407; also H. Rahner, *Ignatius the Theologian* (London, 1968).

[7] *Autobiography of St. Ignatius Loyola* (New York, 1974); cf. the interpretation of L. Bakker, *Freiheit und Erfahrung. Redaktionsgeschichtliche Untersuchungen über die Unterscheidung der Geister bei Ignatius von Loyola* (Wurzburg, 1970), pp. 69–147.

[8] Cf. *Autobiography of St. Ignatius*, nos. 29 and 30.

[9] Cf. Ignatius Loyola, *Spiritual Exercises*, no. 15.

Now this principle is far from being obvious or customary; on the contrary as an explicit principle it is radically modern.[10] In the Exercises a fundamental and free decision of life-long importance should take place. Such a choice essentially comes to be made according to Ignatius not simply by applying general human, Christian and ecclesiastical norms to a specific case, which is merely a concrete instance however complex of a universal principle, but rather by deciding upon the unique, individual destiny willed by God which transcends all general norms.[11] The will of God is not, therefore, simply and entirely transmitted through the objective structures of the world and the Church. The subject goes beyond what is universally valid and seeks through his choice his own unique truth, setting himself at a distance (termed 'indifference') from every particular existing object. This can only be chosen in a free decision as what is here and now important and subjectively accepted by a person, if his subjectivity is set free. By God is meant the guarantee that such absolute

[10] It is of course, possible to interpret this statement of Ignatius in a trivial sense by saying that the direct presence of God is given in the context of the Church and world which is experienced as a prior, valid reality. In practice, this is usually the case in ordinary piety. This priority must be formally considered and recognised by the individual free subject as something which is permanent, and cannot be eliminated or properly thought through. But the subject must (as a solitary individual) experience the rest of the world and the Church as threatened and placed in question by the immediate advent of God and the sovereignty of his will. In this light, the actual world and Church cannot be taken for granted any longer as functionally representative. If subsequently they regain their natural validity, then this is only *because* they have been confirmed in this role by the immediate proximity of God. It remains true, therefore, that the first sentences of the *Spiritual Exercises* assume the uniqueness and historical originality of the individual subject in the sense current in the modern period.

[11] Ignatius developed a logic of existential decision by means of his rules of choice, which had not existed in this form before, despite the traditional doctrine of the discernment of spirits. Since then, there has never been sufficient theological study of the real meaning and presuppositions of this Ignatian innovation. Its importance remains valid today, but it must be removed from the context of the choice of a vocation in the Church and clearly expressed in terms of its general significance for human existence. Hesitation and opposition in the mind of the Church against the spirit of the modern period prevented the real understanding and the proper expansion of this logic of existential and practical reason, which cannot be given an adequate theoretical basis. Cf. K. Rahner, 'The Logic of Concrete Individual Knowledge in Ignatius Loyola', *The Dynamic Element in the Church*, Quaestiones Disputatae 12 (Freiburg and London, 1964), pp. 84–156.

freedom is available to every individual and that it can and should be offered and required of a person.

Naturally in addition to the phenomenon of fundamental choice Ignatius was also familiar with the apparently more rational process of reflection, i.e. with the act of choice as the point of intersection of general human, Christian and ecclesiastical norms. But he regards this as a secondary and derivative version, which applies if and when the fundamental choice is either impossible or unsuccessful.[12] All this highlights the free subjectivity of a person in which the individual himself is directly confronted by the ground and guarantee of his radical freedom, i.e. by God.

The Exercises are an influential factor and an important testament of the modern era, even if they do not at all reject the past heritage of the Christian Church but rather seek to preserve it. But this is done from the typically modern starting point of a transcendent subjectivity radically transformed, we must add, and raised up by grace. Grace should here be understood as the direct presence of God to the unique subject, not as a general principle. In the context of Christianity and the Church the Exercises mean that this subject appears as something genuinely new and is a formative influence in the modern era of the Church. This is not contradicted by the fact that the customary practice of piety usually trivialised this crucial event of the modern era and still continues to do so. Even the Jesuit theology of the high Baroque period only partially and hesitantly studied and developed this modern Ignatian starting point.[13] The battle to preserve what was ancient and permanent in Christian tradition made theology in many ways incapable of using the new point of departure to lay hold of the lasting element in tradition.

The radical point of departure of the modern period allows one to understand why the Church does not figure as the active subject in the Exercises. This fact should nevertheless be a cause of deep interest to the thoughtful reader. 'As *active* subject' is the operative phrase; what is intended here is often treated as a matter of course or accepted without question, and is thus frequently overlooked.

[12] *Spiritual Exercises*, nos. 177, 179–188.

[13] Cf. in this volume, 'Reflections on a New Task for Fundamental Theology'.

Naturally the Church is found in the Exercises as something to which the individual is related as *object*. Ignatius reflects upon the history of salvation and therefore upon the heart of the Church. He aims at a completely personal relationship between the retreatant and Jesus Christ, the Lord of the Church. In this way he brings him to an experience of his calling by Christ to serve the kingdom of God and the Church. According to Ignatius the individual perseveres in his choice which has been made directly before God and his will in the context of hierarchical Church, the holy Mother, the bride of Christ.[14] But this perseverance arises also from the free decision of the retreatant, who in virtue of the direct presence to the subject of God acknowledges these limits.[15] In this sense he accepts the commandments of the Church, papal norms, Church fasts, etc. In Paris Ignatius expressly added to the Exercises as originally conceived at Manresa the rules for thinking according to the mind of the Church.[16] In passing he mentions the retreatant's attendance at Mass and Vespers and the Divine Office. One can see, as did Ignatius, a function of the Church being exercised by the retreat master; there are directions for general confession and confessors aimed to relate the retreatant to the Church. Our Lady and the saints are to pray for the retreatant. But despite all these references and many others the Church is merely a reality to which the individual is related before God. Here the question cannot be discussed how and why the reference to the history of salvation, the life of Jesus and the Church as normative can follow from the modern starting point found in the Exercises, and how much reflection Ignatius gave to the connection between the subject and the Church, a connection which the subjectivity of the modern age made far from obvious. No injustice would be done to Ignatius, living as he did at the break between the Middle Ages and the modern period, if one did not expect too much reflection on his part on this point, even if one must admit

[14] *Spiritual Exercises*, no. 170.

[15] Anyone familiar with the 19th century teaching of the Church on the justification and necessity of a 'rational' fundamental theology, which formally, even if not temporarily and psychologically, precedes the assent of faith of the believer and so his membership of the Church, will not be surprised at this assertion. Church membership is not the primary datum of religious existence. This leaves it open how far Ignatius considered this question, but in this context the ultimate independence from Scripture mentioned above must give food for thought.

[16] Cf. L. Bakker, *op. cit.* (footnote 7), pp. 55–58.

that the well known problems he had with the Church's Inquisition made him sensitive to such questions.

However human subjectivity and the role of the Church are related to each other, the fact remains that the Exercises are a solitary event proper to the individual person and that in this process the Church does not figure as the controlling agent. It is no argument against this claim to say that in the Exercises the sacrament of penance, confessor, Mass and even the Divine Office in choir have a place. As long as one does not read into these practices modern attitudes and interpretations which were certainly foreign to Ignatius, then they do not involve anything more than aids offered by the Church to the individual which operate from without. Retreatant and Church remain different subjects of action, in so far as the latter is active at all. Even external common prayer is at the most an active realisation of the Church *addressed to God*, which remains external to the real heart of the Spiritual Exercises, i.e. the existential choice and the achievement of absolute freedom before God (termed indifference), and the experience of the radical immediacy of God in the comfort of the 'first' and the 'second time of choice'.[17]

So the Church does not emerge as the active subject in the Exercises, or more precisely in the decisive central part of the Exercises. This may perhaps provide some answer to the bemused inquiry how it could work any other way. Can the Church play any other part in the decisive process of the Exercises, i.e. in the act of choice, than the one it actually has, that is to be the context and point of reference for the solitary decision of the individual subject who makes his decision before God himself who alone offers it to him? This is not an obvious query and cannot easily be given a simple negative answer, even if the real problematic can only be clearly seen today. For we are in a position today to ask whether the Church in the form of a small specific community cannot itself be the subject of a religious and existential act of choice, of the discernment of spirits and of the experience of consolation in the sense intended by Ignatius. This line of thought of course would not merely include the official Universal Church and its doctrinal decisions in so far as they affect the life of the individual believer in relation to the world, in the Church's sacramental worship and in the formulation of law; it would also include the Church as subject of a specifically religious decision, of which the individual acknowledges

17 *Spiritual Exercises*, nos. 175 sq.

his membership and in which he finds personal self-expression.

Before pursuing this line of argument and trying to come to some tentative conclusion, two further considerations should be mentioned. One involves a closer examination of Ignatius himself and the other is expressly concerned with the end of the modern era and its effect on the secular world and the Church.

IGNATIUS AND THE 'END OF THE MODERN ERA'

The following assertion is unusual and appears to contradict the traditional interpretation of Ignatius of Loyola and his work and yet it may at least be proposed today as a suggestion: Ignatius in founding his order and in his later life is not only the man of the Exercises in the sense of a solitary spiritual process in which the subject is directly confronted by God and involved in a personal existential decision as it appears in the Exercises. How far he himself was conscious of the additional factor in his life and work whereby he points beyond the modern era of the Church which he helped to found, need not detail us here. But we may note in passing that Ignatius did not regard himself as the single founder of his order,[18] but rather saw the group of his first companions, united by the spirit of the Exercises, as the real founders of the order. We are not, I think, justified in dismissing this notion simply as the expression of saintly humility. For he knew and practised the 'deliberatio communitaria' with his companions (deliberation not only *in* the group but *of* the group),[19] where the logic of existential choice was to apply and operate for the group as a whole. In the same way he treated the static general norms and constitutions of an order not simply as a fixed structure existing prior to behaviour, but rather as something which can and should become valid and effective through a dialectical process of shared testing and decision making

---

[18] Cf. P. Dudon, *Saint Ignace de Loyola* (Paris, 1934), pp. 622–625; A. Ravier, *Ignace de Loyola fonde la Compagnie de Jesus* (Paris, 1973), pp. 96 sqq., 121.

[19] Cf. Dudon, *op. cit.* pp. 335 sqq., 354 sqq.; Ravier, *op. cit.* pp 82 sqq., 230 sqq; D. Bertrand, *Un corps pour l'Esprit* (Paris, 1974). Cf. the following studies from *Studies in the Spirituality of Jesuits*: J. C. Futrell, 'Ignatian Discernment' (April, 1970); J. J. Toner, 'A Method for Communal Discernment of God's Will' (September, 1971); J. C. Futrell, 'Communal Discernment: Reflections on Experience' (November, 1972); L. Orsy, 'Toward a Theological Evaluation of Communal Discernment' (October, 1973). Also, J. G. Gerhartz, 'Vom "Geist der Ursprungs" der Gesellschaft Jesu', *GuI* 41 (1968), pp. 245–265.

which was to take place dynamically in such a group.[20] These facts reveal a tendency in Ignatius which cannot merely be traced back to the text of the Exercises as this now stands; rather they foreshadow a period of time which only now appears to be dawning at the end of the modern age.

What is meant by the end of the modern age, by the new epoch which is gradually but plainly emerging, in which the specific characteristics of the Exercises as they are explicitly contained in the text will embody something of lasting value but will no longer bear the stamp of their age in the same way as before? This is the difficult question which we must now tackle with whatever success, if we wish to discover the proper place of the Exercises in the contemporary Church from a spiritual and practical point of view. In this we cannot rely upon a description of the present epoch which appears to be dissolving the modern period, in so far as this epoch is a general historical and secular phenomenon characteristic of the whole of humanity. Men are searching today for higher forms of social structure, given that western civilisation with its rational and technical methods is becoming dominant all over the world. These social structures seek to reconcile the dignity and value of the individual with the social character of man and also face the social and material demands which are necessary for survival both now and in the future. It should at least be clear by now that these higher social formations are something new, even if their form remains the object of strife between the existing systems of society found in east and west, north and south, in developed and developing nations. Nor is their novelty eliminated by the variety of historical and social conditions under which this struggle is being conducted. This new phenomenon will stamp the emerging historical epoch, however obscure this process may appear now and however much it is interpreted within the framework of understanding proper to the age that is now passing away, i.e. the modern era.

THE CHURCH AFTER THE END OF THE MODERN ERA

There is no doubt that the Church must also enter the new age and its higher forms of socialisation. It may quite correctly appear that the Church of the Second Vatican Council is only now for the first time

---

[20] Cf. A. Ravier, 'Hat die Gesellschaft Jesu das Recht, ihre Konstitutionen zu ändern?', *Gul* 47 (1974), pp. 422–430.

catching up with the backlog of demands raised by the modern period in the various areas of its life (doctrine, liturgy, law, etc.), so that it may come to terms with the spirit of this age while maintaining a critical distance from it. However it is also, we may hope, noticeable that tentative efforts are being made amidst the present changes in the Church to discover new forms of social structure which correspond in the realm of the Church to the characteristics of the era now emerging. There are various signs of this new search which deserve mention. The new discovery at the Second Vatican Council that the Church is not just the hierarchy but is the pilgrim people of God in which each has an active part and a specific task; the search for 'democratic structures' in the life of the Church which are not mere appendages to the democracy of the modern period but embody higher forms of socialisation in the ecclesial community; the call for vital basic communities which build up the Church from below and are not individualistic groups founded on mutual sympathy, but are genuine communities in society based on shared faith in the Gospel and the power of the liberating spirit of Jesus; the liturgy as the real expression of a community's life and not merely an officially conducted ritual which the individual pious Christian attends, a change which the reform of liturgy may have brought about in principle but which is far from being completely carried through. This list could be extended further if one reflects that new structures of law will be developed in the Church in which the freedom of the individual may be safe-guarded without destroying the Church as a body, but rather revealing its unity and its spiritual power to integrate the individual in a new and clearer way. One might also take into consideration that the contemporary Church has the chance to develop within itself models of new social structures for which secular society is also seeking, with the result that the Church would not be forced to follow belatedly the social forms developed by secular society. In all these activities the Church is also seeking higher forms of human socialisation, even if as yet there is perhaps little conscious reflection upon this process.

To grasp this point in a creative and imaginative way, one should concentrate more on local communities and less on the universal Church. One should consider living basic communities, for these are not mere refuges for individual Christians who feel put off by the official institutional system of the Church and suffer from a sense of loneliness and abandonment in their experience of life. Rather they represent new types of genuine community life which correspond to the new groupings in society for which mankind is searching today. These inadequate and vague comments about the new situation emerging in the Church may of course be trivialised by an appeal to prior tendencies supposedly existing in the permanent structure of the Church, which would render the new state of affairs merely a superficial modification of what has always been the case in the life of the Church.

NEW QUESTIONS—NEW PRAXIS

These last remarks cannot receive further elaboration and proof here, but the perspective they have opened up allows us to take a new look at the Exercises of Ignatius. As we have already pointed out, the 'whole' Ignatius is not to be found in the explicit text of his Spiritual Exercises; rather we can discover in him anticipatory signs of community understanding and expression which are important for the notion of the Church and its life which is being developed today. From this the question arises: are we to expect today and in the future the appearance of new forms of the Exercises arising from the cultural and ecclesial demands of the new epoch, in which the Church can act in a previously unknown way? This would imply that the Church would not merely be an objective reality with which the retreatant has to reckon but rather an active subject finding expression in a specific community of believers; it would not consist just of the sum of participants in the retreat, but would be an independent subject to which the individual feels bound in his personal religious existence. This model goes beyond what has been the centuries old practice in common retreats, because in the latter case the retreat master for practical reasons would address many individuals at the same time, without their forming a united group or Church. If one gives an affirmative answer to the question whether such a new form of retreat should exist, despite the formal and vague description of the model, then two other problems immediately become pressing.

How are we to conceive in practical terms of a retreat as the active self-expression of the Church, as an ecclesial event and as something genuinely different from individual retreats happening at the same time? Secondly can and should, in addition to this new form, the type of retreat continue which follows the text of the Ignatian Exercises and corresponds to its original conception? In contrast to these questions it is immaterial whether, if one says yes to the first, one applies the term 'retreat' to this new form of ecclesial expression in which the Church acts as subject. If this form of active community self-expression clearly exists as a living reality, then its title depends upon the history of its development. The fact that nothing can be said on this point at the moment is of no particular importance.

The first question should, I believe, receive an affirmative answer. To grasp this it is important, indeed vital, to take note of what was said earlier about the tendency existing in the Church towards new and higher forms of socialisation. But this is not in itself sufficient. For it is not yet clear whether and why these social formations in the Church and its life should have anything to do with retreats, and whether something which might possibly be called a retreat could be an event in which the Church achieves active self-expression. The first question might be answered from various points of view depending on whether one approaches the matter from an empirical stand-point or from a more fundamental theological angle. Here we will use both methods because this seems unavoidable in the area under discussion.

From an empirical point of view there are today new group activities which are beginning to have an effect on the arrangement of retreats: one thinks in this context of sensitivity training, group dynamics and similar practices, irrespective of whether the word 'retreat' is given to the application of these techniques or other names are preferred, such as days of rest or days of recollection etc. These arrangements make use of discussion or similar types of group dynamic organisation; we will not discuss this question in detail here.

For our task of more fundamental analysis the question is crucial whether such changes and additions which are made to enrich retreats merely involve the use of modern psychological techniques to help achieve the retreat's proper goal which was also the aim of earlier individual retreats, or whether by contrast it is entirely a matter of offering useful psychological and perhaps religious assistance to an individual or a group in solving pressing problems of life. In this latter case the processes of group dynamics, etc. should not be termed a 'retreat', because despite their utility they have little or nothing to do with the nature and goal of the classical retreat. A third conceivable possibility would be that at least in specific cases and under particular conditions they could be in a theological sense what we have called the new self-expression of the Church in a given small community. Here the necessary conditions for 'community' in this sense would not necessarily imply a stable institutional group in the form of a parish or a religious community. One's answer here need not be an exclusive choice of one of the three possibilities as the only one that is feasible and legitimate. The first two can contain continual extensions to the third possibility. Our question is centred upon this third option: does there exist something like the self-expression of a community in the discernment of spirits and the act of choice? Does *this* self-expression apply to the community (Church) as such? Before giving an affirmative reply the question must first be answered whether there can be Ignatian Exercises which would embody, in addition to the permanent traditional model, a new form of spiritual activity to correspond to the specific character of the new epoch which appears to be bringing the modern period to an end?

THE EXERCISES: A POSSIBLE SELF-EXPRESSION OF THE CHURCH

First of all it must be noted that the Church can achieve self-expression over and above the acts of the official institutional Church in doctrinal teaching and legal norms, and this occurs in the life of the ecclesial community. It is immaterial here what sort of concrete structure such a community should have to ensure the claim that its modes of expression are properly acts of the Church as such. A eucharistic celebration in which all members of the community present actively participated is certainly a case of genuine ecclesial self-realisation in a concrete community. No theologian would assert that such eucharistic worship is merely the sum of the actions of the celebrant and the faithful present, regarded as individual worshippers. Rather the Church comes into being in the Mass, although the theologian and the social anthropologist may find it hard to make clear how the community proper, that is the Church, is to be distinguished from the sum of its members in such a shared communal activity. I would hold also that the Church is realised as Church in the choir office of a religious community and that it is not on psychological grounds alone that many individuals come together in common prayer. One common result of discussion of the nature of the Church's liturgy is to raise the question of when to characterise common prayer and celebration as liturgy in the strict sense, i.e. when it should count as the self-expression of the Church as such and is therefore genuinely liturgical. In summary, however, we may say that the Church can certainly achieve self-realisation in the local community.

The further question to be asked is whether a particular community can under certain conditions and in specific situations undertake, in a clearly comprehensible manner, a decision making process, a discernment of spirits in which the community as such reaches a decision and makes the Church a reality in a sense at least analogically related to that occurring in the celebration of the Eucharist and common prayer. I myself would answer affirmatively. As far as I am aware the question has never previously arisen, and indeed could never before have even been posed, since such decisions affecting the life of the whole community have up to now either been taken only on secular matters or have occurred within the framework of a paternalist structure in which one *individual* decides for the group and not the group itself. The problem can be clearly formulated today and reflects a contemporary awareness and a modern demand that decisions affecting a group should be made by the group itself. In this way they possess greater objectivity and clarity, quite apart from the human and formal structure of the group and whether each member of the group is assigned in a formal democratic manner the same role in the decision making process. Certainly one cannot derive from the nature of the Church the conclusion that a group decision is less 'ecclesial', i.e. less the self-expression of the Church, than when the decision is made for the group by an individual (Pope, bishop, etc.) in a monarchical fashion. After all the college of bishops is, with the Pope, a collective entity which is entrusted with the highest authority in its decisions; the Pope is selected by a college in an act of choice which is of fundamental ecclesial significance. Collective acts of decision made by an ecclesial group, a community, can therefore be ecclesial and be, in the strictest sense, self-expressions of the Church.

If these communal acts of decision occur in the religious context of discernment of spirits and involve the Ignatian rules of choice, as they are proposed in the Exercises for the individual's decision, then we would have a form of spiritual exercises proper to the era following the modern period. We cannot find this in Ignatius himself by following the literal text of the Exercises, since there the Church does not appear as active subject. But why today should not communal decisions in this sense be taken in 'spiritual exercises' or retreats. The formation of such a community, which must be an ecclesial body if it is a question of the self-expression of the Church in the discernment of spirits, must obviously involve more than retreats, for otherwise the participants would not come to a common decision but would at most offer mutual assistance in reaching a decision in accord with the method of group dynamics, and this would still leave us on the individual plane. But there are specifically ecclesial communities, involved in the Exercises, which have to make important decisions and could do so in the manner prescribed in the Exercises. Religious orders, secular institutes, etc. would certainly belong to this number.[21]

The question arises whether one could conceive in addition to these ecclesial communities of other groups which might be ready to reach decisions in the way proposed in the Spiritual Exercises, groups such as the presbyterium of a diocese, a Chapter, a parish council, or a group which is gathered together for a religious purpose and wishes to remain together. But this question does not require further investigation here. What is of interest to us is to ask whether the act of decision which can under certain conditions be made collectively could be undertaken in the manner envisaged in the Exercises. One's first impulse is simply to say: why not?! Obviously many changes would have to be made to create a form of Ignatian Exercises which was genuinely collective and much would be done differently from what is prescribed by Ignatius in his handbook. Methods for a practical process of communal decision making would have to be developed in order to preserve the essential character of the Ignatian choice. Only then could one speak of a genuinely religious decision in the sense intended in the Exercises. Any process of group dynamics should therefore be tested to see whether and in what way it can be used as a technical psychological aid to assist communication and thus collective decision making in such Exercises. Given the specific character of a particular group and keeping in mind the goals and subject matter of the decision in question, continual transitions may easily occur between common retreats of a number of individuals or group discussion upon a particular problem requiring resolution conducted with a more secular type of group dynamics on the one hand, and the type of Spiritual Exercises we are speaking of on the other, which involves a process of existential commitment as envisaged by St Ignatius, i.e. the decision of an ecclesial group. The logic of such a decision is specifically Christian and religious in that it is basically 'mystical' and

---

[21] On attempts to form small spiritual groups, regarded as Churches, both within existing ecclesial communities (religious orders, etc.) and outside them (groups of laity and religions, married and unmarried), cf. R. Soullard, 'The Future of Religious Life', *Conc.* 10/7 (1974), pp. 84–92; also M. Delespesse, 'Neue Gemeinschaften und Ordensleben', *Conc.* 10 (1974). In these studies the difficulties are apparent which face religious orders in particular.

leads therefore to the self-realisation of a Christian community and thus to the self-realisation of the Church. We would hold that an entirely new form of ecclesial self-realisation is here being proposed, but that despite its novelty it is just as legitimate as the self-realisation of the Church in the activities of the hierarchy or in the liturgical community. It could indeed be one of the characteristic marks of the Church of the post-modern period, because, as we have noted above, up till now ecclesial groups have either passively accepted decisions affecting them being made by one individual or, in the case of collective resolutions, have used methods common in the secular world.

PRACTICAL CONSEQUENCES

In the Exercises the Church as such can be the active subject of decisions in communities and groups using the method of Ignatian choice; it can therefore achieve self-realisation as the Church. In the actual text of the Exercises this is not the case, but it could occur, as we have shown, in modern Spiritual Exercises. As the Spiritual Exercises in their traditional form, in which the solitary subject faced God and his sovereign will, bore the stamp of the Church of the modern period and deeply influenced its development, so today the Exercises in the form described here could bring about the self-realisation of the Church by preserving what was once new, and so become a characteristic sign and an influential element in the Church of the post-modern era. In this form they would not merely be an arbitrary variant of the earlier Exercises, built up with the help of group dynamics and minor concessions to collective psychological needs; they would rather represent something specifically new. This new element was indeed already foreshadowed by Ignatius himself but it does presuppose the higher degree of socialisation proper to the post-modern age. It also carried this socialisation beyond the purely secular versions and achieves it within the Christian framework. If one takes seriously the process of a genuinely collective discernment of spirits, which takes place in an ecclesial group and is regarded as of crucial existential and religious importance for the members of the group, then one must concede that here there is something which is both new and specifically ecclesial.

Modern movements in the Pentecostal movement often appeal, even within the Catholic Church, to experience of the Spirit, by which is meant an experience which cannot be objectified or controlled. But what is entirely lacking here is the Ignatian logic of existential decision which, while not seeking to displace direct experience of the Spirit, teaches the retreatant to distinguish it clearly from other experiences and thus enables it to operate effectively as the foundation and criterion of a particular decision. An essentially new type of Exercises, which can be envisaged and tried for the first time in the post-modern era, is not meant to exclude the classical format of 'common' retreats which have their own value. Furthermore the new kind of retreat understood as the self-expression of the Church can only be outlined in rather abstract and formal terms; more is impossible at the moment. But whoever has to conduct retreats today may, either because of trends he has experienced and which may seem to him suspiciously fashionable or because of experiments in new collective types of retreat, come to a better understanding through these reflections of what is actually his own real concern, although he has not been fully aware of it until now. He should be encouraged to try to work out with suitable groups a new model in which the Church can achieve new practical forms of self-expression today.

Individual retreats in the original sense also retain their importance, and should be practised and developed in the future. But they are no longer the characteristic mark of the present era of the Church's history, even if they do and must remain the new element of the Church's modern period. But now their novelty has been overtaken by the post-modern state of the Church. The special quality of the Ignatian Exercises can be expressed in the new form of a collective retreat as the self-expression of the Church, without the traditional type of Exercises losing its worth. For individual and social elements remain transcendent human characteristics which are related to each other, although each has its own irreplaceable mode of realisation. Even if the individual person possesses no private existential world which lacks social reference and significance, nevertheless he does have his personal, autonomous life which can find its legitimate place and its proper fulfilment in individual retreats.

In addition modern experience shows that even higher forms of socialisation lead to an increase of individual loneliness which is to be accepted and cannot fundamentally be removed. The acceptance and the existential and religious interpretation of loneliness in the face of the mystery we call God, whose very silence is a mode of speech, form an essential part of individual retreats and can only be properly dealt with in this context and not in group retreats. The life and death of the individual always remain unique events, even if these should be brought into the higher forms of the religious community life and into their self-expression through the new type of retreat, and should be accepted in the group as an element of its own life. There are, then, crucial decisions of an existential and religious kind which must inevitably be borne by the individual on his own. Who, for instance, can decide except the individual person about whether to belong to a particular ecclesial group with its own characteristics which are specific to it and not universally binding? Even given higher forms of socialisation in society and Church, the personal choice of profession, the organisation of one's life style, etc. are matters that fall within the scope of individual freedom. The 'upper room' of the Gospel to which the believer retires in order to speak with God will remain necessary in the future. For men without the courage to pray privately could scarcely be members and representatives of a society containing higher forms of socialisation as these are being sought today. Such people, on the contrary, could only establish mediocre communities in which the individual would not be consciously alert to the radical subjectivity of the modern period, which must also be preserved in the post-modern age and included as part of the groups existing in it. Individual retreats in their classical form do not, therefore, lose their importance and urgency in the new situation.

After what has been said, it should now be plain that the classical type of individual retreat on the one hand, and the group retreat on the other, by which is meant a self-realisation of the Church, mark the two extreme points of what may be termed Ignatian. Between these two points many variations are conceivable which veer in a greater or lesser degree towards one or other extreme. In this basic framework the numerous retreat models proposed today may be more clearly located from the point of view of the history of spirituality and piety. But the primary purpose of these reflections is to encourage both individual retreats and the attempt to work out the new form of retreat outlined here, a form which could bring the Church to self-expression. It is this we are looking for, whether consciously or not.

9

REFLECTIONS ON A NEW TASK FOR
FUNDAMENTAL THEOLOGY

THE following pages, written in honour of J. Salaverri the renowned fundamental theologian, contain no more than a brief and provisional outline of a line of thought which is meant to indicate a new but important task for fundamental theology today.[1] Throughout this essay the provisional character of the present sketch and the rough indications of the direction of thought should be kept in mind. Naturally the existing tasks and methods of fundamental theology are not being questioned nor is any doubt being raised about their importance. This too should not be forgotten. Our concern is rather to point out a new task for fundamental theology which can no longer be overlooked today, and to bring it more clearly than before to the attention of theologians. It follows from the nature of the material that this also indicates a goal for the so-called 'analysis fidei', for this is implied by the close connection between fundamental theology and dogmatic theology caused by the nature of faith and by their mutual interaction.

THE STATE OF FUNDAMENTAL THEOLOGY TODAY

We are assuming here as a definition of fundamental theology that it involves scientific and systematic reflection upon the grounds of credibility of Christian revelation and the obligation of faith. It is not our concern here to examine precisely how this task of fundamental theology is interpreted in particular theological schools and in relation to

[1] For a good general survey of the situation and prospects of fundamental theology today, see H. Bouillard, 'La tâche actuelle de la théologie fondamentale', *Le Point Theologique* 2 (Paris, 1972), pp. 7–49.

156

the various theories of the 'analysis fidei'. We do not intend to enquire either whether fundamental theology should lay claim to other problems and topics. We are primarily interested here in the cultural and human situation which faces traditional fundamental theology today, if on the one hand it tries to be scientific, and on the other hand seeks to make contact with men today whose faith it is supposed to serve.

The history of fundamental theology since the Enlightenment shows that its practioners have always worked upon the material and the problems which were found in the particular period in question and have used the methods available at the time. At least ideally fundamental theology extended its awareness of the problem as far as, but of course no further than, the general cultural problematic demanded and made possible. Thus it was engaged in the questions of the time and made use of the scientific methods, so far as these were available, embodied in' philosophy, history and the social sciences. In the face of these sciences and the results and problems they raised, it sought to justify the credibility and the credentials of faith by using the methods customary in such sciences. This attempt had quite legitimately an apologetic thrust in order to make real contact with men of the times, at least those of the educated classes.

The intellectual world today, which is a conditioning factor of fundamental theology, is such that one must really speak of a qualitative change in the situation facing fundamental theology. The mass of philosophical problems, the range of methods, the variety of starting points and goals, the ever-increasing wealth in the humane sciences are all factors of significance for fundamental theology. In addition, there are the difficulties encountered in the application of methods of analysis, the increasing influence of religious studies, for example the psychology, sociology and history of religion. All this means not merely a quantitative but rather a qualitative change in the situation facing the fundamental theologian.[2]

Today, therefore, the sort of fundamental theology in the form of a handbook does not exist any more, one, that is, which has really covered the intellectual scene and has confronted directly and adequately the problems it raises. The lack of comprehensive expositions of fundamental theology bears eloquent testimony to this observation.

---

[2] Cf. on the question of pluralism in theology: K. Rahner, 'Pluralism in Theology and the Unity of the Creed', *Theological Investigations* XI (London and New York, 1974), pp. 3–23; 'Possible Courses for the Theology of the Future', *Theological Investigations* XIII (London, 1975), pp. 32–60.

There are no fundamental theologians, and cannot be any longer, who could bring together in their own person and in their own head the necessary knowledge, questions and methods required for a modern fundamental theology in the full sense of the term, without failing to do justice to the pluralism of the contemporary situation.

In order to come to terms with the apparently hopeless state of affairs in which fundamental theology finds itself, one may appeal to the possibility of team work. But however necessary such combined efforts may be, they simply do not occur, and in the end it appears an impossibility that they should exist. For in contrast to the natural sciences, the questions and discoveries of one person in philosophy and history cannot be simply taken over by another, if a decision of faith is at stake or the construction with others of a coherent and unified fundamental theology. To take over the results of another assumes that one has oneself worked through the problems under review and come to the same conclusions. We do not mean by this that teamwork has no value or that fundamental theology conducted with the earlier direct methods has become impossible as a science, at least as an ideal to be aimed at. But the present situation is basically new. The goal of creating a comprehensive and well-grounded system of fundamental theology through direct work is no longer feasible. In earlier periods people studying in this area were always conscious of the fact that the work was always open to improvement and clarification, and that in the course of time new questions would constantly arise which would then require new answers. But one could quite justifiably be convinced that one had given satisfactory, positive answers in one's own fundamental theology to the questions raised by the intellectual needs of the day. Even today one can yield to the temptation of wishing to continue in the old style. But this means confining oneself to a philosophical and historical frame of reference which is no longer relevant to the present age. This need not imply that all one's statements and ideas are simply false, but it does mean that one does not make contact with the assumptions and outlook of others. If this were not the case, there could scarcely be so many atheists and other non-Christians alive today.

What fundamental theologian could seriously imagine that he has a comprehensive grasp of existentialism, linguistic philosophy, Anglo-Saxon positivism and structuralism? In this area who could suppose he has such a precise knowledge of Jewish theology at the time of Christ that he can provide an exact scientific exegesis of Mt 16 which is correct from the point of view of fundamental theology, unless of course he specialises in this one narrow field, thereby losing his grasp of the thousand other problems facing fundamental theology? Who can claim as a fundamental theologian, as exegete or as historian of the early Church to be able to give a detailed and accurate account of the history of the Church's early development? In such an account the fundamental theologian must provide the necessary results in this area without giving up the attempt to be an expert in the numerous other fields of fundamental theology which are just as important. One could extend this list of questions indefinitely.

We do not wish to question the value of the labours of earlier fundamental theologians who have tried to gain direct mastery of the problems they have encountered, but nevertheless a sober assessment forces one to conclude that this science with its established methods has ceased to be a practical possibility and has become a limit case, a remote ideal which may be aimed at but can never be fully realised. This situation naturally demands more detailed analysis from the angle of scientific theory but the above description may suffice for our purposes.

INDIRECT METHOD IN FUNDAMENTAL THEOLOGY?

What then is to be done if *the* fundamental theology is no longer available to modern man in the present situation, a science, that is, able to provide answers to the unavoidable problems of pluralism which the individual is no longer capable of mastering adequately in a positive and direct way? A method must be found to enable fundamental theology to study this situation in an indirect manner. Initially this leaves the question of what in fact is meant by 'indirectly' entirely open.

People are often faced by situations in which an absolute commitment is possible and necessary without their being able in advance rationally to reflect upon all the presuppositions and reasons which are involved in the decision. Thus the description of fundamental theology as it affects those who use it to help them reach decisions of faith is not an isolated or unique case. Rather it is obvious and commonplace that a person is often unable to subject the assumptions, reasons and motives of a free decision to sufficient rational reflection and objective analysis. This applies above all in cases when the decision is absolute and irrevocable. This fact does not require extensive explanation here.

Its basic cause is that all reflection which seeks to offer grounds for a decision is conducted within a given horizon of understanding and is affected by particular lines of interest. This does not mean that reflection should not be attempted at all or that it cannot at least be partially successful, but it does imply that it is influenced by psychological, cultural and social conditions which themselves cannot be the object of adequate study without engaging upon an infinite regress. Of course it is often the case that such conditions entirely escape attention and in fact such awareness is not an absolute requirement. But the man who makes a decision is then under the impression that he is aware of the conditions, reasons and motives for his decision, even if this turns out in fact to be an illusion. In other cases a person may be explicitly conscious of the inadequacy of his reflections. In this situation the problem arises for him of how he can legitimately reach a considered and carefully prepared decision, when his process of reflection is incomplete. The decision is more absolute than the reflection, for the latter is inevitably conditioned and provisional.

The fact that decisions are of this sort is confirmed by the theological observation that, according to the teaching of the Council of Trent,[3] no one has absolute conscious certainty about his state of grace, and therefore about the quality of his commitment to a relationship of faith, hope and love to God. There is a disparity in this case between rational reflection prior to a decision on the one hand, and the absolute quality of the decision itself on the other. This disparity is also noted in the 'analysis fidei' when one considers the relationship between the relative human certainty of the arguments provided by fundamental theology for the existence of a divine revelation and the absolute commitment of faith. The same problem is evidently involved here, whatever solutions are offered by the various theories of the 'analysis fidei'. At this point we cannot enter into further discussion of these solutions, nor is there any need to do so.

In any event the various theories are scarcely satisfactory. Either they do not pay sufficient attention to the radical difference between the grounds of faith provided by fundamental theology and faith itself, or they simply appeal to the decision of 'the will'. But today it is precisely the former difference which is most strikingly evident. As regards the latter solution, the will is supposed to overcome the disparity mentioned above but it is never made clear what justifies a man in

---

[3] *Denz.* 1540, 1565 sqq.

making the absolute assent of faith. Recourse is made in this connection to illumination of grace through the Holy Spirit, to the grace of faith; now obviously this is a reality, but one must give some clearer indication what exactly it is, how it works and how it can overcome the disparity.

The question then remains: is there any theological theory to explain how the inadequacy and limitations of one's awareness of reasons and motives for an absolute decision can be overcome in a justifiable and at least 'manageable' way, when it comes to making such a total commitment?

METHODS OF 'CHOICE'

The elements at least of such a theological and spiritual theory seem to me to be present in Christian tradition, although it has not been properly considered in the 'analysis fidei' and in fundamental theology in general, nor fully worked out from a theological point of view. The clearest introduction to it is to be found, albeit more in the form of technical spiritual instructions than of a fully developed theological exposition, in the rules of choice contained in the Spiritual Exercises of St Ignatius.[4] This applies especially to the instructions which are called the first and second time of choice.[5] Naturally we cannot here undertake a detailed exegesis or a theological exposition of the teaching of Ignatius about choice. In fact this teaching has recently been subjected to extensive and penetrating analysis and considerable differences of theological opinion exist among scholars.[6] For our brief sketch it is

[4] Ignatius Loyola, *Spiritual Exercises* (London, 1963) nos. 169–189.

[5] *Ibid.* nos. 175, 176.

[6] A bibliographical survey of the more recent studies is given by D. Gil, *La consolacion sin causa precedente* (Montevideo, 1971), pp. 121–128. In this work the author tries to provide an overall survey by means of a historical investigation of the relevant texts and commentaries. Recent investigations can be attached to the publication of the 'Monumenta Ignatiana'. In general, three important groups of interpretation evolve from this starting point: a Spanish, a French and a German. While the Spanish interpretations seem to concentrate on the exact analysis of the texts themselves, the French and German studies try to confront the contemporary situation. In the French context the *Dictionnaire de Spiritualité* (Paris, 1937 sqq.), initiated by M. Viller, became an important source and point of reference (8 vols. so far). In addition the influence of G. Fessard, *La dialectique des 'Exercices Spirituels' de Saint Ignace de Loyola* (Paris, 1956; new ed. 1966, two vols.), has become steadily stronger. For the present

enough to say that the doctrine of Ignatius in its general outline can and should be used to resolve the contemporary problem of fundamental theology which concerns us here, assuming that the doctrine receives a clearer theological interpretation. For this purpose it is not necessary to go into the differences of theological interpretation given to the ideas of Ignatius; we need only state that this teaching belongs to the study of fundamental theology and the 'analysis fidei', quite irrespective of how particular theologians interpret it in detail.

The above claim requires fuller justification. What does Ignatius intend with his rules of the first and second time of choice? The content of choice which interests him (e.g. a religious vocation) is of course rather different from our concern. But this does not alter the fact that in contrast to the third time of choice, Ignatius's goal is total commitment to the will of God recognised as such, without this knowledge being solely derived from rational reflection upon the legitimacy and necessity of the object of choice itself. An absolute decision to embrace the will of God founded upon rational consideration of the object is left by Ignatius to the third time of choice, but in his view this takes second place to the two others since it applies to cases where no decision has been possible at the first and second time of choice. Thus he assumes that reflection on the object does not provide a clear indication that it is the absolute and unambiguous will of God. In this he is considering a decision situation which corresponds exactly to the one we are discussing. Through rational reflection upon an object the person who has to make a decision considers the object in itself and asks whether it is right for him. The result is a relative certainty of a greater or lesser degree about the will of God. The conviction that it is in fact God's will and demands an absolute commitment arises only from the experience of grace. This

topic, see especially Vol. I, 'Passage de l'avant à l'après', pp. 68–103. Cf. also the investigations in the periodical *Christus* (since 1954). In the German field of studies, see especially E. Przywara, *Dens semper maior. Theologie der Exerzitien*, 3 vols. (Freiburg i. Br., 1938–40). Of this work, H. Rahner said (*ZkTh* 64, 1940; p.171) that it 'leads theologically into the heart of the infinity of God, whence alone everything becomes clear'. H. Rahner should also be mentioned: most of his works on the subject are collected in *Ignatius the Theologian* (London, 1968). In this context, the author's study should be noted, since the basic ideas considered there are applied here to fundamental theology: 'The Logic of Concrete Individual Knowledge in Ignatius Loyola', *The Dynamic Element in the Church*, Quaestiones Disputatae 12 (Freiburg and London, 1964), pp. 84–156.

implies a lived synthesis of the categorial object of choice and the absolute freedom of the spirit directed to the immediate reality of God. God is present in this experience 'without intermediary' and is not displaced by the object of choice.[7]

It is evident that we have here a spiritual guide and at least the elements of a theological theory which can and should be transferred to the 'analysis fidei', and to fundamental theology in general.[8] For the categorial content of faith and its rational foundations which are proposed in fundamental theology certainly form an object of choice of the requisite kind. It can be grasped as the 'will of God', as genuinely willed by God and 'revealed', just in the manner which Ignatius described in the first and second time of choice.

THE SIGNIFICANCE OF THE 'CHOICE' FOR FUNDAMENTAL THEOLOGY

We need not discuss further here the difficult problems involved in the precise theological meaning of the rules of choice. The cultural and historical background and the general conclusions arising from this teaching which are relevant to a theological and philosophical anthropology cannot be dealt with in detail here. The significance of these rules of choice for our problem also depends on the detailed theologi-

[7] Cf. G. Dumeige, 'Ignace de Loyola II. Experience et doctrine spirituelles', *DD Sp* 7, 1277–1306. Apart from the works already mentioned the following should also be noted: J. H. T. Van den Berg, *De onderscheiding der geesten in de correspondentie van S. Ignatius* (Diss. Maastricht, 1958); H. Hagemann, 'Ignatian Discretion', *Woodstock Letters* 88 (1959), pp. 131–138; L. M. Estibalez, *Discernimiento de espiritus* (Bilbao, 1960); L.B. Bakker, *Die Lehre der Ignatius von Loyola von der Discretio spirituum* (Diss. Rome, 1963); F. Marxer, *Die inneren geistlichen Sinne* (Freiburg i. Br, 1963); M. A. Fiorito, 'Apuntes para una teologia del discernimiento de espiritus', *Ciencia e fe* 19 (1963), pp. 401–417 and 20 (1964), pp. 93–123; J. Ayestaran, *La experiencia de la divina consolacion* (Diss. Rome, 1964); P. Sbandi, *Eine Untersuchung zur zweiten Wahlzeit in den geistlichen Ubungen* (Diss. Innsbruck, 1966); E. Hernandez Gordils, *Que su santisima voluntad sintamos y aquella enteramente la cumplamos* (Diss. Rome, 1966); L. Marchand *El Espiritu Santo en los Ejercicios espirituales* (Diss. Rome, 1967); C. Lofy, *The Action of the Holy Spirit in the Autobiography of St. Ignatius* (Diss. Pierre, South Dakota, U.S.A., 1967); G. Bottereau, 'La Confirmation divine d'après le Journal spirituel de S. Ignace', *RAM* 43 (1967), pp. 35–51.

[8] It seems that this was, almost unconsciously, investigated by P. Rousselot, *Les yeux de la foi*. The articles appeared in 1910 in *Les Recherches de Science Religieuse*, pp. 241–259 and 444–475. The fact that he did not make this dependence clear is overlooked even in recent studies: cf. E. Kunz, *Glaube–Gnade–Geschichte*. Die Glaubenstheologie des Pierre Rousselot S. J. (Frankfurt, 1969).

cal interpretation given to the ideas of Ignatius. However the spiritual writers are not themselves agreed today precisely on this point. Nevertheless the truth remains that a theory dealing with a categorial object of choice which is regarded as embodying absolute divine obligation cannot but be of importance for fundamental theology, if it is seriously and realistically to get to grips with the contemporary situation. This applies exactly to the understanding of the object, rational yet incomplete, which in the last analysis is ascribed to God and to the experience of his grace-filled and direct presence.

A task for any genuine fundamental theology is to develop a theology of the Ignatian choice as a precondition of the availability of an absolute decision of faith. Such an openness must at least theoretically contain the process of reflection proper to fundamental theology, a process which never reaches a definitive conclusion. It is not a question of the 'technical' assistance of a 'man of God', if one may put the matter thus. In the Exercises this is the case since the purpose is to bring the individual person to a concrete decision in faith in his own particular situation. Certainly there will always be this task for 'mystagogues' or masters of the spiritual life, and for preachers of the Gospel. But there is also the theoretical demand for fundamental theology to try to bridge the gap mentioned above between the grounds of credibility of Christian revelation and the actual decision to believe. This has always been a topic discussed in fundamental theology but the question was never satisfactorily worked out. Today it seems an impossible task given the methods used up to now. The logical structure of the practical reason operating in matters of faith and the grammar of existential commitment[9] must be subjects for fundamental theology to discuss, but these are materially identical with the rules of choice proposed by Ignatius Loyola. At any rate it is beyond doubt that he tackled the heart of the problem in his Exercises.

Modern theology seeks some connecting link in its treatment of the 'analysis fidei' between the relative certainty of the insights of fundamental theology and the absolute character of the assent of faith by appealing to the illuminating power of the grace of faith,[10] and this certainly provides the elements of a satisfactory solution, but the grace

[9] Cf. K. Rahner, *op. cit.* (footnote 6).

[10] Cf. in addition to P. Rousselot (footnote 8), H. Urs von Balthasar, *Love Alone: the Way of Revelation* (London, 1968). Balthasar regards the interpretation of the Exercises given by G. Fessard as 'very dangerous', and himself agrees with E. Przywara.

of faith must not appear as a theological postulate, a 'deus ex machina' which lies quite beyond verification, and this demands that some indication is given about what exactly the grace of faith is like. It must be made clear how it is to be grasped as the radical reference of the transcendence of man to the immediate reality of God, and therefore as a fundamental element present in human consciousness, i.e. a 'supernatural' formal object. Finally it has to be explained how this grace-filled reference to the immediate presence of God forms a synthesis, in a manner which is basically open to verification, with the categorial object of revelation, so that revelation acquires credibility and thus enables a man, albeit with total freedom, to give the absolute assent of faith.

J. H. Newman attempted to bridge the same gap with his theory of the 'illative sense' which created a unified credibility out of converging but disparate items of knowledge.[11] The positive elements in this doctrine certainly remain of permanent value but the question is still left open of what exactly this spiritual power of synthesis signifies, if it is not taken merely as a capacity proper to practical reason which seeks to retain its independence in every area of life in the face of the logical processes of theoretical reason. Clearly a decision of the practical reason is involved, and one which is directed to God himself and his free presence in the contingencies of history which evade a totally rational analysis. The decision has a quality of uniqueness which cannot be covered by the general structure of the illative sense proper to practical reason. If one seeks to discover the specific character of this sense from a theological point of view, one may be led quite reasonably to consider the theology of the choice of an object in history. This object is recognised as the 'will of God', although the one making the choice is unable to reduce the divine volition entirely to the objective legitimacy of the object chosen. Again we return to the postulate of a theology of decision of a kind at least intimated by Ignatius of Loyola.

Perhaps the somewhat depressing assertion would not be out of place that Jesuit *theology* has not always and in every respect brought the heritage of Ignatian spirituality into effective use in the course of history. One could point to many lines of thought found in this spirituality whose unique qualities have not been translated into theological reflection or accorded the weight which their intrinsic importance merits. One has the impression that Jesuits have regarded

---

[11] Cf. J. H. Newman, *An Essay in Aid of a Grammar of Assent* ch. 9.

Ignatius as a pious and holy man whose achievements earned him an important place in the history of the Church. But he has scarcely been treated in his own right as one of the central figures in the development of spirituality at the beginning of the modern period. Thus Jesuits have a duty towards the founder of the order which has not yet been fulfilled in their theological work.[12] To the retort that Ignatius was no theologian, one should point out that he was more, not less, than a theologian, and that in consequence he can set tasks even for tomorrow's theology. One of these tasks we may have indicated in the brief compass of this essay.

[12] This statement is made without regard to the works mentioned in the above footnotes because these works have had practically no effect in the realm of theology.

PART THREE

Listening to Scripture

10

THE ACCEPTANCE IN FAITH OF THE TRUTH OF GOD

I N every period of history the experience of human need and guilt arouses the expectation among men of an answer from God which would bestow forgiveness and salvation upon man, both individually and in his existence in society and history. This gives depth and clarity to what one can say about the mutual dependence of faith and knowledge.[1] These ideas should now be brought into critical contact with a contemporary situation which may seem to make man deaf to the call of faith, but could perhaps bring him to a more acute sensitivity in a new way.

THE PRESENT SITUATION: A GOD–LESS WORLD.

Until the beginning of the modern period the human picture of the world was so modest and transparent that nearly everywhere the limit was soon reached; its spatial and temporal dimensions were so constructed in human thought that God was for actual experience practically a piece of the world, who dwelt perhaps in heaven but in a sort of heaven which was a continuation, in the same mode, of the spatio–temporal world. Today the picture of the world has been transformed and deepened to an extraordinary degree and the whole situation has altered. The world has become a self-contained whole which is not

---

[1] This essay was originally published as thesis XVIII in the collection, 'Warum Glauben?' Begründung und Verteidigung des Glaubens in einundvierzig Thesen, eds. W. Kern and G. Stachel (Wurzburg, 1967) pp. 169–176. There the author referred to what was said by the other writers, since it was necessary to bring out the transition from the first part of the work, 'Man and God', to the second part, 'Jesus Christ and his Church'.

open to God at particular points and does not flow into the divine sphere; it does not experience the impact of divine causality at specific individual points which are open to human observation (prescinding for the moment from the supernatural history of salvation). It is only as a whole, and therefore in a less demonstrable manner, that it points to God as its precondition. This easily leads to the conclusion that God cannot be found anywhere, for everywhere it is the world that one meets.

Towards the end of the 18th century and during the 19th there existed a theoretical and practical atheism which was so criminally naïve and culpably superficial that it asserted God's non-existence with complete certainty. It produced no men of genius and now it belongs basically to the past, although it is still today a mass psychosis and the dogma of a militant world view. The case is rather different with the 'atheism of anxiety', if the phenomenon we have in mind may be so described. The horror at God's absence in the world, the dismay at his silence, at his self-imprisonment in his own remoteness, at the meaningless secularisation of the world's laws, where this involves man and not nature, this whole experience leads a man to suppose that he must profess theoretical atheism; it is in fact a genuine intuition of the depths of existence with which for long the customary thinking and speech of Christianity has not come to terms. At root it is the experience that God does not belong inside one's picture of the world, that he is really God and not some demiurge or the main spring of the universal clock, and that for every normal event a cause exists which is not God himself.

This experience is falsely interpreted if one supposes that only this-worldy, a-theistic experience is granted to man. The point is to show how man always transcends this experience and that the experience of the 'atheism of anxiety' basically indicates the growth of God in the spirit of man.

PRIOR CONDITIONS

A man never fashions his picture of the world with complete originality or freedom from prior assumptions. He always starts with an inherited world view. We begin with a 'given' world, not only a world of objects but also a mental world. This mental world, behind which we cannot entirely penetrate, has a double face, one metaphysical and one historical. The metaphysical assumptions consist of a series of propositions which are continually being partially 'verified' by experience but can never be actually proved, propositions of the kind that 'worldliness' is a universal phenomenon which always and everywhere conforms to the law of non-contradiction, that everything has a sufficient reason. Such preliminary, a priori structures of thought and being only reveal their legitimacy to those who freely entrust themselves to them; there is no point of reference outside them from which they can be justified.

We do not inherit merely a set of metaphysical principles; we also receive an already formed world picture which has been moulded by tradition. Even if we regard it with the greatest mistrust, engage in revolutionary protest against it, we are nevertheless not free of it; we are still involved with this world view and not with another. Even in the natural sciences we only discover what can be found in the direction in which investigation has been conducted. The discovery can never disclose what was overlooked or missed, or prove that the missing element would not have been of greater importance than the one found. Neither an individual nor a historical period can break out in every direction simultaneously and make a total discovery of everything; every conquest is also a renunciation. The only question is, how to make the sort of renunciation in one's conquests which does not involve a *fatal* loss.[2]

THE BASIC FIRST PRINCIPLE

If the scientific picture of the world is so conditioned, then it cannot claim to be the primary and most fundamental element of human existence. The truth of religion, the knowledge of God and faith in his historical revelation comes before it. We must always hold fast to the conviction that there are not two truths, which contradict each other and are mutually exclusive. In fact in cases of apparent conflict both sides must engage in honest self-criticism and try to discover the cause of the seeming contradiction. But religion is not simply to be handed over to science and its world picture. Religion is a higher reality since

[2] Only in this sense may the shortened form of the doctrines of faith be used, a 'dangerous' expression in theological discussion. In any event a lively awareness is required which basically admits that every gain is bought at the price of a loss and that, in consequence, the vital preservation of the Christian message in a living form is only to be expected from the community of believers as a whole.

it arises from a prior and more fundamental level of existence. Every process of constructing and imagining a world, every attempt to order and comprehend the multiplicity of things occurs within the prior horizon of understanding, is directed to the incomprehensible, the unimaginable reality we call God. This reality is not a part of the world or of a picture of the world; it is an incomprehensible infinity[3] lying behind the world's multiplicity. In so far as it is the transcendent source and goal of knowledge and cannot be conceived in objective categories, it must be thought of as a personal spirit,[4] since it is also the foundation of all personal beings existing in the world.

The transcendence of God has been an explicit and permanent theme of Christian metaphysics. It has been realised that God does not belong to the world picture as the ultimate hypothesis, but rather forms the precondition of the world and knowledge of the world, in such a way that direct human perception of God is impossible and only indirect knowledge lies open to man. He is grasped as the unconditioned, to which the experience of multiplicity and its limits points without consigning its inner reality to human comprehension. Nevertheless it is only in the contemporary situation that this knowledge is explicitly entering the realm of lived emotion and the real heart of human existence.

CHRISTIANITY AND RELIGIONS

Set in the general context of religion and the encounter with God, Christianity does not stand as a rival to the scientific picture of the world which so deeply marks our contemporary thinking. But Christian faith does not merely consist of the silent worship of the nameless God; it is also the word of God addressed to man in human language which must name in a range of particular conceptual propositions the reality of God which lies beyond names. This faith consists, therefore, of history, institution, authority, commandment.

[3] Cf. W. Kern: Human knowledge always goes beyond itself to the infinite mystery of God, which only God himself can reveal to us. Thus, knowledge and faith are dependent upon each other. *Warum Glauben?* (Wurzburg, 1967), pp. 151–159.

[4] Cf. J. de Vries: The intentional ordering of life proves the existence of a spirit which transcends the world; also O. Muck: Human knowledge and will, which naturally strive for infinite being and value, are only possible if God is the goal of this striving. Both in: *Warum Glauben?* (Wurzburg, 1967), pp. 100–109 and 118–127.

In this more concrete sense competition is more evident between Christianity and a world picture, and this seems to produce antinomies and conflict. The revelation of God is expressed in human words and concepts which are in part conditioned by pictures of the world. We do not need at this point to discuss the well known tensions which over the past centuries have burdened the relationship between the Catholic doctrines of faith and modern science, the question, for instance, of the post-Copernican system, the age of the world, the theory of evolution as applied to the physical nature of man, and similar topics. Over the years the apparent contradictions between the two sides which these questions contain have been overcome, and the topics themselves are today only of methodological interest in that they constitute a warning to each side against the transgression of proper limits.

More fundamentally we can say that we are more sensitive than earlier and less complex generations to analogical terms applied to God, his truth and his saving acts. Expressions such as 'Jahweh roars', 'it grieves God', which appear quite naturally in the Old Testament, are not so easily employed today. Whether this is altogether an advantage is a matter we can leave open at the moment. To lessen the imaginative clarity of an expression represents a more serious danger than is often supposed. But in general the constricting sense of the inexact and pictorial character of talk about God, even if it appears in revelation, is simply an unavoidable fact of our times, and one which may in some ways be a blessing. For to grasp that God is an incomprehensible and inexpressible being who transcends all our propositions is a blessing, and means a growth in the knowledge of God. This knowledge is bought at the cost of the sadness of wandering in shadows and images, in the words Cardinal Newman had written on his tomb. But this is no justification for doubting the truth and importance of the meaning intended by these inadequate propositions. The knowledge they contain is more valuable than all worldly knowing. To be able to stammer about God is in the end more important than to speak precisely about the world. Theology knows well enough that stammering is all it can do. The difficulty attributed to theology by men today is seldom as novel as they imagine since they are unaware of the centuries of labour and effort which has been expended in the attempt to expound and interpret the revealed word of God.

But however untiring the efforts to provide clarity and meaning, theologians also realise that *fundamentally* they are reduced to stammering when it comes to speaking of God. All possible explanation leaves the mystery of God intact. Theology is not the unmasking of the mysterious in the self-evident but rather a gaze into the bright darkness of divine mysteries. Total clarity would be a sure sign that the spurious self-evidence of human rationalism had been mistaken for the truth of God.

THE LANGUAGE OF THE BIBLE

There are other ideas arising from the inadequacy of *all* human concepts in speaking of God which have a closer connection to the scientific picture of the world of an earlier age. When we say, God is in heaven, the Son of God came down to earth, descended into hell, etc., then a world picture is evidently assumed which is no longer ours, although it retained its validity in theology until the 18th century. The collapse of this picture of the world seems to demand a 'demythologisation' of the biblical message. This question takes us into the territory of exegesis but one basic observation is in order as a preparatory move to make one more sensitive to the word embodied in historical revelation. Considered from a more fundamental standpoint, demythologisation is not required for two reasons: first 'mythological' statements retain their meaning even after the disappearance of the world picture in which they originated.[5] Secondly this meaning is the same as that originally intended. It can be shown that even at the time the intended content of the statements were not basically identified with the material provided by the current world view. It is true that in past ages there was little conscious reflection on the distinction between the form and content of propositions. But it was realised, even if on the edge of consciousness as it were, that such a distinction was both possible and necessary. In the case of eschatological statements, for instance, which presuppose the ancient cosmology, such freedom and so little consistency is employed that even at the time it was clearly recognised that not everything could be taken with absolute literalness. Today indeed, the intended meaning can be given a more valid sense, which is independent of the shift of world view. Just as the ancients evidently realised that 'sitting on the right hand of God' is an

[5] On the exegetical validity of a limited demythologisation, cf. A. Vögtle: not every form of a 'demythologisation' of the New Testament is false to Scripture; in, *Warum Glauben?* (Wurzburg, 1967), pp. 209–220.

imaginative construction, and yet still expresses genuine meaning, so we can recognise today that the ascension into heaven does not mean a change of location in our physical space, and yet has a valid significance.

Plainly, then, these statements have not become poorer in content for us, and yet the awareness of faith today does share the increasing opacity common to the general scientific level of consciousness (the developments of modern physics would be a case in point). But the fact of diminishing transparency does not need in the long run to lessen the vital impact of statements of faith. But, as was suggested earlier, greater opacity betokens a gain as well as a loss. It lessens the danger of the naïve reduction of religious realities; the inexpressible greatness of God and of human existence before God become clearer. Certainly modern man must first settle down to this new situation and such a process of change demands time.

LISTENING TO THE WORD OF GOD

The change we have described does not mean the escape from the limits of history into a non-historical mastery of the message of revelation; rather it points in a new way to the necessity for man of grasping the word of God in so far as it bestows meaning from within his given situation. He cannot embrace this situation totally in advance by reflection. The reverse is in fact true: revelation first answers the question for him which is signified by his actual situation. The specific historical and metaphysical existence of man cannot be constructed by scientific reflection even on the intellectual level. Religion, seen as the knowledge of God and reception of his revealed word, is prior to the reflective, scientific picture of the world. The 19th century belief that science by itself could provide a basic structure for human existence which was free from any prior assumptions expresses an outlook which, historically speaking, is now dying. That in fact the enterprise could not succeed is not of any particular importance. It has become plain that to expect science to serve as a 'creed' for the foundation of human existence is to overburden its capacities.[6] A scientific picture of the world cannot manufacture a picture of man. The reverse is in fact true: prior to and behind science there lie metaphysics and faith, higher

---

[6] Cf. K. Rahner, 'Science as a "Confession"?' *Theological Investigations* III (London and Baltimore, 1967), pp. 385–400.

and more comprehensive forces which with all the knowledge belonging to them are essentially ordered to freedom and commitment.

A serious attempt to come to terms with this insight necessarily yields a directive of crucial importance: to prevent reflective science becoming a poisonous and random curiosity and a relativistic capacity of instant creation, the roots of the unreflective understanding and harmony of being must not be cut off; rather they must penetrate at least as deeply into the subsoil of existence as the objectifying reflections of science which range ever further in the world of secular experience in all its extent and variety.

The remarkable thing about the present situation is that science itself is coming to this realisation and does not have to be forced to accept it from outside. In the same way philosophy is aware of its limits, without the constant reminder of an opposing religious faith being necessary. By referring to history and tradition in this way man learns to listen to the word of God which is the object of his hope, the saving answer given by the living God in human history which offers meaning to man. It is spoken in the shadows and parables of human language, for how else could it be understood? But it contains the promise of absolute truth which justifies and makes possible all the creative thought and action of man.

11

THE OLD TESTAMENT AND CHRISTIAN DOGMATIC THEOLOGY

THE title of this essay might arouse expectation for an exegetical study.[1] The following reflections, however, are concerned with the question of how a dogmatic theologian can deal with the books of the Old Testament, given that he maintains the dogmatic principles of inspiration and inerrancy in the Old Testament and has an impartial attitude to the results of modern exegesis.

It is not an easy matter to bridge the gap between dogmatic theology and exegesis in the case of the New Testament, and so it is hardly surprising that the same task is still more difficult in the case of the Old. The question is one of course which has occupied the attention of Christian theology at every period. From the very beginning the Church claimed the Old Testament to be its own holy book and proclaimed *its* God, i.e. the father of Jesus Christ, to be the author of the history and book of the Old Testament.[2] In this connection rules of hermeneutics necessary for the understanding of

---

[1] On the problem of the relation of exegesis and dogma, cf. K. Rahner, 'Exegesis and Dogmatic Theology', *Theological Investigations* V (London and Baltimore, 1966), pp. 67–93; on the importance of the Old Testament, 'Old Testament Theology', *Sacramentum Mundi* IV (London and New York, 1969), pp. 286–290 (bibliog.). 'Theos in the New Testament', *Theological Investigations* I (London and Baltimore, 1961), pp. 79–148; 'Christianity and the Non-Christian Religions', *Theological Investigations* V (London and Baltimore, 1966); 'The Secret of Life', *Theological Investigations* VI (London and Baltimore, 1969), pp. 141–152.

[2] This was especially important against Marcion; cf. H. Rahner, 'Markion', *LThK* VII (Freiburg, 1962), 92 sq.; J. Quasten, *Patrology* I (Utrecht and Brussels, 1950), pp. 268–272; B. Altaner, *Patrology* (Freiburg and London, 1960), pp. 143–144.

the Law and the Prophets, as the New Testament described the Old,[3] had to be thought out; various suggestions were put forward to solve the problem. In the same way the biblical encyclicals of the last hundred years from Leo XIII to Pius XII were intended to facilitate the understanding of the Old Testament by emphasising the basic criteria of interpretation, so that modern exegesis of the Old Testament and dogmatic teaching about the bible should be in harmony. It should not be doubted or disputed that these pronouncements of the Church's magisterium and the theological opinions they support were quite justified and still retain their value. The basic idea that none of the very diverse literary genres present in the Old Testament is necessarily an obstacle to its being the inspired word of God naturally retains its significance, and its application resolves a whole series of questions are connected to the problem mentioned above. The same applies to the important notion that the meaning these literary genres express is in harmony with the inspiration and inerrancy of the bible, given an unbiased, precise and correct understanding of the genre in question.

THE RANGE OF THE TOPIC

Does this idea really solve all the relevant questions? Or must the answers gained by its use be considered within a larger and more comprehensive framework, without diminishing their importance in the slightest, in order to find a really satisfactory solution. From this point of view it must be verified whether the usual appeal to the various literary genres in the case of problems raised by the Old Testament can give adequate and convincing weight to the inspiration and inerrancy of these books. If not, then it would be necessary to propose explicitly another principle in addition to the literary genres. This principle is often overlooked, although its application can alone make the idea of biblical inerrancy, as this is traditionally deduced from inspiration, clear and intelligible. Of course such efforts would be superfluous from the start, were we to adopt the position taken by many Catholic theologians today, which is opposed to the pronouncement of the magisterium, or at least to its manner of formulation, and which allows for the occurrence of error even in the inspired text. The distinction used to be made between propositions of a historical and scientific kind and those of a properly religious type, and the

[3] For this expression, cf. Mt. 5:17; 7:12; 22:40; Lk 16:16; 24:44; Jn 1:45; Rev 24:14; 28:23; Rom 3:21.

possibility of error was allowed in the former case but not in the latter. Today, however, this distinction is frequently not drawn. If it is allowed or asserted that erroneous propositions can and do occur in the bible, then this usually includes statements of any kind, and it is only the substance of Scripture as a whole which is regarded as free from error.

This tempting possibility of resolving the problem in one swift blow will not be pursued here since we share the traditional view that in the Old Testament, at least statements of moral and religious import do not contain error. Of course this means excluding errors only on condition that the properly intended meaning embodied in the literary genre under consideration is correctly understood. With this proviso genuine errors which concern religious truths of the Old Testament cannot be admitted. The question, however, remains open whether in fact the solution proposed here is not in harmony with the true intentions of those who support the possibility of scriptural error. It would then simply be a matter of a difference of terminology and of the binding force, if any, of the official terminology of the Church upon a theologian.

SPECIFIC DIFFICULTIES IN THE OLD TESTAMENT

The solution we propose has grown out of consideration of specific difficulties which arise for the dogmatic theologian today in dealing with the Old Testament. Our first task is to point these out in order to make the ensuing line of thought intelligible. The difficulties we mention can be overcome by means of the solution which should be added to the traditional theory, or, to put the matter slightly differently, should be worked out on the basis of the latter theory. This does not mean that the theologian wishes to offer the exegete new material. Rather he is simply presenting the problems in a straightforward manner without providing the complete body of exegetical proof. Certainly the theologian will put in some reflections of his own here and there in course of his exposition, in order to clarify the difficulties as he perceives them on the basis of his theological convictions. The modern exegete may of course take a different view, since he has been accustomed to leave the task to the theologian of showing how the Old Testament text can be reconciled with the dogmatic principle of scriptural inerrancy. Here we are not claiming to enumerate all the problems or to arrange them in an enlightening systematic structure.

A first well known problem for the theologian is the *heno-theism*[4] contained in the older parts of the Old Testament which stands in a certain opposition to the monotheism proper of the Jewish religion. For these early texts provide evidence that Yahweh was the only God to be worshipped by the people of his covenant, but that this position did not exclude the existence of other gods belonging to other nations. It is true that many Old Testament passages merely bear witness to the *historical fact* of henotheism and in this sense are true; one cannot derive from these statements any conclusion about the objective validity of henotheism, since it is here a matter of historical narrative and not of theological truths. This explanation may apply in a number of instances, especially in cases where elements from an earlier understanding of the world and from a more primitive language were used as poetic texts at a later period. But all this does not rule out the view that there are henotheistic assertions in the Old Testament which, at least at an early stage, were meant in a theological sense. To point out in answer to this that such texts would have received a new meaning when included in the broader framework of God's inspired word seen as a whole is merely, in my view, to push the problem one stage further back. For if such statements are transposed into a new context which relativises and transforms them, if, that is, an appeal is made to the 'analogia fidei',[5] then it would still be necessary to work out their meaning more clearly and explain how the text in question was in origin essentially open to such new interpretation and suited for it. But this already leads us to the theory which we wish to offer as a solution.

A second question affecting the inerrancy of the Old Testament arises from the fact that the more ancient layers of these books know nothing of individual survival after death regarded as a positive phenomenon. In this case, too, the lack of knowledge does not necessarily imply that the unknown state of affairs is denied. Further it could be shown that pessimistic assertions about death and sheol do not refer to the condition of the dead *after death*, but rather to the experience of death itself. Or we might say that such statements may

---

[4] Cf. W. Holsten, *RGG* III (Tubingen, 1959), 225; J. Haekel, *LThK* V (Freiburg, 1960), 233. For the Old Testament question, both general and particular, see Fr. Heiler, *Erscheinungsformen und Wesen der Religion* (Stuttgart, 1961), pp. 323, 460.

[5] Cf. L. Scheffczyk, 'Analogy of Faith', *Sacramentum Mundi* I (London and New York, 1968), pp. 25–27. More fully, E. Mechels, *Analogie bei Erich Przywara und Karl Barth* (Neukirchen-Vluyn, 1974).

be regarded as entirely correct in that they express a permanently valid and tenable notion of the 'limbus patrum'[6] in the history of salvation. But even so explanations of this kind do not offer an entirely convincing answer to the problem. For the pious Jew in the Old Testament experienced death as his exclusion from the saving history of God and his people, and so from the saving power of God himself. He gave religious expression to this feeling and drew moral and religious conclusions from it. So his ignorance of existence after death and its positive worth passed over to a direct denial of such an existence. This on the face of it appears a case of basic error.

A third problem centres quite understandably on the egoistic nationalism which is given religious expression in the Old Testament and for which theological justification is sought. Leaving aside the later prophets, we see Yahweh taking so primitive and exclusive a stance in favour of the people of his covenant that political and military victories are quite naturally treated as acts of Yahweh, and the ensuing death and destruction of other nations accepted without question as the simple consequence of his partisan support for Israel. Even the cruelties of the contemporary war ethic are quite logically traced back to the positive will of God, who desires the extermination of his enemies and watches over obedience to this commandment with threats of punishment. Earlier attempts have been made to answer these questions by saying that God is the sovereign Lord of the life of all men, and therefore can champion the cause of one nation in order to forward his providential designs for salvation; thus he is able not merely to allow the extermination of enemies but even to command it.[7] In this connection there can be no doubt of the moral quality of this seemingly egoistic nationalism: the people of the covenant were positively allowed to act in a way which was held to be immoral for other nations. On this ground we are justified in regarding this as nationalism. The conception of the covenant was not that of an ideology which merely sought to give positive value to a normal antagonism between nations.

Finally there are the well known difficulties arising from the prophecies and the historical and theological interpretations made by prophets living at the time of the fall of the kingdom and after. The

[6] Cf. P. Gumpel, LTHK VI (Freiburg, 1961), 1057–1059.
[7] Examples of this line of argument are to be found in moral theology text books; cf. also, N. Peters, 'Die spezielle Sittenlehre', in G. Esser and J. Mausbach, Religion – Christentum – Kirche II (Kempten, 1923), pp. 83–96.

future they proclaim contains contradictions which cannot be simply resolved by an appeal to the element of freedom constituted by faith or apostasy which would determine the actual shape of these future events. In conclusion we should mention the problem which stems from the acceptance of religious and theological conceptions found in the world surrounding the Old Testament, for these have an influence upon the theological statements contained in the Old Testament and lead to results which cannot easily be given internal consistency. This brings us to the question whether such assertions and laws can really claim to be divine revelation.

All these difficulties have only been briefly noted here but they can scarcely be resolved by means of literary genres alone without doing violence to the facts, even though the latter principle does in general offer a solution to numerous problems.

THE HIGHER UNITY OF THEOLOGICAL TRUTHS

Where can we discover the appropriate principle and context by which to understand and explain the difficulties we mentioned, in such a way that error is not included? The answer presupposes that the theological character of the statement in question is taken into careful consideration. For only as theological assertions can they claim to express divine revelation in the proper sense of the term. It is only, too, from this perspective that the meaning of inerrancy and error can be accurately defined with reference to these statements. Of course they can be declared true or erroneous in so far as they correctly describe the object to which they correspond. But it remains to be shown nevertheless that the intended object in theology is *God* and nothing else. All that is other than God can in principle only constitute the material content of a statement of revelation and therefore possess a corresponding inerrancy if and when this content is related to God. Taken in isolation by itself it cannot be the object of revelation since, as an inner worldly state of affairs, it is in principle open to secular human understanding and is thus not the right sort of object to be revealed in a personal, divine self-disclosure.

For this reason perception of an inner-worldly reality can only be an instance of revelation if, and in so far as, the object itself and knowledge of it are set within the spiritual movement by which a man accepts in faith the personal self-communication of God through grace and the Spirit which constitutes the primary event of revelation. In this way he can appropriate the inner-worldy reality, since in it the relationship to the self-revelation of God unfolds.[8] The description of such an inner-worldly state of affairs would not in this case be erroneous, in the sense of a revealed truth, to the degree to which the statement and its content did not displace the openness of the spiritual movement to the direct reality of God. With regard to revelation inerrancy of this sort does not demand essentially and in every instance that such a proposition, considered by itself apart from its place within this spiritual movement, i.e. according to purely secular standards and criteria, should correspond to the facts and in this sense be free from error.

The positive inclusion of such a statement and its content within the primary revelation, i.e. the movement of the spirit caused by God's self-revelation and directed to the immediate divine presence, can occur in a provisional way if the statement is experienced and accepted, without reflective awareness of its goal, as an ongoing process open to an unplanned future. In addition, however, the absolute goal of this movement, i.e. the immediate divine reality, can be explicitly and consciously recognised as the fundamental horizon of understanding and of interpretation of all inner-worldly propositions. Furthermore it is possible that the successful attainment by this spiritual movement of the direct presence of God may be affirmed and experienced as a reality and not merely as a possibility. In the first case where the ultimate horizon of understanding, which constitutes revelation and inerrancy, is grasped and made actual in particular objects of knowledge, we find the manner of revelation proper to the Old Testament. If one goes beyond this to the direct presence of God, then we encounter the mode of revelation proper to the New Testament.

THE OPENNESS OF THE OLD TESTAMENT

To gain a better understanding of what has been said, we should note that only Christianity possesses, or rather establishes, a single binding canon of Old Testament books.[9] The extent and the binding theological character of the books collected in the Old Testament can only be

[8] Cf. K. Rahner, *Hearers of the Word* (London and Sydney, 1969); 'Theology and Authoropology', *Theological Investigations* IX (London, 1972), pp. 28–45.

[9] On the canon of scripture, cf. K. Rahner, *LThK* V (Freiburg, 1960), 1283 sq.; on the Old Testament, P. Katz, 'The Old Testament Canon in Palestine and Alexandria', *ZNW* 46 (1956), pp. 191–217.

defined for us, and indeed in itself, by reference to the New Testament, even if this collection of books existed before Jesus Christ and was respected as sacred scripture in pre-Christian Judaism. However the canonicity which may be attached to them cannot for Christians pass over, independently of Jesus Christ, to the sacred writings of other religions despite the recognition that these books are in some measure special.

We must also reflect that the individual books of the Old Testament, and still more particular statements within them, can only be interpreted as possessing theological significance in so far as they are read and understood within the framework of the whole of the Old Testament. The inclusion of a particular writing in the corpus of the Old Testament can be recognised as valid for us by reference to Christ, in that this corpus forms a written expression and description of the history of salvation, which, though pre-Christian, leads directly to Christ and possesses normative value for a Christian. In this process of inclusion the actual event of inspiration is to be located; only within the totality of the Old Testament can the particular statements of particular books be correctly interpreted and understood as being free from error.

Thirdly we should remember that the Old Testament collection is a record of the history of God and his people and thus expresses a spiritual movement which is open to the uncontrollable activity of the God of history. Theoretical assertions should not be separated from this record, if they are to be correctly understood and are true. Of course the absolute goal of this open-ended movement is not consciously grasped on this level, as it is later in the New Testament when the goal is achieved in Jesus Christ. If the openness of the history, contained in the covenant and promise and governed by the sovereign and unpredictable freedom of God, is recognised as the basic principle of understanding proper to the Old Testament,[10] a principle which is explicitly expressed and widely assumed, then there is available a hermeneutical principle by which to understand the particular statements of the Old Testament and to make intelligible the real inerrancy of these truths. This inerrancy is to be found in the fact that the particular phenomena and the statements referring to them are always open to the spiritual movement of history ordered to the sovereign mastery of God. This openness is permanently present and is accepted in faith.

[10] This concept is intended to cover both pre-Christian Jewish history and the book which witnesses to it.

The spiritual movement is of course brought about by the self-communication of God in grace.

What has been proposed so far may seem more or less self-evident. The position, however, we have adopted becomes more critical when it is assumed that there can be statements about inner-worldly phenomena in this positive revelation which can be 'true', although considered in themselves outside this ultimate horizon of understanding they do not correspond to the intended inner-worldly reality, and on this level are false. In other words inner-worldly states of affairs which in themselves are not grasped correctly and 'false' interpretations of them can nevertheless positively assist the absolute movement towards God. In so far as they achieve this, they can and should be rightly described as true in the sense of truth which consists in the open-ended movement to God arising from God's own self-communication and the grace and revelation it contains. Thus, to put the matter briefly, inner-worldly error can lead to absolute truth. This error must then be itself 'true' because it is taken up into the movement directed to the absolute divine reality.

This possibility seems to me to be the critical point of the theory put forward here. And yet nothing new is being proposed except the application of a well known and accepted principle to our basic problem. It cannot seriously be denied that an inner-worldly confusion and the error attached to it can be the medium of saving action, through which faith, hope, and the love of God come to fulfilment. In consequence it can and should be called true in cases where it is properly established that it is positively integrated in the spiritual movement directed to God himself. Of course in most instances in real life we cannot have certain knowledge of this. We can only, therefore, measure the inner-worldly misinterpretations according to inner-worldly criteria, understand them in a secular horizon of meaning and ultimately treat such confusions and our comprehension of them as cases of error.

But if it is established in a particular case that something which is mistaken and incorrect from an inner-worldly standpoint positively assists the absolute movement towards God, then we are justified in declaring such an interpretation to be true, as long as we do not intend to use the analogy of 'simul justus et peccator'[11] and prefer to call these propositions simultaneously 'true and false'. The latter option appears

---

[11] Cf. K. Rahner, 'What is a Dogmatic Statement?', *Theological Investigations* V (London and Baltimore, 1966), pp. 42–66.

untenable both because it creates a scarcely intelligible paradox and because the linguistic usage of the Church stands against it.

Since the history of the Old Testament from Abraham on is the direct pre-history of Jesus Christ, it is positively directed as a whole to the immediate presence of God. In so far as particular events and propositions are recognised as legitimate parts of this history, the propositions must be treated as true; their legitimacy means here that the historical movement can only find practical realisation through particular phenomena and their interpretation.

THE APPLICATION OF THE SOLUTION

The solution we have reached to the interpretation of particular Old Testament statements which can be considered true, despite all the difficulties attached to them, should now be applied to the line of thought to which the fact of their truth gives rise. Thus it should be made clearer how the assertions in question can be made intelligible and shown to be true. Here we can only offer a few brief and simple comments on the practical application of this theory. For example, is a man who regards himself only as a henotheist not nearer to the God of salvation history, and therefore closer to the truth, if a state of polytheism exists around him which he cannot personally remove, than a person who attempts in this situation the impossible task of being a monotheist? Under these conditions the latter could perhaps mean no more than the abandonment of the God of a specific history of salvation, the God, that is, of Abraham, Isaac and Jacob, in favour of the shadowy figure of the God of the philosophers. If, on the other hand, he declares his exclusive loyalty in a henotheistic sense to the God of the covenant, then by maintaining the contrast between theoretical henotheism and exclusive allegiance to Yahweh he achieves the clearest recognition of the living God open to him. In this situation henotheism is the goad of absolute acknowledgement of Yahweh and as such possesses greater truth than the abstract form of monotheism.

The history of truth is one which cannot satisfactorily be organised by means of our system of logic. If we are placed because of this history in an existential situation in which we are explicitly summoned by the hope of eternal life, whether we wish it or not, then there is no way back for us to the condition in which the people of the Old Testament found themselves and which prevented them from looking beyond their collective and inner-worldly concept of salvation history. If we did do so, we would be denying our ultimate destiny in the direct experience of God. By contrast, in the context of the Old Testament, this state of affairs possessed a positive function in the history of salvation, for it was the means of achieving a relationship of total surrender to the sovereignty of God's freedom. At that period it could be an expression of the truth since it was the only real way available of treating life with absolute seriousness.

The egoistic nationalism of Old Testament Judaism was certainly not revealed as such and was only willed by God in the sense in which the whole history of the world is willed; here, however, we cannot without ambiguity apply the distinction between 'willed' and 'permitted' to specific historical periods. But in a particular historical period exclusive, egoistic nationalism could, at least partially and over a long stretch of time, be one practical way in which a man could put himself totally at the disposal of God as Lord of this history. Thus statements about such a form of nationalism could be true. The war ethic, with all its cruelties, was perhaps the only means, given the circumstances of ancient Israel, of enabling Israel to assert its identity as the people of the covenant, so that the war ethic could be perceived at that time as the will and revelation of God. In that period it could be the only possible, and therefore the true, medium of obedience to the God of history. The predictions of particular prophets made as a result of the national catastrophe in Israel may be contradictory taken in detail. However in the circumstances of the time the individual prophet could only perhaps give expression to his hope in the saving Lord of history and the absolute future through these particular prophecies. Despite their internal contradiction they could, then, be counted as true in a deeper and more comprehensive sense, just as if the material content of their predictions were in simple harmony with each other.

The truths brought into the Old Testament from alien religions and cultures over a long historical period cannot easily be reconciled either with each other or with the basic assertions of belief in Yahweh. In addition the difficult problem can arise, for instance in the case of belief in angels or the devil, that conceptions originating outside the Old Testament could either be asserted absolutely or only within the hypothesis, which was in the end left undecided, that they were valid in themselves. The questions we have mentioned demand further investigation. However, whether the material content, which came from a variety of sources, is correct in itself or only assumed as a hypothesis, the statements under discussion did express the religious truth of radical openness to the sovereign freedom of the grace of God.

The interpretation of religious truth we have briefly sketched assumes a certain concept of truth which, though not opposed to the formal notion of truth in the usual sense, has nevertheless a specific character in the realm of religious truth. The conformity of a proposition to the reality it signifies, i.e. the general nature of propositional truth, refers in our case to the conformity of reality and proposition (with respect to the concrete, free self-surrender of man in faith) to the direct self-communication of God. The material and categorial content of the corresponding proposition cannot always be reconciled, either for the individual or for the human community, with the innermost personal act of commitment to God's self-communication. To this extent, therefore, propositions, even taken in a religious sense, can be false with respect to their material content and should in consequence be rejected. But on the other hand not all material content which is incorrect both in itself and with reference to the reality it signifies need be irreconcilable with a successful and authentic commitment of faith to God. This is certainly true, for example, in the case of practical judgements which lead to an action which is *subjectively* right but whose categorial content is *objectively* wrong.[12]

To show that the use of traditional terminology without such a conception of truth cannot solve the problem we are considering, we need only mention the 'expectation' of Jesus. Jesus may, though the issue is not important, have rejected the demand to give the exact time of the coming of the kingdom of God, but he did presumably operate on the assumption in his preaching that the kingdom would come soon. We can then ask whether taken as it stands this assumption was true or false. If one considers the 'soon' in isolation and does not integrate it into a higher unity with the unknown character of the day

[12] Cf. on 'situation ethics', K. Rahner, 'On the Question of a Formal Existential Ethics', *Theological Investigations* II (London and Baltimore, 1963), pp. 217–220; 'Zur "Situationsethik" aus ökumenischer Sicht', *Schriften zur Theologie* VI (Zurich, 1968), pp. 537–544. For the idea of 'mental concupiscence', cf. K. Rahner, 'On the Relationship between Theology and the Contemporary Sciences', *Theological Investigations* XIII (London, 1975), pp. 94–102.

of Yahweh, – a synthesis for which scarcely any evidence can be discovered in the consciousness of Jesus –, then one can speak of an 'error' in the expectation of Jesus. In this 'error' he would then have merely shared our human lot, for to err is better for historical man, and therefore for Jesus, than always to know everything. But if one assumes the concept of truth we have outlined *here* and maintains it consistently out of respect for the terminology of the magisterium, then there is no reason to speak of an error in Jesus' expectation. A genuine human consciousness must have an unknown future before it; the expectation of Jesus was the right way for him in his situation of realising an absolute commitment to the call of God's proximity. Only if human propositions are located in a static realm with no regard for history, on the assumption that human commitment for or against God can take place beyond time and history, only then can Jesus' objectification of the decision of salvation cause surprise or be regarded as erroneous. [13]

THE SOLUTION AND THE NEW TESTAMENT

Finally we must add a cautionary word against wishing to apply the theory we have used to explain Old Testament statements to the theological truths of the New Testament in too naïve and hasty a manner. This does not mean that the theory has no significance at all for New Testament writings, though we cannot develop this point more fully here. But in the ultimate analysis Christianity appeals to the fundamental assertion that Jesus has surrendered himself to the incomprehensible reality of God in his death, i.e. in the destruction of the categorial, and has been accepted by God in this radical self-surrender. This statement contains a categorial, and therefore falsifiable, content if it is taken by itself, but its content is guaranteed in a radical and a priori manner from factual falsification in that it explicitly enables the categorial content, both in its appropriation (faith) and in its objective referent (fides quae: the victorious death of Jesus) to be handed over to the incomprehensible being of God. There is a basic difference between the statements of the New and Old Testaments, and so the specific concept of truth proper to the New Testament must be treated on its own. We must assert that the hermeneutic of the Old

[13] On the notion of truth, cf. K. Rahner, '*Zum Problem Unfehlbarkeit. Antworten auf die Anfrage von Hans Küng*, Quaestiones Disputatae 54 (Freiburg i. Br., 1971), pp. 9–70.

and of the New Testament, in a theological and not a philological sense, must be distinguished, even though God is the author of both Testaments.[14] The propositions of the Old Testament are true on condition, and for the reason, that they signify the realisation of a commitment to the God of an unknown and open-ended promise; the propositions of the New Testament are true in that they proclaim the death and resurrection of Jesus, in which the absolute future has already arrived and is no longer a mere possibility presented to the freedom of man.

---

[14] Cf. the confrontation with Marcion, summarised in the works referred to in footnote 2; more recently, B. Aland, 'Marcion, Versuch einer neuen Interpretation', *ZThK* 70 (1973), pp. 420–447.

12

ON THE 'HISTORY OF REVELATION' ACCORDING TO THE SECOND VATICAN COUNCIL

THE relationship between exegesis and dogmatic theology[1] labours under considerable difficulties. Scholars on both sides seem to grow further apart rather than come closer together. What can a dogmatic theologian say to an exegete in these circumstances?[2]

An important area of common effort could be the dogmatic constitution of the last Council which more than any other is relevant to exegesis: the dogmatic constitution on Revelation, *Dei Verbum*.[3] In this study only the short section 3 from the Ist Chapter of this conciliar text will be considered and a few critical remarks formulated to serve as a stimulus offered by a dogmatic theologian for an encounter between the two disciplines.

We do not intend here to dispute or doubt the central statement of this short passage; the purpose or our critical comments is rather to

[1] This essay was originally written for the Festschrift for R. Schnackenburg, *Neues Testament und Kirche* (Freiburg i. Br., 1974). It has been revised for publication here, but the original occasion of its composition influenced the choice of topic and the formulation of the question.

[2] On the topic of exegesis and dogmatic theology, cf. K. Rahner, 'Theology in the New Testament', *Theological Investigations* V (London and Baltimore, 1966), pp. 23–41; 'Exegesis and Dogmatic Theology', *ibid.* pp. 67–93; 'Scripture and Theology', *Theological Investigations* VI (London and Baltimore, 1969), pp. 89–97; 'Scripture and Tradition', *ibid.* pp. 98–112.

[3] A scholarly commentary is given in: *Commentary on the Documents of Vatican II* III (London and New York, 1968), pp. 155–272. Introduction and Commentary by J. Ratzinger, A. Grillmeier, B. Rigaux. Cf. also the highly readable commentary on the introduction and ch. 1 by H. de Lubac, *Dieu se dit dans l'histoire – La Révélation divine*, Foi vivante 159 (Paris, 1974).

make plain the degree to which such a conciliar text leaves open questions which demand an answer, if the concept of the *history of revelation*, which is of fundamental importance for the exegesis of scripture as written revelation, is to be clarified, so that it can in some measure be integrated into the contemporary horizon of human understanding. These remarks may serve to pinpoint the relevant questions without attempting to offer a solution.

THE TEXT AND ITS PRESUPPOSITIONS

For the sake of convenience the section in question will be given in the official translation, although when compared with the original Latin text it is not entirely satisfactory.

'3. God, who creates and maintains all things through the Word (cf. Jn 1:3), offers men of every age evidence of himself in created things (cf. Rm 1:19–20). Because he willed to open the way of supernatural salvation, he made himself known, in addition, to our first parents from the beginning. After their fall he restored them to hope for salvation by promising the redemption (cf. Gn 3:15). Without intermission he concerned himself for mankind in order to give eternal life to every man who seeks salvation by persistence in good works (cf. Rm 2:6–7). Later he called Abraham in order to make him into a great people (cf. Gn 12:2–3). After the patriarchs he brought this people through Moses and the prophets to recognise him as the only living and true God, as a loving father and a just judge, and to look forward to the promised saviour. So through the ages he prepared the way of the Gospel'.[4]

In the context of the Ist chapter, the place of this section is easily intelligible. There the topic discussed is revelation and its acceptance in faith, to which the teaching of the transmission of revelation can then be attached. This in turn introduces the main theme of the Constitution, i.e. Scripture. The earlier sections of the Ist chapter offer a brief formal account of the nature of revelation; the section following then speaks of the climax of revelation in Jesus Christ. The text quoted above describing the history of divine revelation from the beginning right up to the climax in Jesus Christ discussed in the next section is quite understandably placed between the two. If one ignores the fact that the schema has an 'objectivist' structure, i.e. it deals with revela-

---

[4] Cf. og. lit., III pp. 172–175.

tion in itself without then or previously answering the question of how a man can expect or recognise in the realm of his own existence something like a divine revelation at all, then the external sequence of the topics considered in this chapter seems quite reasonable. If one then turns to the text itself, one is struck by the way in which the very first clause speaks of what is usually regarded as the 'natural revelation' of God in his creation.[5] This implies that the text confirms the view, not explicitly but as an unspoken assumption, that the natural revelation of God is an obvious and universal phenomenon. This phenomenon provides a man with the best starting point from which to gain an understanding of divine revelation in the strict sense. Behind this line of thought there lies a mental model of the relationship of nature and grace, i.e. of the natural knowledge of God and the self-disclosure of God in revelation proper, a model which has remained constant in the development of theology since the Enlightenment. While recognising a legitimate distinction between nature and grace, one can no longer assert that this model is self-evident in modern theology or indeed wholly valid. For beyond space and time there exists a saving will of God which is universally effective and which directs man everywhere to his 'supernatural goal', i.e. the direct possession of God. This relationship to God is given a radical orientation by divine grace to God's self-communication and self-revelation, at least as an offer presented to man's free decision. This fact highlights the essential unity, ordained by God, of the relationship to God in spirit and in grace, which man experiences. In the factual order the so-called natural knowledge of God and the self-revelation of God in the strict sense are *inter-related*. For these reasons the divine revelation proper should not be assumed a priori to be a phenomenon located in a particular space and time. On the basis of this assumption the section we are considering can too easily take natural knowledge of God as a self-evident starting point.

STAGES IN THE HISTORY OF REVELATION

The account of the *history* of revelation (presupposing here the general character of revelation given in section 2) divides this history up to the climax in Jesus Christ clearly into three stages: the original revelation of God to the first parents; the period between them and the Old

[5] On the idea of 'natural revelation', cf. H. Fries, 'Die Offenbarung', *MySal* I (Zurich, 1965), 159–238, esp. 163–165.

Testament history of revelation starting from Abraham and Moses; the Old Testament history of revelation itself up to Jesus Christ. Let us take a brief look at each of these three very different sections of the history of revelation before Jesus Christ.

First of all the primal revelation:[6] we may pass over here the break which in the text is built into the original revelation as a historical event, namely the fall of the original parents. This event separates the revelation of the 'way of supernatural salvation' and the revelation of hope and promise of redemption. Even if we abstract from this point, the text raises a number of questions for contemporary man which remain unanswered, although a genuine understanding of this passage can scarcely dispense with either the questions or the answers. To register a critical note is not, to make the point clear from the start, to demand that a conciliar text of this type should itself offer answers to such questions, in so far as the answer is still an object of controversy amongst theologians, or for a variety of reasons is not fit material for an official statement of the magisterium. The purpose of the critique is merely to point out that the text might have been formulated in such a way that it would have been clearer to the modern reader that at least these problems were recognised and taken into account, and that a traditional formula had not simply been chosen, a formula which taken literally may seem somewhat naïve and far removed from a contemporary horizon of understanding. How is one to conceive of this revelation to the 'first parents', when they lived perhaps two million years ago, originated from the animal world by evolution and so must be imagined as 'primitive' beings? And yet they are supposed to recognise the path of 'supernatural salvation'. Furthermore what is one to make of this account if, with some justification, one assumes a state of polygenism with regard to the origins of mankind?[7] Why should not the whole story be an incredible myth? Has our knowledge of this original revelation been transmitted from the revelation itself by an unbroken tradition right from the beginning, or is the descrip-

[6] On the 'original revelation', cf. J. Heislbetz, 'Uroffenbarung', *LThK* X (Freiburg, 1965), 565–567 (bibliog.); also K. Rahner and J. Ratzinger, *Revelation and Tradition*, Quaestiones Disputatae 17 (Freiburg and London, 1965), pp. 9–25.

[7] On 'Polygenism', cf. K. Rahner, 'Theological Reflections on Monogenism', *Theological Investigations* I (London and Baltimore, 1961), pp. 229–296 (bibliog); also *HThTL* 5, Herderbücherei 455 (Freiburg i. Br., 1973), pp. 100–104.

tion of it an inference projected back to the origins, an aetiology[8] (either mythological or empirically justified, or a mixture of the two)? Such an aetiology might come from a later experience of salvation and revelation and contain the insight that, because of the unity of human history and universal salvific will of God, the basic structures of human history must have been present right from the start. As an extrapolation with a universalist thrust of the Israelite experience of salvation and revelation in relation to the God of its later history, the subsequent aetiology could also have influenced the account of paradise and the fall of the first parents given in Genesis and so make intelligible the development of this account and the precise limits of its meaning. But can one put this original revelation, which is an inferred postulate projected into the past, on the same plane as the later, historical and articulate revelation in the way evidently proposed in the text here? A further query is whether one can blithely assume that this revelation explicitly referred to 'supernatural salvation' in the modern sense of the term. The same questions could of course also be asked with regard to the fall of the first parents. In summary the portrayal of the original revelation is located in a traditional framework of meaning and ignores too many questions to allow a contemporary reader to make sense of it.

The second stage of the history of revelation which is described in our text is the period of time between the first parents and Abraham and Moses. The first thing that strikes us about this account of an enormous stretch of time, which makes the period from Abraham until today seem a brief moment by comparison, is that there is no mention of revelation taking place in this period, but only of a history of the saving providence of God, which is not necessarily the same thing at all. Did a genuine history of revelation take place in this time? How is it be conceived? Can one operate here with once feasible notions derived from a time when the history of mankind was understood to have lasted a mere few thousand years, and imagine that revelation during this vast stretch of years consisted in the transmission of the original revelation? If not, then did some *new* history of revelation occur in the course of this enormous period of time? Or was there at this stage a history of supernatural salvation without revela-

---

[8] On 'aetiology', cf. K. Rahner, 'The Sin of Adam', *Theological Investigations* XI (London and New York, 1974), p. 247–262. Also, *LThK* I (Freiburg, 1957), 1011–1012; *HThTL* I, Herderbücherei 451 (Freiburg i. Br., 1972), pp. 148–150.

tion? But then how could faith in a strict theological sense conceivably have happened in this period? At this point the dogmatic constitution is not as advanced in its theology as other conciliar decrees, in that it treats the question of faith and revelation in this period, understood as the conditions for salvation operative even at that time, with much greater caution and timidity. In the decree on the missions it is regarded as self-evident that faith leading to salvation (and therefore revelation which is its precondition) is both possible and necessary,[9] even though the decree declines to explain more clearly this possibility of faith. In the dogmatic constitution on the Church and on the pastoral constitution, saving faith is assumed and stated to be a possibility for every man who follows the demands of his conscience.[10] It would thus have created no problems to affirm the existence of revelation in the true sense in the period stretching from the beginning up to the Old Testament patriarchs, and so to assert the possibility of genuine faith in revelation. But in fact this is not to be found. Why? The need to treat salvation and revelation history of this period very briefly hardly explains by itself the restriction to the mere saving providence of God in a passage which really required mention of the history of revelation. It does seem as if the issue was passed over too lightly and questions left aside to which the modern reader requires at the least the first elements of an answer, or at the minimum the explicit statement that no answer was possible. To fail to do so is to frustrate a legitimate interest in the unity of man and his history. What is more important, the present account makes the history of revelation following this period seem a quite new and unexpected age with no connection with the whole history of mankind. To the modern man such an age appears then as a sheer miracle, even if he is basically ready to grant the occurrence of new and unexpected events in history.

We have now come to the third phase, which is presented in our text as the history of revelation up to Jesus Christ. We may leave aside here the fact that the history of Old Testament from the time of Abraham seems to have been regarded perhaps in a rather too optimistic light, and conceived practically as the uniform and unbroken preparation of the chosen people for Jesus Christ. We can also overlook

---

[9] Cf. *Decree on the Church's Missionary Activity*, no. 3. cf. *Commentary on the Documents of Vatican II* IV pp. 87 sqq.; cf. in same decree nos. 8,9,14, 15, 17.

[10] Cf. *Dogmatic Constitution in the Church*, no. 16 and 17. cf. *Commentary on the Documents of Vatican II* I, pp. 182–185. Also, *Pastoral Constitution on the Church in the Modern World*, nos. 22, 26, 38, 41, 57.

the total lack of reference to the dualism of law and Gospel (promise) which is characteristic of the Old Testament period. What does, however, demand our attention is the fact that revelation to Abraham and the prophets occurs in a manner quite unrelated to the universal history of salvation and revelation which has certainly taken place. Now a person schooled in the history of Old Testament scholarship will ask whether it is possible to attribute so easily to an 'Abraham' the *historical* role which is given him here following the fashion of an age which was quite unaware of modern critical study of the Old Testament. In our text the intention is to portray genuine history in the modern sense. Can Abraham simply be made the father of the nation which is the bearer of the history of revelation available to us in the writings of the Old Testament? Can one adopt the style of e.g. Gen 12:2–3 and merely repeat formulae, if one wishes to explain the reality, origins and significance of the Old Testament history of revelation to Christians today, who can approach the Old Testament in faith only on the basis of Jesus Christ? Even if one does not just speak of an Abraham saga and is prepared to grant a genuine historical core to the figure described in the Old Testament, even so the failure to take into account the enormous temporal gap between Abraham and Moses and the consequent silence on the subject remains somewhat surprising. One could make the same comments about Moses: he is fitted rather too smoothly in our view into a continuous list with the prophets of a far later period, who can be grasped even by us today as historical figures, each with a particular individual stamp. Is not Moses also conceived in a rather naïve and unsophisticated manner, following the style of Old Testament presentation and without regard to the results of contemporary study of the history of the Near East and modern exegesis? And is not the whole history of Old Testament revelation presented without any connection with the rest of the history of religion, which can readily be understood as a single history of revelation, even if corrupted by sin and error? For without in any way wishing to dispute the dignity and value of the Old Testament, we may say that in this general history the revelation of the Old Testament is clear and verifiable in so far as it forms the immediate (regarded, that is, from the point of view of the history of man and salvation) and quite short preparation and context for the Christ event. It is this latter event which provides the only guarantee of the continuing validity and normative status of the Old Testament for us even today.

In conclusion we want to repeat that this critique of the text contained in section 3 does not demand that all the questions raised by this passage should be answered. The point of these critical remarks was to show that, if the authors of the text had clearly perceived and reckoned with these questions as ones which are urgent and necessary today, then they would have composed the text differently. In all probability they might have altered the entire conception of the pre-Christian history of revelation and not presented it, as they have, in the framework of a simple *time* series, a model which is not intelligible to us. Instead they might have treated it retrospectively, taking as their starting point Jesus Christ,[11] who alone makes the event of revelation intelligible to us. From this view point they could have looked backwards and offered a survey of the whole of human history as the history of salvation and revelation, providing a careful outline of the particular history of salvation which we call the history of the Old Testament. This section, quite small in spatio-temporal terms, of the universal history of revelation still affects us in that it forms the immediate and proximate history of the Christ event. It would then perhaps also have been feasible to have developed the theme of section 3 on the assumption that the saving will of God is both supernatural and universal. On this basis the necessary and universal character of revelation in every age (despite our inability to say exactly how this occurs) could have been presented as a theological deduction and not as a piece of historical description. The exegesis of the New and Old Testament did not play the part it should have done in the Council. In general an honest effort was made to give expression to traditional theology and to strengthen these statements with traditional proof texts. Of this our text is a good example.

---

[11] Cf. also the speculative methods mentioned below. The author has tried to combine both methods in: K. Rahner and W. Thüsing, *Christologie – systematisch und exegetisch*, Quaestiones Disputatae 55 (Freiburg i. Br., 1972), 'Grundlinien einer systematischen Christologie', pp. 15–78. This also provides a practical example of collaboration between exegesis and dogmatic theology.

13

THE ONE CHRIST AND THE UNIVERSALITY OF SALVATION

THE purpose of this enquiry is to throw some light on the question of the one Christ and the universality of salvation as a theme of systematic theology.[1] The precise meaning of this topic may become clearer in the course of these reflections.

Our method here will be to use both the binding statements of the Church's magisterium and broader theological opinion to underpin the ideas presented. For it is in fact impossible to formulate a systematic account of the teaching of the Church, in a form that can be personally appropriated in a contemporary setting, without free theological opinion playing a role whose limits can often not easily be separated from dogma proper. Christian faith at any particular historical period needs theological opinion in order to be given appropriate expression; no theology can be made up of the defined propositions of the Church's magisterium alone, for theology must be explained and explanation necessarily requires the use of concepts, assumptions and contexts of meaning which are subject to chance. At any rate theological opinion does enter in either explicitly or in a disguised form; the boundary between it and the binding dogmatic truths may be clearly marked or ill-defined and the theological weight of this opinion may be of various types. But such opinion is always present, even for instance in the 'Credo of the people of God' of Paul VI.[2] Here, however, we can dispense with explicit definition of the

---

[1] A student of the author has investigated the question of the universality of redemption from a historical perspective in a dissertation: A. Bsteh, *Zur Frage nach der Universalität der Erlösung*. Unter besonderer Berücksichtigung ihres Verständnisses bei den Vätern des zweiten Jahrhunderts; Wiener Beitrage zur Theologie XIV (Vienna, 1966).

[2] Published in *AAS* 60 (1968), 436–445.

various theological 'notes', in as much as the topic under discussion directly embodies only one statement of a dogmatically binding sort and even this has perhaps not been explicitly defined as such. I refer to the truth that the achievement by any man of his proper and definitive salvation is dependent upon Jesus Christ. How that is to be conceived is the subject of this enquiry.

Naturally other propositions possessing either dogmatic force or a high theological 'note' will be employed in the course of this investigation. But to clarify the truth of the universal significance of Jesus for the salvation of every man, any meaningful and reasonable proposition can rightly be used which is appropriate for the explanation of this dogma.

THE THEOLOGICAL MEANING OF THE QUESTION

We are speaking in the first place of the basic possibility of the salvation of all men and not of the extent to which, according to Christian understanding, salvation will in fact be achieved, i.e. whether the 'apocatastasis' of all men is a legitimate hope or not.[3] Here the question is the *possibility* of salvation, not its actual realisation. Contrary to the view of St Augustine, this possibility is a real one in a fallen world: no man is excluded from salvation simply because of so-called original sin; a man can only lose the possibility of salvation through serious personal sin of his own. Salvation here is to be understood as the strictly supernatural and direct presence of God in himself afforded by grace. This, of course, excludes, despite the statement of *Pius* VI[4] on the subject of limbo, a purely natural state of blessedness. The direct 'vision' of God is the only salvation for all men. How the many stages of this long journey to the final union with God are to be conceived is not a matter of concern here. Indeed in certain cases the journey may not even be terminated by death. The traditional teaching about a 'place of purification' embraces a multitude of assumptions and modes of interpretation whose possibilities have by no means been exhausted and which can substantially alter the common popular notion of purgatory.

The fundamental proposition which is the proper subject of theological investigation refers therefore to the universal possibility of supernatural salvation for all men after original sin. This possibility

[3] Cf. J. Loosen, *LThK* I (1957), 709–712.
[4] *Denz.* 2626.

must really be given to *all*. By this is meant all those throughout human history who have come to a free realisation of their existence. The question is here excluded of the salvation of those who are clearly human beings but who have probably never achieved the full exercise of their freedom. Theological reflection upon the universal possibility of salvation involves, then, all those who have reached complete self-determination as free persons and have thus explicitly or implicitly taken a free decision for or against God. Whether this definition implies a real restriction of universality or not is a matter about which we have no certain knowledge. In any event it means all men who have existed from the beginning of human history proper, even if this beginning can scarcely be defined with any theological precision. To this group all men of course belong who have never had direct tangible contact with the Gospel and its preaching. In this context the question raised by Billot[5] is of fundamental importance, whether, that is, every man who did not die as a child and could lead a more or less normal life, given the changing cultural circumstances, was capable of reaching the realisation of freedom necessary for the achievement of supernatural fulfilment. In the light of the actual historical and cultural conditons of life experienced by many individuals and groups, one may doubt whether many so-called adults do in fact reach a level of freedom which is effective for salvation. There is no simple means of resolving this question. Either one can appeal to the fact that subjective freedom in certain circumstances can be achieved despite lack of thematic reflection and scanty material, which means that the number of adults 'under age' with respect to their salvation is of no importance. Or one asserts that many so-called adults do exist who, with regard to their salvation, never go beyond the stage of unbaptised children who die young. We know as little about the fate of such men as about the destiny of those who die as embryos or infants.

Without proper evidence one can only say about such men that we are entirely ignorant of their fate. If one were to claim knowledge, one would merely be projecting theological data, in itself correct enough, into the absolute future in a one-sided and inadmissible manner, and the outcome of such a procedure is questionable. The significance of this is to indicate the limits of any theological proposition about the universal possibility of salvation.

[5] L. Billot S.J. (1846–1931), Professor at the Gregorianium, Rome and important speculative theologian.

GOD'S SALVIFIC WILL IN THE CONTEMPORARY UNDERSTANDING OF FAITH

Given these assumptions the theological truth of the universal possibility of salvation may be taken without reserve to possess binding dogmatic force. It may be that it has not been defined but there is no doubt that it belongs to the contemporary understanding of faith and may be considered as the explicit and official teaching of the Church. As such it is to be regarded as absolutely binding. The truth in this matter was not always seen with such clarity to be part of the faith of the Church as it is today, despite the numerous scriptural passages[6] which are used today by theological textbooks to prove the universal salvific will of God. For even if the notion that God's salvific will is limited to the predestined is rejected as heretical[7] and even if God's salvific will is taken to apply to non-believers and St Augustine's particularism about salvation is considered a restriction which is now overcome, nevertheless the truth that God wills the salvation of all men can be so loaded with 'ifs' and 'buts'[8] that it can hardly be characterised as a formal dogma in the sense intended here.

Now, however, the Second Vatican Council has recognised the possibility that even non-Christians, polytheists and atheists can live in a subjective state of freedom from serious sin. At the same time the Council reckons with the possibility of supernatural salvation in such cases. Thus it is an evident part of the contemporary understanding of faith that there is no human state which allows one to draw definite conclusions about the personal sinfulness of a man and thus deny him the possibility of salvation. This is the meaning of the proposition that all men have the possibility of being saved, as this proposition is understood today. This implies that there is no human situation which can be empirically verified and conclusively established, that certainly rules out salvation from the start. At the same time salvation is only achieved in fact when a man acquires faith, hope and love, and so overcomes the contrary tendencies in him. The Second Vatican Council, in contrast to the previous tradition of the schools, reckons with the possibility of the saving activities of faith, hope and love being found even in the case of atheists who remain attached to their belief. So the possibility cannot be denied to any other group of men, whatever their externally verifiable attitudes and beliefs. A man may be

[6] Cf. 1 Tim 2:4.
[7] Cf. *Denz.* 623 sq., 1567, 2005, 2304 sq.
[8] This must apply at least until the Second Vatican Council.

disposed in whatever way he will as far as empirical criteria are concerned, but the direct possibility of salvation cannot thereby be denied to him. Only if we grant this, can we take seriously the biblical injunction that we can judge no man.[9] How the real and direct possibility of salvation can co-exist with a human situation which objectively ought not to be[10] is a matter to be considered later.

The Second Vatican Council offered no definition of the truth of the universal salvific will of God, but this truth has never before in history been so clearly a part of the understanding of faith as it is today. One can, therefore, either offer the sort of theological description we have provided above or define the proposition as 'sentientia fidei proxima',[11] with L. Ott for example. The topic of our deliberations is not the proposition in itself but rather its Christological reference; thus the above remarks may be considered sufficient explanation of its theological significance, its limits and its theological 'note'. Further proof of its validity and a more detailed treatment of its history are not in any event necessary here.

THE DIRECT AND SAVING PRESENCE OF GOD

In every conceivable historical and social situation of life a man can have direct saving access to God without necessarily being required to leave his objective situation 'de necessitate medii absoluta', in order to be able to discover the direct reality of God somewhere else. Naturally the actual discovery of this immediate presence demands 'metanoia', faith, hope and love, but the universal possibility of salvation, as it is understood here, means precisely that the necessary turning to God can be achieved, either reflectively or unreflectively, from any conceivable existential standpoint, in so far as it is the given historical, cultural or religious situation which is in question. This possibility is a categorial one and belongs to the basic structure of human freedom and human self-realisation. It may often occur in the case of a particular human life that the refusal freely to alter his own existential situation means a denial of God and the destruction of the chance of salvation. But this assumes that the prior historical situation of a man is directly open to the saving presence of God, in so far as it is not

[9] Mt 7:1; Lk 6:37.
[10] E.g. an objective sin, a theoretical or practical atheism.
[11] Cf. L. Ott, *Grundriss der Katholischen Dogmatik* (Freiburg i. Br. 1959), pp. 288 sq.

formed or maintained by the personal sin of the individual. In purely human terms we can never assert with total certainty of any situation that its existence is only possible because of the personal guilt of the individual living in it, and that it is therefore a sign of the loss of God's direct saving presence.

In an *ultimate* sense God is equally near everywhere. The narrow gap can everywhere be bridged through faith, hope and love with the help of whatever aid the particular historical circumstances provide. Conversely the faith which is effective for salvation never enters so clearly into any situation that its presence or absence enables one to make a certain judgement that the situation is open or closed to salvation. In saying this I do not at all mean to question the importance or the objective value of a moral act, the validity of the confession of faith, or of actual membership of the Church, or to relativise these values with regard to the subjective salvation any man. However a more thorough treatment of these questions would divert us from the topic under discussion.

The world is drawn to its spiritual fulfilment by the Spirit of God, who directs the whole history of the world in all its length and breadth towards its proper goal. This means that every man, whatever his situation, can be saved. The Christ event, however, seems at first glance to be the effect and not the cause of the dynamic of divine spiritual communication to the world. How can one claim, then, that salvation comes entirely from Jesus Christ? This question forms the focal point of our reflections, given the necessary clarifications we have provided.

THE PROBLEMATIC

We live in a world in which each and everything is inter-dependent, in which every event is in some way important for every other, at least if it comes later in time, a world in which Sirius wobbles in its course when a child throws a doll out of its cradle, to quote the telling remark of one modern physicist. But this physical unity of space and time does not offer a suitable basis for the solution of our question. For we are not dealing with a framework or a unity in which every element is significant for every other, but rather with a single, specific, historical event which is supposedly important even for the periods of history before it. This event, taking place within history, is meant to be absolutely fundamental for every other event occurring at any time from the beginning to the end of that same history. And yet this must be understood as a history of freedom operating at every particular moment, i.e. events continually occurring which cannot be dependent for their very essence, the decision for or against God, on other events, however much these latter may form the conditions and context for the exercise of freedom. In the realisation of salvation the freedom of the individual is irreplaceable.

One could offer the answer that freedom must be exercised under prior conditions and circumstances which are independent of it, since human freedom is finite. One might add that the 'objective redemption' through Jesus Christ forms part of the condition of freedom as far as salvation or damnation are concerned. But this raises at least the question of how redemption understood in this way can apply to those who lived *before* Christ. Furthermore how can this situation be of relevance for the free action of those who, though living after the time of Christ, have either no knowledge of him at all or knowledge of a kind which does not impel their freedom to an ultimate decision? Finally in what way is the objective redemption to be analysed as constitutive of human freedom and its exercise?

The 'objective redemption through Christ' can be a specific and characteristic element in the basic structure of human freedom, which includes numerous other elements as well. It would then possess a unique place among these elements, which is higher than all others, since it forms part of the predestination of freedom ordained by God. This predestination is assumed in all schools of Catholic theology, whatever their exact interpretation, to be something which can be reconciled with human freedom. But this is merely a statement of the real problem. Whether we should speak of a general (or particular) predestination of human freedom to salvation or simply of the saving will of God does not make any difference to our investigation. Our enquiry concurs the *how* of the connection of such a saving will, or divine predestination, with the Christ event.

A quick and easy answer to our question which consists in an appeal to the 'cosmic Christ' should be avoided. Of course the pre-existing Logos of God can be conceived without difficulty as a creative, sanctifying, reconciling and divinising force operating in the world and in history. Human salvation depends on the Logos and all salvation is related to it. The eternal Logos of God gives himself to the central core of human freedom as the condition of possibility of a supernatural response to the self-communication of God. He thus constitutes the redemption or the redemption event. On the basis of the 'communicatio idiomatum' one can say of Jesus that he is the salvation of the world, just as he can say he is creator of the world.

But all this does not provide a satisfactory answer to our question, for the self-communication of the divine Logos to the world is conceived not as a single event within history but as the ultimate dynamic orientation which operates universally and is the ground of the whole of history. One may leave aside here the further problem of how the function of the Logos in its work of salvation and its guidance of the world is related to the activity of the Holy Spirit, and how, or rather with what justification, the disciples of Jesus moved from the experience of him as the one crucified and risen (cf. the letter to the Colossians, the writings of John and the letter to the Hebrews) to the pre-existent, creative and saving Logos embodied in Jesus. But that still leaves the question unanswered how the particular historical event of the death and resurrection of Jesus, which happened at a particular time and place, can be of fundamental importance for the salvation of all men. It may be that the question cannot be answered without reference to the pre-existent Logos in Jesus, but this appeal by itself does not provide the solution we are looking for.

SELF–REDEMPTION AND REDEMPTION BY ANOTHER

In Christian apologetics a distinction is usually drawn between self-redemption and redemption by another. We mention this point in order to avoid the danger of making greater demands than are theologically necessary upon the redemption of all men in Christ and upon his death and resurrection. Otherwise people today are forced into a situation of meaningless confusion from which they cannot escape. The Christian doctrine of faith, hope and love, of the union in grace with God and of the free reception of God's self-communication can well be understood in the sense of a true self-redemption. The person who redeems himself in freedom, i.e. places God in the centre of his own free existence, is a creature who is constituted by the creative freedom of God and is therefore given the capacity to accept God's self-communication. God, however, shares himself with man both through uncreated grace which forms his very being and through the supernatural capacity which arises from grace and belongs to man in his freedom. God is himself the condition of possibility of human salvation from which man freely realises his salvation. Naturally it is taken for granted in Christian theology, in contrast to any form of Pelagianism, that the free acceptance of salvation is also a gift of God's grace and thus forms the very core of the human person and of human freedom.[12]

If, however, self-redemption means that a man can achieve his fulfilment without God, then any form of self-redemption is foreign to Christian teaching. Christian salvation can only be understood as self-redemption in the sense that a man does not merely receive his salvation in a passive manner but rather realises it with total, and not just partial, freedom. The very possibility of freedom, however, is established by God through nature and grace. To gain a proper idea of this grace one should not conceive of the grace in which a man achieves salvation as an external means but rather as the innermost core of human freedom which is freely constituted by God.

If self-redemption is presented in Christian faith in the above sense, and if the cross of Christ (rooted in the incarnation of the Logos and reaching fulfilment in the resurrection) is made the cause of our salvation as the 'redemptio objectiva', then the causality of the cross must be understood in relation to the general and the individual conditions of possibility of self-redemption. But how this is to be conceived still remains unclear.

CROSS: CONSEQUENCE OR CAUSE?

It follows from what we have said that the event of the crucifixion, taken as 'redemptio objectiva', cannot be the cause of the uncaused salvific will of God, at least not in the usual sense of the term. For according to common understanding, cause means a physical or moral operation which brings something about. By contrast we must say: because God wills salvation, therefore Jesus died and rose again, and not: because the crucifixion occurred, therefore God wills our salvation. God is not transformed from a God of anger and justice into a God of mercy and love by the cross; rather God brings the event of the cross to pass since he is possessed from the beginning of gratuitous mercy and, despite the world's sin, shares himself with the world, so overcoming its sin.

[12] Cf. A. Hamman, *LThK* VIII (1963), 246–249. Also the more recent study of the position of Pelagius by G. Greshake, *Gnade als konkrete Freiheit. Eine Untersuchung zur Gnadenlehre des Pelagius* (Mainz, 1972).

What mode of 'causality' is to be attributed to the cross for the salvation of all men, is precisely the question which is at stake here. This is also a version of the real difficulty of the so-called Anselmian theory of satisfaction,[13] which in a crude or a more subtle form has determined the doctrine of the redemption in western Christianity, at least where the crucifixion has not been denied any form of causality and the cross and resurrection treated only as ground for *our* faith and *our* trust in God. The satisfaction theory requires a series of tortuous distinctions in order to make plain that the one making satisfaction and the one accepting it are in our case one and the same. This seems to make the theory untenable as a model for the understanding of the causality of the redemption. We can see from the history of preaching and theology how this theory consistently obscured the simple fact that the event of the cross did not originate in an angry God who demanded reparation, but from a God of gratuitous and merciful love. This is not to deny that God's holiness and justice are evident on the cross or to dispute the value for religious teaching of certain elements of the satisfaction theory, which are entirely to be approved. But the theory, almost of necessity, introduces the metaphysically impossible idea of a transformation of God and obscures the origin and cause of the crucifixion which is the mercy and love of God. This love can only include sin in the world because, as God's yes to man, this love was meant to prove itself victorious over man's no to God.

The satisfaction theory requires the ultimately inconceivable notion that Jesus is man's representative and is opposed to the correct understanding of self-redemption outlined above. In addition the Pauline formula '$\dot{v}\pi\grave{\epsilon}\rho$ $\dot{\eta}\mu\tilde{\omega}\nu$' is interpreted in an unconvincing manner which forces the sense of Paul's words.[14] But how could the apostle of the gentiles know and speak of this '$\dot{v}\pi\acute{\epsilon}\rho$' in the light of the experience of the death and resurrection of Jesus of the first disciples?

THE MERIT OF CHRIST

Official doctrinal pronouncements of the Church as well as traditional theological opinion both refer to the fact, e.g. in connection with the doctrine of the Immaculate Conception of Mary,[15] that grace and salvation were guaranteed man 'intuitu meritorum Christi'. Yet this

[13] Cf. W. Kasper, *Jesus the Christ* (London, 1976), pp. 219–221.
[14] Cf. 2 Cor 5:21; Gal 1:4; 3:13; 1 Cor 1:13; 11:24.
[15] Cf. *Denz.* 2803.

comment, while perfectly correct in itself, expresses no more than the truth from which these reflections originated and which requires further elucidation. This line of thought connects human salvation with the cross of Christ, without explaining how the connection is to be conceived. At least it makes it easier to understand how pre-Christian mankind and men living outside Christianity could be dependent for their salvation upon the cross of Christ, in that the idea of God's eternal fore-knowledge of this event in time is brought into play. This makes intelligible a possible effect of Christ's cross operating before the time when he himself became a historical event.

There is here the problem that the elements of the history of salvation, which should be inter-connected to form a single salvation history, are in this account bound together by forces operating outside history, that is, by the eternal fore-knowledge of God. This foreknowledge does not belong to salvation history as such, since all historical and temporal moments are equally and eternally present to it. But even if we leave this difficulty aside, the fact remains that the proposed 'intuitus meritorum Christi' does not explain the real meaning of the statement that God wills human salvation 'because of' the cross of Christ.

In the light of what we have said the cross of Christ cannot be the cause of human salvation in the sense that it brought about the will to save in God which otherwise would not have existed, or that it bestowed upon men a type of salvation which takes no heed of human freedom. Despite all these objections does a connection exist between the cross of the Lord and the salvation of all men, a connection which is more than an appeal to the moral impact which the death and resurrection of Christ has on us? Any attempt to discover such a connection should not ignore the fact that *all* men are involved. Let us start our investigation with Jesus himself and then turn to ourselves; the double perspective will open up questions which otherwise might have been overlooked.

JESUS AND ALL MEN

The relationship of *Jesus* to all men raises a series of questions relevant to exegesis and fundamental theology which cannot be systematically investigated here. Only one will be mentioned: how did the pre-Easter Jesus conceive of his death? Did he approach it with full knowledge and consent and accept it in ultimate unconditional faith and trust? Did he realise the soteriological significance of his death? Under what assumptions and in what framework of meaning can Jesus' knowledge of the soteriological importance of his death be conceived? What is the minimum required by dogma and fundamental theology to enable us to attribute to the pre-Easter Jesus a soteriological value for his death in a historically tangible form?

Without being able here to go further into these and similar questions, we will simply assume that the death and resurrection of Jesus, taken together, *do possess* soteriological significance. We take this to be the teaching of Scripture and the Church, and there is sufficient evidence to connect its content with the reality of the pre-Easter Jesus. Here the only question to be asked is how the connection between the death of Jesus and the salvation of all men can be imagined without our getting enmeshed in the conceptual tangle we mentioned earlier.

Of course we should remember first, that Jesus possesses *that* relationship to every man which connects all men together in the many dimensions of life within the framework of a single humanity and history. The existential, ontological, historical, philosophical and theological grounds for this assertion cannot be listed or developed here, except to say that humanity and history form a genuine unity and do not merely consist in a sum of individual human beings and isolated biographies put together by our thought processes. This unity affects not only the common physical and biological basis of man and his world, but also the human reality of man and his freedom and history, which cannot easily be explained. It is obvious that such a specifically human unity, and not one with merely material and biological foundations, is important for the soteriological connection between Jesus and the whole of humanity and should not be obscured or undervalued. It plays a role in the doctrine of redemption found among the Greek fathers, in that in their view humanity has a form of existence which enables the eternal Logos to enter into communion with the single race of mankind. But even the western theory of satisfaction presupposes a unity among men to which Jesus belongs as well, irrespective of whether this unity, in which Jesus in his representative function can act for all, is thought of as the result of divine decree rather than as a natural unity of mankind to which the incarnate Logos of God also belongs. Yet however necessary it is to reflect upon the unity of man and his history, nevertheless it is not sufficient by itself to make what is meant here intelligible.

If one wanted to say that the redemption was achieved through the incarnation alone, then the universal significance of the Christ event could be explained on the basis of the unity of mankind alone. Humanity is one and is saved as a single whole through the incarnation of the eternal Logos in this unity. He must share the ultimate salvation with man which necessarily belongs to him as the Logos of God; otherwise the unity of human history would be destroyed, if the necessary salvation of one of its members were irrelevant to the destiny and possibility of salvation of the whole of mankind. Certainly these considerations have positive meaning and validity and they should therefore be included in a theology of the cross and its significance for salvation. But if the cross of Christ, his death and resurrection, are regarded as a saving event affecting all men, then even the notion of a universal communion of race and history shared by the Logos is not sufficient by itself. The death and resurrection of Jesus must possess universal importance in themselves for salvation and cannot merely be regarded as isolated events, of no significance in themselves, in a life which only has universal relevance for salvation in being the life of the eternal Logos. It is this Logos which entered the unity of mankind and took on a human nature, thus taking on and saving the whole of humanity.

As we have seen earlier, the 'causality' of the saving death of Jesus for the salvation of all men must be the consequence and not the cause of the self-giving of God to the world in grace. It does not mean a transformation in God, for God brings the crucifixion to pass out of grace not out of anger, although the meaning of the cross does not consist alone in its power to convince us of the love and forgiveness of God. If the causality of the cross with regard to salvation were exclusively interpreted in this way, then any universality would be out of the question, since the majority of mankind have no explicit knowledge of the cross and since, according to Paul's notion of the saving effect of the cross, the death of Jesus is set within the category of sacrifice. However we may here with caution assert that the Pauline ideas of 'sacrifice', 'ransom', 'reconciliation through blood' do not reflect the original understanding of the saving significance of the Cross of Jesus for all men; they are legitimate ideas but they are secondary notions which must be explained in the light of the primary and original data and are aimed to bring home the significance of Christ's death for our salvation. In other cultures and historical periods such ideas do not so easily achieve this goal, even if we do not mean to imply by this that, for us today for example, these models of thought should be entirely rejected.

The question, therefore, of the mode of causality remains open. One is tempted to demand from the start the abandonment of the idea of 'causality' altogether. But the fact remains that it is part of the Christian confession of faith that the death of Jesus *means something* for the salvation of all men, that it was *for* us that he died. Such formulations express the same content as the 'causality' of the death of Jesus with regard to the salvation of all men. The problem remains the same whether one speaks of 'causality', 'meaning' or 'for us'. In any event all forms of causality of a physical or moral type fail, so that a causality of the death of Jesus is suggested which is precisely one that should not come into question.

To resolve this dilemma one may pursue a number of paths. Here we will choose one which discloses the causality of Jesus' death we are seeking with a concept which is familiar in a different theological context and has been extensively investigated.

We may assert the following: the cross (together with the resurrection of Jesus) has a primary sacramental causality for the salvation of all men, in so far as it mediates salvation to man by means of salvific grace which is universally operative in the world. It is the sign of this grace and of its victorious and irreversible activity in the world. The effectiveness of the cross is based on the fact that it is the primary sacramental sign of grace.

SACRAMENTAL SIGN AND GRACE

The salvific causality of the cross should not be *subsumed* under the sign causality of grace which is characteristic and familiar from sacramental teaching, or rather from *one* possible and legitimate version of that teaching. The specific character of the effect of the cross must be obtained from theological investigation of the cross itself. Of course this can lead to a notion of causality which evidently agrees with the sign causality of the sacraments. Such a conception can then easily be adopted, although the proposed causality is not to be found elsewhere and is not to be subsumed under the other familiar notions of causality. Sufficient proof of this is provided by the fact that the new concept in sacramental theology is recognised as sign causality, a type of causality, therefore, which is proper to the sign as such and is not something added to the sign. In sacramental theology it is not that the qualities sign *and* causality are attributed to the sacramental processes with regard to grace and then other categories of instrumental causality of a physical or moral type are applied to cover this sign causality and interpret it. It is rather the case that the sign is the cause. 'Sacramenta causant gratiam, quia et prout significant gratiam'. We are not of course assuming here that every sign of a thing can also be treated as its cause. But in so far as a sacrament can and should be conceived of as a 'real symbol', as a historical and social embodiment of grace, where grace achieves its own fullness of being and forms an irreversible gift (opus operatum), to this extent the sign is a cause of grace, although the sign is caused by this grace.

The mutual inter-dependence prevents one regarding grace and the sign of grace as two quite separate realities set over against each other as cause and effect. We should rather speak of two moments in a process of historical and ontological fulfilment, even if the conditions of each are different. In this sense the sacramental sign is a cause of grace. The sign belongs to the essential actualisation of this grace which thereby finds irreversible historical expression. The sign is in fact brought forth by grace as its 'real symbol', so that grace itself achieves fulfilment. The ontological and pneumatological implications of sign causality and its connection with the bodiliness and the historicity of man require fuller clarification but these remarks about the notion of sign causality must suffice. Its legitimacy in any event is independent of the following reflections and thus can serve as theological evidence in their favour.

What is to be said in our case? God's saving will embraces everything and so permits even the sin of the world. His self-communication which consists in an offer made to human freedom touches the innermost nature and goal of man and therefore of salvation history. In this process each thing is important with and for every other, since every individual in this single salvation history is willed by God's saving purpose *as* an element within it. The solidarity of man in salvation history is not of the same character for every individual as this history unfolds in time, nor does it consist merely in a temporal succession of individual histories of salvation. It tends towards a goal and a fulfilment of the whole of salvation history, in which the being of God as self-giving love and the freedom of God find an irreducible and historically tangible expression. Under these conditions it is at least conceivable that the ambivalence of human and divine freedom which is a primary feature of this history will be resolved by a free and historical act before the universal culmination of the total historical process. The outcome would then be fixed and irreversible from within history.

The logical possibility is assured if the irreversible outcome, appearing within history, of the historical process of human and divine freedom is positive, i.e. signifies the salvation of the world which could not then be totally lost. This would be possible if God were to communicate himself to a man in such a unique manner that this man would become the definitive and irreversible self-gift of God to the world. He would also freely accept the divine self-gift in such a manner that this too would be irreversible, i.e. through his death as the definitive culmination of his free actions in history. If salvation history is irreversibly directed in this sense to salvation, and not to damnation, through a concrete event, then this historically tangible occurrence must be a sign of the salvation of the whole world in the sense of a 'real symbol', and so possesses a type of causality where salvation is concerned. To this we wish to apply a well known theological concept and call it 'sacramental'.

Christian faith sees in Jesus, his cross and resurrection just such an event. Given the unity and solidarity of mankind, we have here before us the sign of an irreversible positive outcome of the one historical process. Before this event took place the positive ending of salvation history was not assured with tangible historical certainty, but was obscured by the ambiguity of human and divine freedom. Thus we may predicate of this sign of the salvation of the whole world the type of sacramental causality which was mentioned earlier. *Because* Jesus died and rose again, therefore salvation is offered and given to the whole of mankind; taken together cross and resurrection are the 'cause' of the salvation of all men. To avoid the problems alluded to above, this 'causality' must be thought of in terms of 'sacramental sign causality', which is brought about by the prior divine will to save mankind and is not itself the cause of this divine will. If the Second Vatican Council emphasises that the Church is the sacrament of the world's salvation[16] and explains this statement by describing the Church as the basic sacrament of salvation,[17] then Jesus Christ may be

---

[16] Cf. *Dogmatic Constitution on the Church* (LG), nos. 1, 8, 48, 59; *Decree on Eceumenism* (UR), no. 2; *Decree on the Missionary Activity of the Church* (AG), no. 1; *Pastoral Constitution on the Church in the Modern World* (GS) no. 45.

[17] Cf. K. Rahner, 'Kleine Vorüberlegung über die Sakramente im allgemeinen', *Die siebenfaltige Gabe. Über die Sakramente der Kirche* (Munich, 1974), pp. 7–18.

called the *primary* sacrament ('Ursakrament'), which is the original 'sign and instrument of the innermost union with God and of the unity of the whole of mankind'.[18] In this way the Constitution on the Church speaks of the Church, deriving its description from the nature of Christ.

The quotation refers to 'sign and instrument', which can be easily interpreted according to a particular sacramental theology as, 'instrument because sign'. The objection may be raised that a sign, which can only be directed and addressed to men, may possibly be a significant cause of their awareness but cannot be the cause of the reality signified, i.e. the salvation of men. In reply to this it should be pointed out that a notion of 'sign' is here being assumed which is quite inappropriate for a sacramental sign. Certainly this form of explanation does not do full justice to the causality of Jesus and cross where salvation is concerned, or entirely explain the dogma of the redemption through the cross. But in a sacramental sign the saving will of God and grace find historical expression. Sign and signified are essentially one, in contrast to the above assumption, so that the reality signified comes to be in and through the sign, and the sign therefore, in this specific and limited sense, causes the reality signified.

This applies in a fundamental way to the relationship between the saving will of God and grace which is the innermost purpose of the whole history of the world, on the one hand, and the cross of Jesus on the other. In consequence the cross can and should be understood in this sense as the cause of the salvation signified and not merely regarded as the cause of our awareness of salvation in faith. Of course the cross possesses this latter function for us and our faith as well, but the cross of Jesus as the universal primary sacrament of the salvation of the whole world expresses more than this, and indeed says everything, always assuming that 'sacrament' is correctly interpreted and is seen to possess the specific type of causality which is proper to the cross as the instrument of salvation for all men.

The explanation we have offered does not of course exhaust the subject matter. Much has been left without proper proof or development, e.g. the solidarity of all men and the history of individual freedom within the totality of human history, the connection between God's self-communication in grace and the death of Jesus, the theology of death, the unity of the death and resurrection of Jesus, etc. On

[18] LG, no. 1.

many of these topics we have spoken elsewhere; others are deliberately left open here. For the thesis we have proposed is not meant to include at any price under the notion of the primary sacramental causality of signs all that objectively belongs to the salvation brought about by Jesus and the universal significance of his cross and resurrection. Our theory does not in the least exclude other factors which have not been mentioned here and which could not be included under this concept, as long as the thesis is not itself placed in doubt by such alternative possibilities. Our purpose here is to show, by moving from Jesus to humanity as a whole, how a single historical event may be seen to possess universal meaning. This meaning is unique and does not arise simply from the importance which any particular occurrence in history possesses for the totality of human history.

MAN AND THE CROSS OF CHRIST

It was stated at the start of this enquiry that the universal significance of the cross of Jesus for human salvation must be seen from the point of view of the whole of humanity. It is plain that this significance is only present and intelligible if the relationship is *mutual*, if, that is, not only is Jesus related to mankind but also mankind is related to him. In part this is presupposed, in part proposed as a thesis. But this poses new problems which acquire proper focus and depth if we leave on one side those with faith who believe explicitly in Jesus and redemption on the basis of the Christian Gospel and concentrate on those who, for no fault of their own, have never really been touched by the explicit message of Christianity. To this number belong the whole of mankind living before Christ as well as non-Christians since the time of Christ and all those who consciously and explicitly believe that they are required by their conscience to refuse the Gospel of Christ as this is presented to them. In this last case it is not a question of sin offering a threat to salvation. All these groups ultimately belong to a single category, since for a variety of reasons they have not been reached by the Gospel of Jesus and yet their rejection of the Christian message does not mean an existentially serious sin. Seen from this point of view, therefore, such people form a single group as far as our topic is concerned despite all the differences amongst them, for their problem is a common one.

To answer this question two assumptions must be made: first, that all men only achieve salvation through Christ. This is not self-evident and is sometimes not given sufficient consideration in contemporary theory when the question of non-Christian religions and the universality of salvation is being discussed. Further treatment of this point is not needed here, however, since we have already shown how the universality of salvation may be conceived in relationship to Jesus.

The second assumption is still less obvious and both as fact and possibility requires clearer proof. It states that all men who reach salvation must have a relationship to *Jesus Christ* in their saving faith and that the fact that Jesus is the universal cause of salvation implies that all men are related to Jesus by means of the faith that is necessary for salvation.

The fact and possibility of this raise two different questions of which the 'how' question will receive most of our attention. On the fact itself a few prior comments will be made so that its possibility can be intelligibly discussed. As a result of the Second Vatican Council it must be accepted that salvation is open to any adult human being on the basis of a strictly supernatural faith in revelation brought about by grace. This is true of all men, even for 'heathens', and this means that in no case can faith in any way be replaced by anything else, as could be proposed at the beginning of this century by Straub,[19] for example. All such suggestions contradict the teaching of the magisterium. The theological difficulties this raises are made plain by the repeated assertions of the Council that God alone knows how such a faith is in fact possible in certain circumstances and under certain conditions. Specifically this applied to pagans and those living before Christ who were untouched by the Old Testament. But despite this evident embarrassment the Council held fast to the conviction that supernatural faith in revelation in the proper sense of this term was necessary for all men and rejected the view that in place of faith a purely metaphysical knowledge of God, freely accepted, would suffice. A free self-revelation of God is thus demanded, which is to be accepted by man. Without going any further into this problem, the possibility and intelligibility of a supernatural faith in revelation for all men must simply be presupposed. Otherwise we would have to discuss the possibility of salvation and faith for atheists and the question of anonymous theism, as was done at the Council.

Let us suppose, then, that a faith which is directed to the self-revelation of God is possible even when a person has not been in

[19] Cf. A. Straub, *De analysi fidei* (Innsbruck, 1922).

contact with the explicit revelation contained in the Old and New Testaments. We may note in passing that this does not mean accepting the theory of an 'original revelation in the Garden of Eden' in the usual sense, or supposing that this primitive revelation was transmitted through several million years of human history. The only matter to be discussed is whether the faith, whose possibility we are assuming, may conceivably contain, in a manner analogous to the implicit and unthematic presence of God, an implicit but still genuine presence of Jesus Christ, especially in the case of so-called atheists. Only under this condition would such people not only be drawn into the redeeming action of Jesus, but would also possess a relationship to this act of salvation through their faith, thus creating a two way connection.

This brings us to the often discussed question of 'anonymous Christians',[20] a topic which in the space available here can only be briefly touched on. Recently the phrase has occasioned massive objections, which sometimes contain considerable misunderstandings. It is absurd and ridiculous, for instance, to assert that supporters of this notion merely want to use it to console Church members for the diminishing number, both in relative and absolute terms, of those confessing explicit Christian faith. It was never just a matter of a 'tranquilliser' to counter the disappearance of Christian belief. In fact the theory arose from two facts: first, the possibility of supernatural salvation and of a corresponding faith which must be granted to non-Christians, even if they never become Christian; and secondly, that salvation cannot be gained without reference to God and Christ, since it must in its origin, history and fulfilment be a theistic and Christian salvation.

One can only escape this conclusion if one adopts the pessimistic outlook common in the past and disputes the possibility of supernatural salvation for such people, thereby consigning them to hell or limbo, or if one grants salvation merely on the basis of human respectability without reference to God and Christ, or if, finally, one refuses to think about the Christian character of salvation in these cases, thus endangering the universality of Christ's redeeming action, which should on the contrary be firmly maintained.

As we said years ago, it is not a question of the name, 'anonymous Christian' or 'anonymous Christianity'.[21] The issue clearly arises from

[20] Cf. K. Rahner, 'Observations on the Problem of the "Anonymous Christian"', *Theological Investigations* XIV (London, 1976), pp. 280–294. Bibliog. and references given there.

[21] Cf. the introduction to the article referred to in footnote 19, *op. cit.*, pp. 531 sq.

the teaching of the Second Vatican Council. In addition we should have learnt enough from psychology, depth psychology and a genuine metaphysical understanding of human knowledge and freedom to realise that a man does not know and deliberately put into practice only those things which he can state in words as objects of his conscious awareness or can freely affirm. It is obvious that a contradiction can exist between the way a person takes free possession of himself in an unthemetic and unreflective manner and the way he interprets himself as an object in words and concepts, and this contradiction does not have to be noticed by the person concerned, who may indeed expressly deny it. Is it surprising that in certain circumstances the real situation and the basic self-understanding of a person may be grasped more clearly by someone else than by the person himself, who may in fact strongly resist the other's interpretation? This fact must be accepted; it cannot be avoided or explained away, since it frequently happens that one man interprets another differently from the latter's own reading of himself.

I must assert as a Christian and a metaphysician who holds that the spiritual element in man cannot be reduced to matter that even a materialist philosopher does those free, spiritual activities which I objectify in a philosophy of spirit, even if the empiricist affirms that such activities do not in fact exist. A Marxist philosopher of history certainly interprets my role as a priest differently from the way I do. From a formal point of view, then, there is no problem in my treating someone as an anonymous Christian, even if he energetically denies my interpretation and rejects it as false or incoherent; Nishitani the well known Japanese philosopher, the head of the Kyoto school, who is familiar with the notion of the anonymous Christian, once asked me: What would you say to my treating you as an anonymous Zen Buddhist? I replied: certainly you may and should do so from your point of view; I feel myself honoured by such an interpretation, even if I am obliged to regard you as being in error or if I assume that, correctly understood, to be a genuine Zen Buddhist is identical with being a genuine Christian, in the sense directly and properly intended by such statements. Of course in terms of objective social awareness it is indeed clear that the Buddhist is not a Christian and the Christian is not a Buddhist. Nishitani replied: Then on this point we are entirely at one.

Of course an anonymous Christian is different from an explicit Christian. Otherwise he would be an explicit Christian and not an anonymous one. He lacks nearly all or most of those characteristics which on the level of objective understanding and social life go into making a Christian. The idea of the anonymous Christian does not mean that the realities which the anonymous Christian lacks, such as the explicit profession of Christian faith or baptism, are unimportant for salvation and for being a Christian, even if it is not possible here to explain more clearly their significance for salvation.[22] It is more important that the heathen in his polytheism, the atheist in good faith, the theist outside the revelation of the Old and New Testaments, all possess not only a relationship of faith to God's self-revelation, but also a genuine relationship to Jesus Christ and his saving action. It is in fact not easy in the case of the relationship to God to solve the question why such men do not merely have an unthematic, transcendent relationship to the God of philosophers but also possess a relationship to the God who communicates himself to man in grace and bestows a supernatural self-revelation on man.

A CHRISTOLOGY OF QUEST

The actual history of Jesus Christ, the particularity of his cross in space and time, makes the relationship to him difficult, more difficult at any rate than the transcendent relation of man to God. In contrast to the possibilities open to believers, Jesus cannot be meant to be an explicit theme in the cases we are considering, nor be presented as a concrete historical point of reference which would make possible an encounter with his unique spatio-temporal location. Otherwise the reference to Jesus embodied in faith of this type would not differ from that possessed by an explicit Christian. One way out of the cul-de-sac created by the demand for a relationship to Jesus for which a concrete historical possibility cannot seemingly be discovered, may be offered by the suggestion that such a relationship can actually be established by a person's alignment, correct in terms of faith, to realities which are objectively and historically connected to Jesus and his history. This would mean that a man would be related to Jesus without this involving any subjective implications. This notion need not be false, but it leaves the proposed relationship so 'thin' that it does not suffice by itself. For the relationship would have, in part at least, a purely objec-

[22] The importance for salvation of the realities which constitute explicit Christianity may be explained as the response to a command or as a necessary means of salvation or in a variety of other ways.

tive character and would not enter at all into the existential realm of the life of faith, or at least not in an intelligible fashion. The objective part of the relationship remains so general and abstract that it provides less explanation than is here required. Finally the whole theory is based on the single truth that, given the unity of history, each part is connected to the whole.

We can only find a real way out of this difficulty if in such cases we attribute a 'Christology of quest' to all men of good will and regard it as sufficient to answer our question. A person who is searching for something which is specific and yet unknown has a genuine existential connection, as one alert and on the watch, with whatever he is seeking, even if he has not yet found it, and so cannot develop the relation to the object of his quest to its full extent. The reality of the relationship to this object and its inner connection to the goal becomes clear, since the relation to the goal is always characterised by a new and more radical search. If this were not true we could not speak of the growth of faith and the quest of hope in the case of the justified. If searching belongs to the essence of the pilgrim state of having found what is being sought, then the real connection of the search to its object cannot be denied, even if the object of the quest has not yet been found. At this point it will be clear that the search is brought about by grace, which has found its historically tangible expression and its irreversible force in Jesus. This means that if the search is caused by this grace, a person engaged on such a quest is directed in some measure to this goal. We are assuming here that such a Christology of quest involves hope and expectation of an Advent kind and that a person who is caught up in the actual process of history demands some factual guarantee of the successful fulfilment of his eschatological hope. Its realisation means the end of his history, the fulfilment of his own transcendent nature which consists in the reference to God and his own self-realisation in freedom. This realisation, however, does not occur in an isolated transcendence apart from history, but takes place in the specific and common history of all men.

For further clarification of the relationship of eschatological hope to Christ, as it is found in the actual fulfilment of human existence transformed by divine grace, three different claims upon human existence should be distinguished. Human existence is always directed to the freedom of man. In accepting freedom a man gives assent in his quest to the absolute source of salvation which is tangible in history, although these three claims do not in themselves exhaust the basic structure of human existence.[23] They are united by the fact that a man who approaches them without reserve is always engaged upon a 'Christology of quest' in his human existence. The difference between such a person and an explicit Christian is that in the Christology of quest a man does not know that it is in Jesus of Nazareth that what he is seeking is to be found. Because a man engaged upon the Christological quest is prepared without conditions or qualifications to accept the goal wherever and however it can be found, this Christological search is in fact directed to Jesus, for it is Jesus who in reality is its proper goal. This means that the Christological quest possesses a relationship to Jesus, even if a man does not know how to call him by his proper name. This relationship plainly differs from that of a professing Christian to his Lord.

THE CLAIMS UPON HUMAN EXISTENCE

First of all there is the demand for an absolute love of neighbour, in the form presented in Mt 25. This must be taken with radical seriousness and approached, as it were, from 'below', from the love of the particular neighbour. If one adds an 'as if' to the statement of Christ that *he* himself is genuinely loved in a neighbour, or if one adopts a theology of purely legal attribution, then one distorts the sense of Jesus' words which is taken from the real experience of love. The true meaning is that through radical and unconditional love of another, a man makes an implicit act of faith and love in Christ. This is indeed true, for any man, being both finite and unreliable, cannot rationally justify from his own resources the offer of absolute love in which a person dares to commit himself without reserve or qualification to another. In himself he could only be the object of a limited love, a love in which the lover either holds himself back or ventures into a realm which may be without meaning. If this dilemma could be overcome *purely* by an appeal to God as the guarantee and limit of the absolute character of love, then this might be feasible in an abstract and speculative sense with reference to the general concept of absolute love. But if a man experiences the absolute quality of love, it is plain that love demands

[23] Similar ideas, though from another point of view, form the basis of the author's study, 'Das konkrete Verhältnis zu Jesus', *Ich glaube an Jesus Christus* (Zurich, 1968), pp. 49–65. They have also been used for various proposals for a short formulation of faith; cf. R. Bleistein, *Kurzformel des Glaubens* II (Wurzburg, 1971), pp. 86–94.

more than the permanent and transcendent guarantee of God. Love does not find its full realisation out of its own resources but from the radical unity it has with the love of God in Jesus Christ. It implies a unity of the love of God and the love of neighbour, in which the love of neighbour is the love of God and so has an absolute quality, even if this lacks thematic expression. Love searches for the God-man, i.e. for the one who can and may be loved as man with absolute commitment proper to the love of God, not as an idea but as a concrete reality. Ideas cannot be loved: it is the reality which is desired, whether this be already present or lies in the future. This notion depends of course upon the assumption that men form a single totality and that genuine love is not an isolated, individualistic affair. It always tends rather to embrace all men with all the practical implications demanded by love, and conversely it must find concrete expression in the love of the particular individual. Furthermore we are saying that the existence of the God-man within the single totality of mankind makes possible absolute love of another person.

Secondly there is the demand to be prepared for death. Normal preaching tends to concentrate in the case of the death of Jesus, despite its crucial significance for salvation, too much upon the particular, categorial event which takes place alongside many others on the world stage and has its own specific character. But the particular character of this death does not make plain much of the innermost being of the world and of human existence, or bring it to fulfilment. One moves too quickly to a consideration of the external causes and the violent nature of this death and treats it in the context of a theory of satisfaction as the purely external and meritorious cause of the redemption. But in a theology of death the event of Jesus's death can be more closely related to the basic structure of human existence. Death is the one act governing the whole of life in which a man as a free being has total self-determination. This means, or should mean, the acceptance of absolute control in the radical powerlessness which is acutely experienced in death. If a man, whose freedom signifies being responsible for his own destiny and the desire to control it, freely and willingly accepts this radical powerlessness, and if this is not an acceptance of the absurd which could be rejected with justifiable protest, then in this acceptance a man is looking forward to death as reconciliation with expectant hope, or giving assent to it in these terms. For a man does not give assent in the ultimate analysis to abstract norms and concepts but rather to that present or future reality found in his own history as the basis of his existence, in which the enduring dialectic between action and powerless suffering is finally reconciled in death. But this is only possible if the dialectic at the root of human existence is resolved through being attributed to the one who is himself the ultimate ground of this duality.

Finally we should mention the demand for hope in the future. A man has hopes and plans and at the same time projects himself into the unforeseeable which lies ahead. In so doing he moves towards his own future. In this process he is continually striving to overcome the inner and outer self-alienation and to lessen the gap between what he is and what he wishes and ought to become. Does this absolute reconciliation, both individual and collective, remain a distant goal, ever approached but never reached, or can it be achieved as the absolute future, without its achievement destroying the finite and being swallowed up in the absolute being of God? If the absolute future of God is really our own future, does the reconciliation still lie ahead of us as a final goal, or does it already belong to history, so that history even now embodies the definitive pledge of the goal and, though still incomplete, is moving *within* its final purpose? The man with authentic hope must hope that the reality of history gives an affirmative answer to the second alternative in each question. This hope offers a Christian an insight into that which faith in the incarnation and resurrection of Jesus, understood as the definitive beginning of the coming of God, professes to be the absolute future of the world and of history.

PART FOUR

Questions About God

14

THE HIDDENNESS OF GOD

'GOD is dead' is a modern slogan which is now beginning to ebb and fade away. 'How should we speak about God?' is a question raised by not a few theologians in the attempt to come to grips with the actual realities of understanding, thought and intelligible language on this subject. 'God is hidden', 'He is a mystery, indeed he is the absolute mystery'. So speaks a long theological tradition, and it is on this tradition that a dogmatic theologian would like to offer a few reflections here.[1] The paucity of the data, familiar to every school of theology,[2] allows no more than an abstract treatment

---

[1] For the relevant statements of the Church's magisterium, cf. *Denz.* 294, 501, 525, *800*, 804, 3001.

[2] See the remarks which are usually made in the chapter on the possibility of knowledge of God. These ideas are normally proposed for the knowledge of God after death only as an appendix. M. Premm, *Katholische Glaubenskunde* I (Vienna, 1951), pp. 86–88; J. Pohle and J. Gummersbach, *Lehrbuch der Dogmatik* I (Paderborn, 1952), pp. 151–155; 174–176; Joh. Brinktrine, *Die Lehre von Gott*, I (Paderborn, 1953), pp. 39–42; Fr. Diekamp and Kl. Jüssen, *Katholische Dogmatik* I (Munster, 1958), pp. 129–131; *Die Katholische Glaubenswelt* I (Freiburg i. Br., 1959), pp. 396 sq.; H. Lais, *Dogmatik* I (Kevelaer, 1965), pp. 43–45. The topic is easier to grasp and is approached by different authors in *Mysterium Salutis* II 'Die Heilsgeschichte vor Christus,' (Zurich, 1967), pp. 35, note 7; 289 sq., 300, 345, 349.

Our reservations in embarking upon the Protestant treatment of the question are based on the great diversity among different writers which seems to have existed in discussions of the 'hiddenness of God'. Even a cursory glance at the following accounts by dogmatic theologians gives evidence of this: W. Elert, *Der christliche Glaube* (Berlin, 1940), pp. 176–184 (Gotteserkenntnis); P. Althaus, *Grundriss der Dogmatik* (Gütersloh, 1959), pp. 31–33 (Der verborgene Gott); W. Trillhaas, *Dogmatik* (Berlin, 1962), pp. 97–119 (Gottes Verborgenheit und Gottes Erkenntnis); above all, the extensive treatment by Karl Barth is to be noted: *Church Dogmatics* II pt. 1 (Edinburgh, 1957), pp. 179–204 (The Hiddenness of God).

of the subject. All the striking and concrete information drawn from biblical and historical theology must here be omitted. Still this investigation will be undertaken in the hope of presenting a somewhat more radical analysis of the problem which lies behind the phrase, 'the hiddenness of God'.

First of all we should review the traditional data found in manuals of theology on the topic. By the theology of the manuals is meant Catholic theological endeavour in so far as this has influenced contemporary textbooks without achieving any very penetrating investigation into the richer and more colourful history of this theological proposition about God.[3] If such a phenomenon should also be found in the realm of Protestant theology, then this must be left aside since the author is not competent to deal with it.

The second stage will be to consider the problematic, raised by the propositions found in this theological school, which has not itself received sufficient attention within the school. Finally some attempt will be made to bring together the contributions of a systematic theologian into a positive synthesis.

'THE HIDDENNESS OF GOD' ACCORDING TO CLASSICAL THEOLOGY

If I am not mistaken, the concept 'hiddenness' is less frequently used in Catholic theology than that of 'incomprehensibility'. This fact is of some significance. Does it mean that a metaphysical treatment of the question is preferred to an investigation from the perspective of the history of salvation and revelation? Of course the theologian knows from revelation that vital knowledge of God is given to man through the revealed word, knowledge of which he would otherwise be quite ignorant despite its crucial importance for salvation. God emerges, as it were, from his hiddenness in revelation and makes himself known to man as the author of salvation.[4] And yet the revealed word of God

---

[3] Cf. the references given in footnote 2. In general one may say that on the Catholic side there is a tendency to treat the question in a narrow and restricted way. At any rate there is little attempt to go beyond the statements of the magisterium. On the Protestant side, however, a whole range of topics are touched on under this heading, so that the meaning is hard to grasp clearly. The treatment is normally extensive and almost indeterminable. Here only the textbooks in German are considered, but they scarcely differ from works in other languages, at least on the Catholic side. *Mysterium Salutis* is also available in other languages.

[4] Cf. Vatican II, *Dei Verbum* nos. 2 and 3, where however our question is

is seen from the point of view of the 'incomprehensibility of God' as something which is hidden and can only be illuminated through the word of revelation, in so far as this is intrinsically possible. Here the metaphysical or essential aspect is dominant. The basic assertion of classical theology refers to the incomprehensibility, the 'incomprehensibilitas' of God. This incomprehensibility follows from the essential infinity of God which makes it impossible for a finite created intellect to exhaust the possibilities of knowledge and truth contained in this absolute fullness of being.

This does not mean, however, that in God some things are known (at least in the final vision of heaven), while others simply remain unknown. Rather one and the same God is known and is at the same time fundamentally incomprehensible, even if the investigation of the question is not normally taken any further, i.e. how one can speak in the same breath of the 'knowability' and the 'unknowability' of one and the same 'object'.

The incomprehensibility of God is then defined more precisely by the observation that the being of God and the mystery of the Trinity are not 'transparent' to man. This applies at least in the case of the possibilities of knowledge open to man during his life of pilgrimage when his natural intellectual capacities do not permit him to obtain a speculative and philosophical grasp of the Trinity. He can only know of the Trinity through the word of revelation which man does not naturally merit and which in this sense is supernatural. Even then, after revelation, the Trinity escapes conceptual mastery and remains a mystery.[5]

In addition the attempt is made to ground the necessity of revelation in the fact that God is free with regard to the world, and that even through the act of creation God has not experienced any restriction of his freedom. Thus the possible realm of free divine decisions is not completely exhausted by creation and its structures. God can behave as a free agent towards the world once it is a given reality. Such free decisions could on this account only be known by man through revelation. In so far as a sort of hiddenness is attached to these free 'decrees' precisely because of their origin in freedom and as long as they are not

---

not explicitly mentioned.

[5] Cf. K. Rahner, 'The concept of Mystery in Catholic Theology', *Theological Investigations* IV (London and Baltimore, 1966), pp. 36–73; *The Trinity* (London, 1970).

objectified, God remains in this free relationship to the world the one who is hidden. Why and how far the free decisions of God retain their hidden and incomprehensible character after revelation are questions which scarcely receive any detailed analysis. Wherever such a free self-disclosure of God reveals something which is and remains a mystery in virtue of God's own inner nature, a quality of mystery is evidently attached to these decisions because of their content. Essential incomprehensibility and the necessity of historical revelation are closely connected in such a viewpoint.

The reference to the free decrees of God in relation to a world which is already created make it possible to pursue the theme of salvation history in the question of the hiddenness of God, for God freely emerges from his hiddenness into history. But the doctrine of God's free decisions with respect to the world is not very clearly related to the fact of God's ontological incomprehensibility. In consequence the theme of God's hiddenness in relation to salvation history, though briefly touched on, remains secondary to the main idea of his essential incomprehensibility.

Classical theology adds a second crucial assertion: God remains incomprehensible even in the beatific vision. One might remark that this notion is already covered by the way in which God's incomprehensibility is grounded in relation to the human mind. For this line of reasoning rests less upon the special features of human existence in its earthly form than upon the incommensurability of the finite capacity of knowledge proper to man with the infinite nature of God. In other words the argument is conceived in terms of metaphysics and not of salvation history. But the fact that classical theology holds firm to God's incomprehensibility even in the beatific vision must nevertheless be underlined. For scholastic teaching differs from Scripture in that the state of human salvation, of ultimate blessedness, is more radically centred upon the beatific vision. This is conceived as the fulfilment of man's theoretical intellect. In this perspective the absolute and direct contact between the human intellect and the being of God is stressed and this contact is no longer mediated by any finite reality. This the difference must be brought out and emphasised between the pilgrim state on the one hand, in which knowledge of God remains obscure and is mediated through the created world and finite language in riddles and images, and the radical and direct self-disclosure by God in the beatific vision on the other hand. If the incomprehensibility of God is still affirmed despite the emphasis laid upon his self-revelation in the beatific vision, then this is a striking assertion of God's mystery which is far from self-evident. Of course it poses the question how God can still be incomprehensible if he is directly perceived and if, at least in this state, man is said to be 'capax infiniti'. The problem, then, is how such a vision can exist and what it is supposed to entail, if God still remains incomprehensible.

THE PROBLEM OF GOD'S INCOMPREHENSIBILITY

These propositions of classical theology are not free of problems. In this theological endeavour one is struck by the predominant desire for theoretical understanding. From the start the incomprehensibility of God is so firmly based upon a certain conception of knowledge and of truth obtained by such knowledge that God's incomprehensibility merely forms the presupposition for a negative assertion of the finite nature of man. Man can never entirely or exhaustively grasp God. One might almost add, unfortunately! The horizon of understanding which is assumed here, the criterion by which human knowledge is measured so that God remains incomprehensible, represents a conception based on a model of knowledge in which an object is penetrated and mastered. In comparison with this paradigm of knowledge, human perception of God on earth and even in the state of final fulfilment remains deficient. God is, unfortunately, always incomprehensible, however much a man may know of him and however directly he may perceive him in heavenly beatitude.

In such an ideal of knowledge the Greek desire of absolute gnosis and the modern understanding of knowledge as a process which leads to the mastery of an object come together, whether the mastery in question is conceived in terms of German idealism or of the natural sciences. In this context the incomprehensibility of God is the ground for the permanent finitude of the creature negatively conceived, even though it must be granted that the assertion of such finitude gives God the glory which, in an absolute sense, is proper to him alone. This must be stated in the face of any temptation to make human subjectivity the event of absolute consciousness or to suppress the pain of being finite in any other way. It only remains to ask whether with the predominance of the desire for theoretical understanding the radical recognition of God's utter incomprehensibility does not naturally lead to an indifference on man's part towards something which he cannot understand, that is, to a kind of practical atheism. And how can the state of human beatitude be conceived if man is thrown headlong into direct contact with God's incomprehensibility which is utterly beyond his powers, and if his capacity for knowledge is not meant to be directed to the experience of incomprehensibility[6] but rather to comprehensive mastery? This means that he must be resigned to being trapped within his finite capacity of knowledge in the face of the incomprehensible God.

This theology raises a second problem about God's incomprehensibility. It is quite understandable that the free decisions of God with regard to the world must remain hidden as long as they are not communicated through specific verbal revelation. But it seems that the hidden character of God's personal freedom in relation to the world is not so easily intelligible as classical theology apparently imagines. One need only recollect that the free decisions of God towards his world must, it seems, be given objective expression in terms of worldly realities in a manner similar to the divine purpose in the creation of the world. But then the free decisions of God seem to possess no special hidden quality beyond that belonging to any free personal decision before it is made known through a freely created objective form. As long as the free decrees of God are not related to his intrinsic reality of incomprehensible glory, then they are necessarily linked to those realities which he freely creates (e.g. the salvation of men). Such realities belong to the finite realm and cannot be more incomprehensible to a man with a finite capacity for knowledge than other realities in the world. Being finite they are intrinsically commensurable to a finite intellect of a fundamentally unlimited, transcendent kind. If one wanted to understand the incomprehensibility of God from the point of view of the freedom of his decisions and the necessity of revelation it implies, then the 'deus absconditus' must come out of his hiddenness in order to become 'deus revelatus' in such a way that his whole revelation would be comprehensible. It would then be a matter of indifference to us what he might perhaps keep hidden, for the 'incomprehensible' element of the 'deus revelatus' would merely consist in the human fear that God could behave towards men differently from the way in which he in fact does behave. The God who treats sinners with mercy and grace could also be a God of pure anger and judgement, or, to put the matter in Catholic and scholastic terms, he could be a God who denies the chance of supernatural destiny. But this fear

[6] In this experience the issue is the incomprehensibility itself and not what is grasped and known.

must be removed by the experience that in reality God *has* freely acted as the God of forgiveness and absolute nearness. But this would be intelligible as a statement about us, even if it rests upon the freedom of God, and so cannot be any more incomprehensible than we are ourselves. At any rate this is how it seems until it becomes clear that the actual content of God's free decisions in relation to us consists precisely in the presence of his incomprehensibility. Only in this way can the doctrine of essential incomprehensibility and the idea of the divine hiddenness of salvation history be mutually related.[7] For this to occur it is not enough to say that through revelation God has freely determined to manifest those mysteries which lie hidden in him and which retain their mysterious quality. For the question still remains open, what is the exact relationship between the process of revelation and the content of revelation, between 'revelatio qua' and 'revelatio quae'.

In general it is not clear in classical theology that the problem arising from the direct vision of an incomprehensible God can only be solved in the context of love. It is not a matter here of the scholastic dispute, whether the essence of beatitude consists in the intellectual fulfilment as such, i.e. in the 'visio', or in the fulfilment of the will in love for which direct vision merely provides the precondition in the form of knowledge, or in both. The traditional diversity of opinion and the various scholastic theories are of no interest as long as one does not realise that knowledge of the incomprehensible God himself in direct vision can only cease to be the opposite of fulfilment, if knowledge itself achieves perfection by being 'raised up' into love. Otherwise knowledge, taken in the sense usual in western tradition, would itself founder on the alien and inhospitable rock of God's incomprehensibility. If the fundamental character of knowledge is understood, not in the sense of 'seeing through' an object, but rather as a possible openness to the mystery itself, then the question becomes at once more straightforward. Knowledge in the traditional sense would then be regarded as a derivation of the basic meaning of knowledge. The mutual perichoresis of knowledge and freedom occurs naturally and settles the question of the primacy of knowledge or love by focusing upon a more fundamental and essential spiritual unity which finds expression in the duality of knowledge and love. In the traditional conception of the direct vision of God[8] no answer is usually given to

[7] This is not only possible, or merely provisional and only factually overcome.

[8] Here one must overlook Bonaventure and a few other theologians who

the question of why knowledge does not come to grief when faced with the vision of God's incomprehensibility, or of why it does not despair and give up when confronted with his enduring hiddenness. If it is assumed that knowledge means comprehensive mastery, then the object grasped in such knowledge, even when it reaches fulfilment, must be qualified with the negative predicate of incomprehensible. Vision in this account can only be a radical version of the insight that we never reach God.

Finally we should notice a further problem inherent in the classical doctrine of God's incomprehensibility. Whenever the necessity of a supernatural verbal revelation is grounded in the fact that God is hidden in himself from the human spirit, distinctions are made between various grades of 'mysteries'. We do not want to pursue this point further here, but it is clear that it is simply assumed even in the case of the highest level of the mysteries of faith and revelation that there are a specific *number* of such mysteries. It is asserted of 'mysteria stricte dicta' that they could only be made known through the revelation of God and even after this revelation they remain impenetrable to man. There is scarcely any attempt made to answer the question whether this impenetrability is maintained for *each* of the 'mysteria stricte dicta' in the direct vision of God. It is supposed rather that the number and type of mysteries communicated through divine revelation depends simply upon the free decision of God.

The concept of divine incomprehensibility, as this is grasped by the human mind, naturally implies that it can be spelt out in an indefinite number of mysteries, always assuming of course that such a 'multiplication' does not contradict the basic notion of incomprehensibility. This assumption, however, hardly receives any explicit consideration. Scholastic teaching takes it as a matter of course that 'mysteria stricte dicta' in the sense outlined above can refer not merely to the explicitation of the incomprehensibility of God, as for example, the mystery of the Trinity. They can also be present in realities which embody God's actions 'ad extra' such as transubstantiation. We have already said that such an assumption is far from obvious or illuminating. In any event it is evident that the doctrine of the *multiplicity* of 'mysteria stricte dicta' is not related in this account to the primary mystery of divine incomprehensibility. No answer is given to the question, and perhaps it is not even seen as a question, of how any finite reality, created by God

---

were aware of the value of the 'ecstatic' in the being of man.

and distinct from him, can be a 'mysterium stricte dictum' for an intellect possessing unlimited transcendence. If the axiom is valid that being, intelligibility and knowledge increase and diminish in the same measure and are ultimately identical, as St Thomas took for granted and regarded as self-evident,[9] then a finite reality of this type cannot be fundamentally impenetrable. If one starts from the position that the quality of mystery in the sense of a 'mysterium stricte dictum' can only be predicated of God alone and of no other reality, then the question of the 'number of mysteries' is seen in a new light. If such a number exists, then it must in any case be related to the incomprehensibility of God himself.

OUTLINE OF A SYNTHESIS

We should now address ourselves to trying to give a positive answer to the problems we have found in classical Catholic theology with regard to the incomprehensibility, hiddenness and mystery of God.

In such an attempt to discover a positive synthesis we should not be worried about whether we are concerned with philosophy or theology. The following reflections may seem philosophical and speculative but in fact they proceed from a conviction of faith, that is, from a strictly theological proposition. This states that perfect beatitude granted to man by God consists in immediate access to God, i.e. God is himself the fulfilment of man. All communication in the created order, in so far as this can be conceived or is to be found in traditional theology (lumen gloriae), must be understood in relation to the direct access to God as communication with his immediate presence. It cannot be a question here in any sense of a created reality originating in God which merely represents God and only makes him indirectly present to man as the cause of the fulfilment which is properly ours. Of course this theological assertion can be taken as an interpretation of the experience of faith which can be directly grasped in Scripture. The proposition as defined by Benedict XII,[10] which counts as dogma for Catholic theology, cannot be anything else than the expression of a *radical* human hope in the Spirit of God, despite all the other possible formulations of this proposition. God himself in his own very being wills to be the beatitude of man. This fulfilment of the 'capax infiniti'

[9] Cf. K. Rahner, 'Thomas Aquinas on Truth', *Theological Investigations* XIII (London, 1975), pp. 13–31.
[10] Cf. *Denz*. 1000–1001.

through the 'infinitum' may not be weakened by an appeal to other modes of communication which are of a more finite and intelligible nature. This 'metaphysic' need involve no more than the assertion that God himself and nothing else is our eternal life, however he may be understood by us here and now. This theological proposition forms the basis of all the reflections which are contained in this essay. However philosophical and speculative the line of thinking may appear, its only purpose is to make the primary theological statement intelligible and to prevent it being weakened or undervalued.

'*The* Truth' occurs in the basic experience of the mystery itself. Such knowledge is not in origin a defective mode of real knowledge, in the usual sense of the term. For such knowledge is directed to what can be comprehended and penetrated and only fails in this endeavour in a particular instance, without the object which is partially perceived becoming something totally unknown. What is called knowledge according to the common usage originating in the western tradition of philosophy, i.e. comprehension and mastery, consists in the ordering of data in a horizon of understanding and system of coordinates which is evident to us as the object which we possess identically with ourselves. But it is this which is a defective form of the true knowledge in which the mystery itself unfolds. If knowledge in the ordinary sense is regarded as a secondary and defective form of the real nature of knowledge, then it is of no importance whether ordinary knowledge is understood in the sense of the creation of functional connections between the primary data of an original experience, or treated as the vision in which what is seen is comprehended. For the essence of knowledge lies in the mystery which is the object of primary experience and is alone self-evident. The unlimited and transcendent nature of man, the openness to the mystery itself which is given radical depth by grace, does not turn man into the event of the absolute spirit in the way envisaged by German idealism or similar philosophies; it directs him rather to the incomprehensible mystery, in relation to which the openness of transcendence is experienced. Man as transcendent subject is not the shepherd of being but the one protected by the mystery. In the primary realisation of his being (dasein) and in the philosophical reflection derived from it, man comes to be himself and here he does not experience himself as the dominant, absolute subject, but as the one whose being is bestowed upon him by the mystery. *This* is the reason why, in forming any concept, he understands himself as the one who reaches out beyond the conceptual into the nameless and the incomprehensible. Transcendence grasped in its unlimited breadth is the a priori condition of objective and reflective knowledge and evaluation. It is the very condition of its possibility, even though it is ordered to the inexpressible. It is also the precondition for the freedom which is historically expressed and objectified. Thus the experience of the nameless mystery as both origin and goal is the a priori condition of all categorial knowledge and of all historical activity; it is not merely a marginal phenomenon at the end of the road. Otherwise it would merely be a matter of a journey into the bright light of categorial and ultimately scientific understanding, a journey on which a man grows weary in the pursuit of knowledge, leaves what is still unknown to itself and gives the name of mystery to this unmastered realm of the intelligible. In contrast knowledge in the primary sense is the presence of the mystery itself. It is being addressed by what no longer has a name, and it is relying on a reality which is not mastered but is itself the master. It is the speech of the being without a name, about which clear statements are impossible; it is the last moment before the dumbness which is needed if the silence is to be heard, and God is to be worshipped in love. If one insists that knowing in the basic sense consists in a piece of clear and ordinary understanding and in the science based upon it, then what we have said would have to be formulated in a different way. The manner of formulation is ultimately of no special consequence. The origin and goal of knowledge in the mystery is one of its constituent elements. In an unthematic way this is experienced in day-to-day knowledge and may be called 'primary' in the sense of the a priori condition of possibility of all knowing, even though it only becomes thematic in a secondary sense through subsequent reflection upon its own a priori presuppositions. There may be many truths. They can be clear and can guarantee control over reality. But they all stem from the unfolding of the mystery itself, from the *one* truth. This is not merely a later collection of truths but precedes them as the condition of their possibility. The presence of the one truth is of course unthematic, since it exists in the first instance as the condition of possibility of spatio-temporal and categorial-historical experience. It can therefore be overlooked and suppressed; its silent presence can be ignored in the face of immediate phenomena which in their variety and particularity can fill the space of life and consciousness. Where, too, this one truth is expressed in word in the ultimate courage of existence and, almost against its own nature, finds objective form, it can be confused with other objective expressions and so lack truth and credibility. But this does not alter the fact that the one truth is the primary event of the spirit; it is the mystery which endures and unfolds and establishes the essential human capacity for truth.[11] In other words the 'deus absconditus' is the source of truth for man, which is freely bestowed upon him and determines his identity. Man always stands before the 'deus absconditus', even when he tries to look away and refuses to accept the truth that clear knowledge of the reality of the world, which gives him mastery over the world, comes from this 'deus absconditus'. Knowledge is primarily the experience of the overwhelming mystery of this 'deus absconditus'.

Divine revelation is not the unveiling of something previously hidden, which through this illumination leads to an awareness similar to that found in ordinary knowledge of the world. Rather it means that the 'deus absconditus' becomes radically present as the abiding mystery. This mystery presents itself through revelation as the source of forgiveness, salvation and an eternal home. Revelation does not mean that the mystery is overcome by gnosis bestowed by God, even in the direct vision of God; on the contrary, it is the history of the deepening perception of God *as* the mystery. This continues in the direct presence of God afforded by what we call the beatific vision and can only be sustained in the loving surrender to the enduring mystery. It is the lost and not the blessed soul who perceives everything as infinite variety and so perceives nothing at all. The blessed abandons himself unconditionally to the direct self-communication of the mystery of the 'deus absconditus' from which come love and salvation. If the theoretical intellect is understood as the capacity for conceptual mastery and comprehension, then beatitude means that the theoretical intellect is set free to love the mystery, which lays total hold of us by its direct presence. The history of revelation, then, consists in the growing awareness that we are involved with the permanent mystery and that our involvement becomes ever more intense and exclusive. If revelation is seen in this perspective, there is certainly a great deal more to say about it than we usually find in discussions of revelation. But if the climax of revelation, the communication of the Spirit of God himself, takes place when a man loses everything in death except God, and *in*

---

[11] Cf. The author's studies in the metaphysics of knowledge: *Spirit in the World* (London and Sydney, 1968); *Hearers of the Word* (London and Sydney, 1969); 'Thomas Aquinas on Truth', *Theological Investigations* XII (London, 1975), pp. 13–31. All these studies were written in the same period.

this way achieves blessedness,[12] then the history of revelation can well be written in the manner proposed here. In any history nothing can ultimately be explained without reference to the ending. In our case the ending is the advent of God who is the enduring mystery and is accepted in love. In that history, therefore, the mystery is not removed by a slow process of attrition; rather all the provisional realities are dismantled which can lead to the belief that we can only achieve a relationship to God through what we believe we know about him. But such knowledge only offers figures and images, either good or bad, which represent and shape him to our needs. This process only lasts until we finally let go of everything in the assurance that God, the one who fundamentally cannot be shaped to our needs, becomes through his self-gift the being who alone is fitted to us. For through his own very being God has granted to us that the measure of our knowledge, desire and activity need not be ourselves but is the immeasurability of God himself. The fulfilment of the created order consists in the fact that God, who is our absolute future, is the incomprehensible mystery. This incomprehensibility is not to be taken as the limit of fulfilment but rather signifies its limitlessness which is loved and experienced as such. Of course this doctrine represents a danger for man. If he derives enjoyment from its theoretical and objective expression and turns it into a secret idol, then the highest fulfilment is distorted into a terrifying disorder. Only if the incomprehensible mystery is itself the object of love, if knowledge goes beyond the self and knowledge and love penetrate the mystery through such ecstasy, no longer returning to the self, only then is the final and greatest danger removed, the danger, that is, of turning the doctrine into a sublime gnosis in which once again a man replaces God with self. One cannot escape this danger by refusing really to accept that it is the will of God to be *himself* the absolute future of man and to be his proper fulfilment. He desires to be the beatitude of man in his incomprehensibility and not despite it, and this is the key to man's own self-understanding. The incomprehensibility of God as the blessed fulfilment of man, if one wished to develop the metaphysical line of thought any further, is the same reality as the incomprehensibility of God in his own being and in the free gift of the mystery to man in his individual concrete history. This is realised in the single 'free decree' of God, which is at root beyond understanding since once again it is identical with God

[12] Cf. K. Rahner, 'Ideas for a Theology of Death', *Theological Investigations* XIII (London, 1975) pp. 169–186.

himself, who is the fulfilment of man and his reconciliation and for-giveness. This applies to the sinner as well as the justified, for the sinner is resolved in himself to reject God, because he wishes to escape from the incomprehensibility of God and seek refuge in the intelligibil-ity of his own knowledge and action.

One further consideration must here be added, if we are to give a positive and systematic answer to the problems arising from the classi-cal treatment of the hiddenness of God, and this concerns the manner in which an appreciation of God as the mystery which always lies beyond knowledge can be related to the understanding of other theological statements within a Christian dogmatic system, in order to give them new depth. Thus, for example, we must confront the doc-trine of the Trinity with the notion of the hiddenness of God. It would then have to be shown that the 'Father' as the original source of both the processes within the godhead and of the creation of the world, means the being who transcends conceptual mastery and cannot be subordinated to any overarching system. He persists in this mode of being when he unfolds his identity through grace and vision in becom-ing totally present to man. 'Pater immensae majestatis'. The 'Spirit' would then signify the divine possibility of direct self-communication to man as mystery. The 'Son' means that God can give historical shape to this ultimate truth, which is himself, and bestow it upon humanity in a man who freely accepts his salvation in death and thus makes the divine self-gift of the mystery a definitive and credible reality. Because God himself and not some created representation of God is involved in the free self-gift of God as mystery, the three-fold form belongs directly to God in his relationship to man. Thus the economic Trinity of salvation is ipso facto the immanent Trinity.[13] What knowledge we possess from the history of revelation and faith about the threefold relationship of the single divine self-communication, which confronts us directly with the mystery itself, also applies to the immanent divine Trinity, whose 'mystery' is none other than the 'mysterium' which communicates itself to man and endures for eternity.

For a systematic Christology we should also reflect that Jesus stands as a human being in faith before the inexorable mystery which is an object of love precisely in its incomprehensibility. This makes it intel-ligible that his death is not just one of a series of events in his human

---

[13] Cf. K. Rahner, *The Trinity* (London, 1970); 'Remarks on the Dogmatic Treatise "De Trinitate" ', *Theological Investigations* IV (London and Baltimore, 1966), pp. 77–102.

life but is the climax of his existence. For as long as a man accepts death unconditionally with faith and hope, he comes naked before the incomprehensibility of God, since all else has been destroyed. Classical Catholic theology, in dealing with the question of the knowledge and self-consciousness of Jesus as man, has a strange, if touching, tendency to ascribe as much positive and specific knowledge to the mind of Jesus as possible, while refusing to predicate divine omniscience of Jesus' human consciousness. In this theological account it would in fact be more important to stress the humanity of Jesus and emphasise that he surrendered himself unconditionally in his mind to the incomprehensibility of God and accepted with love, and without any attempt at repression, the ultimate 'beata ignorantia'.[14] Seen in this light the ignorance of Jesus, for which there is ample evidence in Scripture, does not point to a deficiency, but rather to a positive merit in his acceptance of this ignorance.

We have already alluded to the significance of the doctrine of God's incomprehensibility for an investigation of revelation and its history in theology. In the teaching on grace and justification, the fact and reason for God being in himself the justifying grace of man would be illuminated by treating the incomprehensibility of God as the positive goal and definitive fulfilment of man. It could then be shown that the doctrine of 'gratia increata', which is found in classical Catholic theology, is central to any radical treatment of grace and justification. Unfortunately the doctrine is usually presented as a mere effect of grace understood as a created characteristic of man. The Tridentine teaching of the infused 'habitus' of divine virtues in justification can and should be regarded as expressing the fact that the direct self-communication of God genuinely reaches man, without the 'infusi habitus' being a replacement or substitute for the self-communication of the mystery.[15] This might perhaps lead to a better understanding within classical Catholic theology of the forensic notion of justification found among the Reformers, always assuming that this

[14] Cf. K. Rahner, 'Dogmatic Reflections on the Knowledge and Self-consciousness of Christ', *Theological Investigations* V (London and Baltimore, 1966), pp. 193–215; 'The Two Basic Types of Christology', *Theological Investigations* XIII (London, 1975), pp. 213–223.

[15] Cf. K. Rahner, 'Some Implications of the Scholastic Concept of Uncreated Grace', *Theological Investigations* I (London and Baltimore, 1961), pp. 316–346; 'Gnade', *LThK* IV (Freiburg i. Br., 1960), 991–1000; 'Selbstmitteilung Gottes', *LThK* IX (Freiburg i. Br., 1964), 627.

conception is itself not given a false mythological interpretation, but is taken rather to express the fact that man is justified by God if God *himself* acts directly towards man and makes him just through his own being.

The connection between the enduring incomprehensibility of God as the source of beatitude and eschatology has already been made clear in this essay. Only if eschatology points to God himself as the absolute future of man can it avoid being unmasked as a mythological (and therefore open to demythologisation) presentation of the tasks and goals which man should achieve through his own powers, albeit in an unending evolutionary process. The human future only becomes the true God in himself when man recognises it as always lying beyond his comprehension, or better, places his hope in it. Otherwise the future would merely be the object of human comprehension and control and so be immanent in the world. Alternatively it would be a cipher for the endless human progress into the future which can never be said to have reached its definitive goal.

These reflections should make it clear how vital the doctrine of the abiding incomprehensibility of God is for a theology of history,[16] not only of the individual but of humanity and society as a whole. The critique posed by Christians of the historically given state of any society comes from the power of hope in the absolute future[17] which one cannot dominate or plan. The absolute future is to be trusted and not treated as an enemy which one should reject or escape. Such a critical stance can be radical, patient and courageous; it implies neither a conservative glorification of the present situation, underpinned by ideology, nor a destructive impatience which seeks violent means to force a new world into existence by sacrificing the men of today.[18]

Finally the doctrine of the incomprehensibility of the absolute future of man, which is a promised gift, must be seen in connection with the meaning of the word 'God'. One might, for instance, enquire whether

[16] Cf. A. Darlap, 'Fundamentale Theologie der Heilsgeschichte', *MySal* I (Zurich, 1965), pp. 3–156; 'History and Historicity', *Sacr. Mundi* II (London and New York, 1969), pp. 31–39.

[17] Cf. the author's collected studies, *Zur Theologie der Zukunft* (Munich, 1971).

[18] Cf. K. Rahner, 'The Function of the Church as a Critic of Society', *Theological Investigations* XII (London, 1974), pp. 229–249; 'The Church's Commission to bring Salvation and the Humanisation of the World', *Theological Investigations* XIV (London, 1976), pp. 295–313.

the content of the scholastic idea of the infinite being of God, which could very easily be misunderstood as an inadmissible exaggeration of the experience of the finite, could not better and more clearly be explained with reference to the incomprehensibility of our divinely inspired hope in the absolute future.[19] If the classical Catholic theology of the incomprehensibility of God were seen in this radical perspective, it would also be plain that a genuine 'theologia gloriae', for which Catholicism is often criticised, is still, if rightly interpreted, a theology of 'deus absconditus'. The 'gloria' is nothing other than the loving surrender of man to the incomprehensibility of God which is now a directly present reality. This is not to deny that essential differences exist between the theology of the pilgrim condition and that of fulfilment in glory, and that theologians in this world still need to be warned that they must be conscious in their theology of their condition as pilgrims. But the accusation, usually levelled from both sides, of a presumptuous transgression of boundaries could be considerably blunted, if it was mutually conceded that any 'theologia gloriae' always concerned the glory of the incomprehensible God. In every theology there is always the danger of imagining that the 'lumen gloriae' clarifies everything and even illuminates the mystery of God in such a way that at least in this 'gloria' God becomes transparent to the human mind. Conversely, however, it is not true that the 'deus absconditus' is the sort of God who desires that we should not recognise him at all. He does not share one part of himself with us and conceal the other; rather he bestows his whole being upon us. In communicating himself as 'deus revelatus' he becomes radically open to man *as* the 'deus absconditus'. From this mystery man is no longer able to escape: he accepts God as he is, as the mystery of incomprehensibility who, once recognised, is the very truth of man and, once loved, is his blessed fulfilment.

[19] Cf. K. Rahner, 'Observations on the Doctrine of God in Catholic Dogmatics', *Theological Investigations* IX (London, 1972), pp. 127–144; 'On the Theology of Hope', *Theological Investigations* X (London, 1973), pp. 242–259; 'Immanent and Transcendent Consummation of the World', *ibid.*, pp. 273–289. On the question of God, cf. K. Rahner, *Gotteserfahrung heute* (Munich, 1972), pp. 1–16.

15

AN INVESTIGATION OF THE INCOMPREHENSIBILITY OF GOD IN ST THOMAS AQUINAS

HE purpose of the few brief remarks presented here is to supplement and develop various questions connected with St Thomas Aquinas's[1] doctrine of the incomprehensibility of God. We will, therefore, assume the basic substance of his teaching that God always lies beyond the understanding of any finite created mind, even that of angels and of men in a state of ultimate fulfilment, and of the created soul of the God-man. Thus the fact that the state of blessedness can vary with the individual beholder is made intelligible.[2]

[1] This essay, originally conceived as a lecture, appeared under the title, 'Über die Unbegreiflichkeit Gottes bei Thomas von Aquin', in the collection ed. by L. Oeing-Hanhoff, *Thomas von Aquin 1274–1974* (Munich, 1974), pp. 33–45. It was further revised for publication here. The author owes a debt for the ideas it contains to the as yet unpublished dissertation of his student P. Siller, *Die Incomprehensibilitas Dei bei Thomas von Aquin* (Innsbruck, 1963). This topic has engaged the author's attention a great deal recently, for which further evidence is contained in the essay published in this volume, 'The Hiddenness of God', which tackles the question in a more general context.

[2] Cf. a number of studies on this question: R. Garrigou-Lagrange, *Le sens du Mystère et le clair-obscur intellectuel: nature et surnaturel* (Paris, 1934); A. M. Hoffmann, 'Mysterium bei Thomas', *DTh* 17 (1939), pp. 30–60; G. Marcel, *The Mystery of Being* (London, 1950–1); J. Pieper, *The Silence of St. Thomas* (London, 1957); V. Richter, 'Logik und Geheimnis', *Gott in Welt I* Rahner-Festschrift (Freiburg, 1964), 188–206; E. Schillebeeckx, 'The Non-Conceptual Intellectual Element in the Act of Faith', *The Concept of Truth and Theological Renewal* (London and Sydney, 1968), pp. 30–75. P. Siller, 'Unbegreiflichkeit', *LThK* X (Freiburg, 1965), 470–472 (bibliog.); A. Halder, *Aufklärung und Geheimnis* (Freiburg, 1967); G. Ebeling, 'Profanität und Geheimnis', *2THK* 65 (1968), pp. 70–92; J. Splett, 'Hegel und das Geheimnis', *Phil JB* 76 (1968), pp.

The reason for this incomprehensibility lies, according to Aquinas, in the disproportion, even in the case of the beatific vision, between the self-communication of the infinite God, the source and object of direct vision, on the one hand, and the finite character of the beholder on the other, who remains limited even when raised up by grace and the light of glory and given the capacity to have the beatific vision. It is this question which we would like to consider briefly from a hermeneutical point of view, without setting out the whole theory or assembling the numerous texts of Aquinas[3] on the incomprehensibility of God so as to form a single system. The object of these remarks is to caution against too simple and straightforward an interpretation of Aquinas's teaching on this point, for in fact his theory opens up all the heights and depths of Thomist theology and philosophy. In a sense the theory of the incomprehensibility of God is itself an incomprehensible doctrine; the mystery[4] which the doctrine concerns turns back, as it were, upon itself and transforms it into an inexpressible mystery, which is *the* ultimate mystery of man himself.

THE PROPOSITION OF FAITH

In any attempt to assess Thomist teaching on the incomprehensibility of God, it must be made quite clear from the start that for the master

---

317–331; P. Wess, *Die Incomprehensibilitas Gottes und ihre Konsequenzen bei Thomas von Aquin und Karl Rahner* (unpubl. diss. Innsbruck, 1969); P. Wess, *Wie von Gott sprechen?* Eine Auseinandersetzung mit Karl Rahner. (Graz, 1970), pp. 91–109; K. Rahner, 'Geheimnis', *LThK* IV (Freiburg, 1960), 593–597. K. Rahner, 'The Concept of Mystery in Catholic Theology' *Theological Investigations* IV (London and Baltimore, 1966), pp. 36–73.

[3] This is based on the following passages in Aquinas: *Super ep. ad Eph.* c.3 lect. 5; *ibid.* c. 5 lect. 3; *In Evang. Joan. expos.* c. 1 lect. 11; *Super I ep. ad Tim.* c. 6 lect. 2; *In III sent* dist. 14; *In IV Sent.* dist. 49 q.2; *De Verit.* q.2 a. 2 ad 5; *ibid.* ad 6; q.8 a.1 ad 5; a.2; a.4; q.20 a.4; a.6; *S.c.g.* III 51–56; *S.th* 1 q.12 a.7; a.8; a.9; a.10; q.56 a.1 ad 1; q.57 a.5 ad 2; q.62 a.9; q.107 a.3; I/II q.93 a.2. It is unnecessary here to quote the commentaries, especially those on Pars I of the Summa.

[4] On the concept of 'mystery', cf. the author's works referred to in footnote 2; also more recently, 'Theology as engaged in an Interdisciplinary Dialogue with the Sciences', *Theological Investigations* XIII (London, 1975), pp. 80–93, esp. 87–89; 'On the Relationship between Theology and the Contemporary Sciences', *ibid.* pp. 94–102, esp. 96–100. Also, K. Fischer, *Der Mensch als Geheimnis*. Die Anthropologie Karl Rahners (Freiburg, 1947); the review article by K. H. Neufeld, *Std2* 192 (1974) pp. 429 sq.

of Scholasticism this incomprehensibility is a statement of faith which is to be found in the witness of Scripture[5] and tradition.[6]

For Thomas, therefore, the heart of the matter is not a philosophical doctrine which remains within the self-evident horizon of philosophical understanding, even though confirmed by revelation. For Thomas, and here we encounter at once the difficulty of this doctrine, the incomprehensibility of God must always be considered in relation to the possibility of the direct vision of God, which is only made known to us through revelation. The question of how precisely the nature and process of revelation should be conceived is not relevant here.[7] In this vision there is no longer a 'species' in the intellect of the creature which represents the object of the vision. The reality of God himself fulfils the function of a 'species', even though Thomas is firmly convinced that the self-communication of God which causes this vision can only find a human response if the intellect of man is adapted to it through the light and grace of glory, which raises the natural human capacity to a higher level. This statement of faith which affirms the possibility of a direct vision of God alone gives depth to the doctrine of the incomprehensibility of God, as well as causing problems for this doctrine. The incomprehensibility of God should not then be regarded as a distant reality, for it increases rather than diminishes in the vision of God, in which alone it becomes an inescapable event. It does not describe the remnants of something which, sadly, remains unknown, but rather points to the immediate object of the experience of God in heaven, an object which is present in the mind overflowing with the fullness of God's self-communication. From the hermeneutical point of view we must read and interpret the Thomist doctrine of God's incomprehensibility by confronting it with his teaching on the direct vision of God, if its positive qualities and its limitations are to be correctly evaluated. The theory of the direct vision of God poses an incomprehensible mystery for us and conversely the reality (and thus the possibility) of the mystery of this vision in eternal life is experienced precisely in the direct encounter

[5] Cf. Phil 3:12; 1 Cor 9:24; Jer 32:18 sq.; Rom 11:33; Job 11:7.

[6] According to the commentaries of Aquinas on Eph 3; Jn 1; Rom 9; Eph 5; 1 Tim 6, Thomas finds evidence for this idea in tradition in Ambrose, John Chrysostom, Augustine, Denis the Areopagite and John Damascene.

[7] For the idea of 'revelation' in K. Rahner, cf. numerous studies elsewhere; a preliminary account is to be found in: Sacr. Mun. V (London and New York, 1970), pp. 343–355; also 'Offenbarung', Rahner–Register (Zurich, 1974), pp. 144 sq.

with the *incomprehensibility* of God. But if this is so, then in the ultimate analysis the *mystery* of the direct vision of God does not cease to exist in heaven; rather the incomprehensibility is experienced as the reality which offers itself directly to human vision. For it is God in his simplicity *as a whole* who is perceived. His incomprehensibility cannot be understood as a 'part' of God which remains beyond the visual field. The assertion of the direct vision of God and assertion of his incomprehensibility are related for us here and now in a mysterious and paradoxical dialectic. They seem to destroy each other, for it cannot be the case here that God's incomprehensibility means that a particular part of the 'simple' God is clearly perceived, while another remains beyond sight. In its ultimate and most radical meaning the incomprehensibility of God is itself an internal factor in the awareness, through revelation, of the possibility of the direct vision of God. Only if this point is clearly understood, can one scale the heights which Thomas's doctrine possesses in its totality, even if not in every individual text on the topic.

THE INTERPRETATION OF AQUINAS

In dealing with the question of God's incomprehensibility, Thomas makes repeated use of his 'metaphysic of light'. This has of course a long tradition before his time and has a quality of self-evidence for him which makes it readily available as a conceptual and verbal instrument. In the infinity of his unlimited and pure being, God has an absolute identity transcending the duality of subject and object. He is the being who is absolutely in and by himself; in this unity of reality and knowledge he is the pure light who both makes the object intelligible and luminous when finite knowledge exists, and renders the subject capable of grasping the object in his activity and bringing it to the level of his own activity, so that the subject is illuminated as well. The exact meaning of the metaphysic of light in Thomas, how it differs from the theory of illumination in Augustine, its Aristotelian twist and yet its fidelity to Augustine's basic intention,[8] these are all questions which

---

[8] On the question of the 'metaphysic of light', cf. G. Söhngen, 'Thomas von Aquin über Teilhabe durch Berührung', *Die Einheit in der Theologie* (Munich, 1952), pp. 107–139; J. Ratzinger, 'Licht und Erleuchtung–Erwägungen zur Stellung und Entwicklung des Themas in der abendländischen Geistesgeschichte', *StudGen* 13 (1960), pp. 368–378; L. Oeing-Hanhoff, 'Licht II. Philosophisch', *LThK* VI (Freiburg, 1961), 1023–1025.

need not occupy us here. They can readily be left aside without damaging our understanding today of Thomas's doctrine of God's incomprehensibility, as long as one pays careful attention to its real meaning and the extent to which it can be understood even without reference to the concept of light.

To read Thomas properly, of course, one needs to know what is his central concern. Here however the metaphysics of light can be left to one side, since it is no longer helpful in the context of contemporary metaphysics, which inevitably comes into play in any interpretation of the medieval master. Furthermore the real meaning intended by Thomas can be expressed in terms of Thomist ontology which is immediately intelligible today and can be directly related to the modern question of being. If we exclude the metaphysic of light from our considerations and try to state the content of theory by means of Thomist ontology and ontological theology, then one immediately meets a double problem, at once philosophical and theological. The first concerns the relationship between divine being, in which pure existence forms the 'essence' of God, and finite being in which essence and existence are distinct and the essence forms and determines the manner and degree to which the being shares in the divine existence as a 'similitudo' of God. The second question refers to the relation between the self-communication of God afforded by grace and glory, without which the direct vision of God is impossible according to Thomas's metaphysics of knowledge, and the grace-filled, illuminating and elevating disposition, termed the light of glory, without which a direct perception of God is similarly inconceivable for Thomas. Both questions must be recognised and considered if one wants to understand Thomas's doctrine of the incomprehensibility of God. For the direct vision of God must be conceived in such a way in Thomas that the incomprehensibility of God, far from being removed, is in fact opened out to the one who sees God. Conversely the incomprehensibility of God must be thought of in such a manner that it does not contradict the directness of the vision of God. It is obvious that the problems raised by this question necessarily lead back to the larger issues mentioned above.

It is, then, not surprising that Thomas cannot bring fully into play the whole extent of his philosophical and theological anthropology concerning the basic relationship between God, who is pure existence, and a finite being and his knowledge in the realm of nature and grace, whenever he speaks in particular texts of the incomprehensibility of

God. Thomas, like any other thinker, cannot make the whole range and depth of his thought present in every sentence, although his very *formal* model of speech does allow him to maintain an openness to the totality of his theology and metaphysics in individual statements, despite the limitations of the horizon of understanding present in each case. We cannot and should not go more fully here into these two issues here, although they must always be kept in mind for hermeneutical purposes, if the texts of Thomas dealing with divine incomprehensibility as it is found in the direct vision of God are to be properly evaluated and their depth of expression and their difficulties plainly seen. A few remarks may clarify where a discussion of the problems frequently found in these texts may lead.

With regard to the first question: if the whole of Thomas's thought concerning the relationship between absolute being and finite existence is given due weight, then insights into this relation clearly emerge which are of a more radical and discriminating kind than is often apparent both in the school of Thomism and in many texts of Aquinas himself.[9] The relationship between absolute 'esse' and the 'esse commune' of finite reality can be made intelligible in a somewhat over-simplified philosophy and theology, using the notion of creation which is itself modelled, albeit analogically, on the causality known to us in world. On the basis of the idea of creation an ontology of participation can then be built up. But usually the concept of creation is based in too primitive a fashion upon the idea of causality accessible to us in other ways. If one thinks of the idea of creation as a unique phenomenon, then one must ask what is the source of this idea, for it cannot occur subsequently to a genuine knowledge of God in his own existence. Furthermore the question arises about the relationship which must obtain between an agent and an effect when the separation between them is not the precondition of their relationship but is established originally by the agent and the difference is basically maintained by the agent itself. This makes the relation between absolute being and created reality very problematical and means that it cannot simply be inserted into a scheme of general causality. The transcendental uniqueness of the concept of creation and of the relationship between

[9] Cf. L. Dümpelmann, *Kreation als ontisch-ontologisches Verhältnis*. Zur Metaphysik der Schöpfungstheologie des Thomas von Aquin (Freiburg, 1969); J. Pieper, 'Kreatürlichkeit. Bemerkungen über die Elemente eines Grundbegriffes', *Thomas von Aquin 1274/1974*, ed. L. Oeing-Hanhoff (Munich, 1974), pp. 47–71.

absolute being and a finite reality must be brought to light or, to use an alternative formula, taken back into the darkness of its incomprehensibility. Only from this starting point can the ontological relation between the self-communication of God and intellect engaged in the direct vision of God be properly understood, and the incomprehensibility of God in the direct vision be conceived as the climax of that impenetrability which necessarily obtains for finite reality in its ontological relationship to pure being. If the relation of pure being to finite reality is not carelessly conceived on some general causal model, in which the difference between agent and effect already exists as the condition of possibility of the process of cause and effect and is not established by the agent itself, then the ontological intelligibility of a self-communication of the being of God to a created being no longer lies outside the scope of an ontology of the relation between God and creature, even if the mystery of the possibility of the vision of God offered in revelation is not thereby removed. For the absolute being of God freely establishes us *for ourselves* as beings distinct from God *and* maintains this distinction in himself because established by him alone. This means that for the absolute being of God the same distinction does not exist which he imposes upon us as our mode of existence. The vision of God is the radical form of the general ontological relationship between the being on the one hand whose self-communication establishes distinction (for us) and identity (for absolute being), and finite reality on the other hand. This vision involves an *ontological* self-communication of God[10] to the created intellect which is not the result of direct vision but its ontological condition, in the same way that the 'species', as the real actualisation of the intellect, is the condition of possibility of actual knowledge of an object. Thomas sometimes eases the difficulty of showing how a direct ontological self-communication of God to a created spirit is possible, without either making God finite (as the 'form' of the finite intellect) or dissolving the creature in its infinity, by drawing a distinction between the orientation of a creature to *being* and the orientation to *knowledge* (modus essendi-modus cogitandi). But this distinction, though quite valid in its intention, leaving as it does God incomprehensible and infinite and the intellect with vision finite and limited, does not really solve the problem, if the ontological nature of the

---

[10] The author has constantly spoken of the 'self-communication of God'; for a brief summary, cf. *Sacr. Mun.* III, pp. 114–118; *ibid.* IV, pp. 297–305; *ibid.* V, pp. 348–355.

divine self-communication in the vision of God is taken seriously. Of course it is not necessary to 'solve' this problem since it is a part of the divine incomprehensibility which unfolds rather than diminishes in the vision of God. But clearly the general ontological relationship between pure being and finite reality must be thought of in a way that gives some genuine content to the ontological relationship between God and creature in its state of beatitude. Conversely one has only reached a sufficiently radical understanding of the general relationship if it bears the formal characteristic of rendering conceivable a relation between God and the creature which is found in the vision of God as the condition of its possibility. In all these respects hints and suggestions are to be discovered in Thomas in his comments on the incomprehensibility of God, which compel one to go back to the general ontology of the relationship between the pure being of God and finite reality, if one wishes to gain an authentic and creative interpretation of the text. It must be stressed that such a reference must give thematic expression at one and the same time to the conceivability (which does not mean the perspicuousness) of a direct vision of God and to the divine incomprehensibility. Only in this way can one prevent the doctrine of incomprehensibility from becoming an opaque, but sadly inevitable, element in God which remains unknown in the vision of God. At the same time it opens up the possibility of making divine incomprehensibility the positive content of the vision of God, since this vision is the supreme climax of the ontological relationship between God and the creature. This relationship signifies a positive finite state and not a block which fixes the creature in his finite condition in the face of infinity. For then the finite state would always be surpassed and made superfluous by the infinity of God and would in the end become unbearable.

On the second main issue we mentioned, the following observations may be permitted. In a reaction against Peter Lombard, who simply identified the grace of justification with the Holy Spirit, Thomas rightly emphasised that this grace essentially signified a *created* determination of the substance and capacity of the one justified, or at least necessarily implied it. In consequence Thomas correctly postulates a created 'lumen gloriae' which, being finite, makes the permanence of the divine incomprehensibility, even in glory, intelligible. But on closer inspection the relation between the created grace of justification and the 'indwelling' of God in the one justified is much more complex than appears at first glance. It is clear that for

Thomas,[11] as opposed to an over-simplified scholastic theology, 'uncreated grace' is not simply a consequence of finite, created, habitual grace. For, leaving aside all other considerations, this would be impossible for Thomas since the 'visio', the fulfilment of grace, is grounded in an ontological self-communication of the reality of God himself to the created spirit, and this cannot be derived from any created grace. It is no divergence from the Thomist theology of justification and glory to make use of insights hinted at by Thomas and to interpret created grace and created light of glory as a disposition which is formed by the self-communication of God in grace and glory as its effect and the condition of its possibility. As is quite common in Thomas, there is a mutual relationship between act and potency which is fully disposed for the act, so that each is the condition of the other. For Thomas, however, the incomprehensibility of God is not simply and entirely made plain, even in direct vision of God, through the finite light of glory which he postulates. Rather it must be made clear why and how the self-communication of infinite being to the direct vision of a finite spirit does not merely permit the continued existence of divine incomprehensibility but rather demands it of its own essence and that of man. So, despite the doctrine of the created light of glory, which is quite correct in itself, we are still dealing here with the pure mystery of faith, incomprehensible in itself and experienced as such, the mystery namely, that the incomprehensibility of God can make itself directly present in an encounter with a created spirit, for whom there exists the experience of incomprehensibility which gives God his ultimate name.

THE FINITE NATURE OF MAN

Any interpretation of the Thomist doctrine of the incomprehensibility of God should not overlook the fact that this doctrine is primarily a statement about man, about his finite nature and its positive quality. Only in a highly derivative and tenuous sense should one regard divine incomprehensibility as an 'attribute' of God himself. If one starts by making divine incomprehensibility a (negative) attribute of God, then it would simply become one of a number of attributes which we predicate as 'names' of God, despite his simplicity and infinity. The doctrine of divine incomprehensibility could not then be given its proper weight or value for a theological and metaphysical anthropo-

[11] Cf. S. 1 Dockx, *Fils de Dieu par grace* (Paris, 1928).

logy. The most radical and ultimate statement of this anthropology is that man is a being who is endowed through the free self-communication of God in grace with the infinite incomprehensibility and incomprehensible infinity of God, and so shares in his own being in divine incomprehensibility. A closer examination of Thomas's doctrine clearly shows that God's incomprehensibility is a theme of his anthropology. The doctrine presents itself most often in the context of the knowledge of angels, of man and of Jesus. The basic thrust of the Contra Gentiles makes it plain that here too the doctrine of incomprehensibility is fundamentally a topic of philosophical and theological anthropology, since it deals with the 'finis' of man, i.e. the God of men. It is true that in the Summa, in the first section of the Prima Pars, the doctrine of incomprehensibility is included as part of the treatment of the divine attributes, but here we should not forget that in qu.12, and especially art.7 of qu.12, qu.3–11 are repeated with an anthropological twist in which the divine attributes, having first been described with reference to God himself, are once more analysed to see how God 'in himself' is at the same time the God of men. If the crucial significance of the doctrine of incomprehensibility for a genuinely Christian anthropology is overlooked, then it is almost impossible to prevent divine incomprehensibility from appearing merely as an attribute of God, which man, as a result of a purely negative experience of finite limitation, can only accept of necessity with more or less resignation. This obscures the basic truth that divine incomprehensibility is of vital importance for human self-understanding: it affects all man's knowing and does not only emerge when man is specifically concerned with God. If the affirmative synthesis in human thought always and inevitably refers to 'what' to a 'something' beyond it, while necessarily distinguishing the two, then 'esse' itself is affirmed as the point of reference of the predicative statement, as the reality which is not comprehended. Thus the controlling presence of divine incomprehensibility is also affirmed. All human knowing, despite the possible intelligibility of the 'what' which is predicated, is enfolded in an incomprehensibility which forms an image of the divine incomprehensibility where God reveals himself as the one without a name.

'EXCESS' IN GOD

For Thomas the incomprehensibility of God is present in an 'excessus', in an 'excedere'. This 'excessus' should not simply be identified with the 'via eminentiae', even though it is the latter's ultimate found-ation. It is the primary movement of the spirit and of its activity (intellectus agens) directed to the unlimited being and incomprehensi-bility of God, which is the ground of all knowing. It is only if a man permits this 'excess' to operate in the free act of his existence and *accepts* it as the real kernel of his own self-realisation, that he recognises divine incomprehensibility as his own blessed fulfilment. It is not enough to treat this superabundance as a transcendent characteristic of the human intellect operating (even if unthematically) in every act of knowledge, a characteristic which determines the essential nature of the 'intellectus agens' as it shares in the light of God and itself gives illumination. It must be seen, too, as the free human act in which a man accepts his own being ordered in grace to the incomprehensibility of God, and surrenders himself unconditionally to this incomprehen-sibility as the true source of his own fulfilment. Only then do we find the reality we call faith, hope and love, assuming only that the 'excessus' is taken to be direct and immediate encounter with divine incom-prehensibility brought about by God himself. The theological dispute among the Schoolmen about the real nature of eternal beatitude is familiar enough, as is the explicit teaching of Thomas on the question. But in my opinion we should take seriously Thomas's doctrine of a perichoresis (if we may put it thus) of the transcendent determination of a being as distinct from its categorial determinations which are closely connected to one another, and introduce his notion of 'excess' at this point. If we then give full value to his assertion that particular capacities unfold in their multiplicity from the original unity of the essential substance, then the ancient controversy need not be settled by a cheap compromise (as perhaps in Suarez), but can really be trans-cended in an authentic and original way. Freedom and love can be seen as identical in origin with the intellect (given the 'ordo' between them), and the intellect only achieves its own fullness of being when in hope and love, in a freedom which properly belongs to it, it surrenders itself to incomprehensibility as its own beatitude.

16

THE MYSTERY OF THE TRINITY

CHRISTIAN theology must always address itself to the Trinitarian confession of faith. In so far as such statements do not make up a coherent framework, they are open to systematic correlation, explanation and even criticism.[1] Thus a theologian who has developed and expounded these formulations in his theological reflections and wishes to state his opinion about these ideas is faced by considerable difficulties.

We will, however, leave this problem aside, simply because the topic of the Trinity is enormously important and involves a central question of Christian doctrine and preaching. No individual angle or particular theological investigation should occupy the limelight; the quicker individual contributions are absorbed into a general understanding of the mystery which has contemporary relevance and

---

[1] This essay originally appeared in Brazil in Portuguese and formed an accompanying note to the study by M. de França Miranda on the self-communication of God in the trinitarian theology of K. Rahner. Here the personal reflections have been expanded and contents revised. The remarks contained here are an obvious addition to the author's trinitarian theology which is not spelt out here. A few references may help to orientate the reader: 'Remarks on the Dogmatic Treatise "De Trinitate" ', *Theological Investigations* IV (London and Baltimore, 1966), pp. 77–102; 'Nature and Grace', *ibid.* pp. 165–188; 'The Theology of the Symbol', *ibid.* pp. 221–252; 'Theology and Anthropology', *Theological Investigations* IX (London, 1972), pp. 28–45; 'Observations on the Doctrine of God in Catholic Dogmatics', *ibid.* pp. 127–144. The scriptural basis is to be found in: 'Theos in the New Testament', *Theological Investigations* I (London, and Baltimore, 1961), pp. 79–148. For a short summary, cf. 'Trinity' and 'Trinity in Theology', *Sacr. Mun.* VI (London and New York, 1970), pp. 295–308. A more extensive treatment is available in: *The Trinity*, (London, 1970).

pastoral vitality, the happier the theologian should be.[2] For the issue itself should not be forgotten in modern theology or in the contemporary awareness of faith in the Catholic Church, or relegated to a backwater. This is in fact in danger of happening today in one of two ways. Either the Trinity is taught in a way that merely conforms to received formulations and has no interest in, or connection with, the realities of Christian life and spirituality. Alternatively the doctrine of the Trinity is forgotten in an exclusive concentration upon a distorted political theology or a theology of liberation which is unable to see beyond itself, or in a Christology exclusively concerned with Jesus from below. All these attempts fail to do justice to the fullness of New Testament teaching. A few reflections are offered here though they do not provide a systematic or comprehensive treatment of the question.

As we have observed above, it is not a matter today merely of reproducing other people's formulations of the mystery. Any attempt today to present the Christian doctrine of the Trinity must involve a 'liberation' of the usual traditional propositions from their 'splendid isolation', in which they have been encapsulated in scholastic theology. We must try to make the doctrine of the Trinity fruitful for practical Christian living, given that the doctrine has a 'sitz im leben' and that the Trinity is of crucial importance for actual Christian life and spirituality. Furthermore the teaching cannot even have the right 'speculative' content and form, unless it meets these demands in Christian life.

For this purpose a collection and systematic arrangement of the author's theological statements and insights on the Trinity was necessary, since these are scattered in a variety of writings and are not for the most part included in the author's more extended and systematic treatment of Trinity.[3] Because of his age, the author was unable to join together these 'membra disiecta' into a single whole and wishes to express his gratitude for the achievement of this task.

---

[2] This line of reasoning is to be understood in the light of the general theme of spiritual experience which forms the main topic of this volume. This experience, which most of the essays deal with, or presuppose, is certainly not only a private and personal event in the spiritual life of mystics, but is also a social phenomenon, which is clearly evident in the community insofar as the concrete demands of God's will are expressed in the actual faith of Christians, in and through which they find then real salvation.

[3] Cf. K. Rahner, *The Trinity*, (London, 1970).

Such a collection, however, does create a certain problem in that lines of thought and ideas appearing outside the context of the Trinity must be taken into account and these items, being isolated and incomplete, can scarcely be integrated with any clarity into a systematic presentation of the Trinity. This applies, for instance, if we recall the impression given by this systematic approach that Christological data have been neglected, while general anthropological factors have been given preference. But if it is a cause for criticism that insufficient attention is paid to the awareness of sonship in Jesus which is clearly to be found in Scripture, then it should be remembered that in traditional treatises on Christ and the Trinity this awareness of sonship is understood in direct relation to the 'immanent' sonship of the eternal Logos. Now the New Testament evidence suggests that the awareness of the sonship of the Lord is a far more complex and difficult matter than is suggested by this approach, even though it remains the permanent basis for knowledge of the 'immanent' Trinity. From an exegetical viewpoint Jesus' consciousness of divine sonship, whose unique character distinguishes it from that of the justified Christian, cannot simply be identified with the process by which the eternal Logos originates from the Father.

The task of exegesis and biblical theology this entails can scarcely be tackled successfully by one who is an amateur in New Testament exegesis. However he may be able to escape being too severely criticised for the lack of Christological material in the treatment of the Trinity if he explicitly recognises that his reflections could well be deepened and supplemented in this area.

A further objection concerns the excessively formal character of the thesis that the justified possess real relationships to the Trinitarian God and not merely those of appropriation.[4] It is to be welcomed that the thesis of the existence of such relationships is assumed and basically accepted, for even today it is not one that necessarily commands general recognition as part of the common deposit of Catholic theology.[5] Obviously one should have no hesitation in trying to fill out this assertion with more 'material' content and to explain it more clearly. Stress is in fact laid on the eternal significance of the humanity

[4] Cf. M. Schmaus, 'Appropriation', *LThK* I (Freiburg i. Br., 1957), 773–775.

[5] Cf. K. Rahner, 'The Eternal Significance of the Humanity of Jesus for our Relationship with God', *Theological Investigations* III (London and Baltimore, 1967), pp. 35–46.

of Christ as the mediation of the direct contact between God and those in a state of grace and even of final beatitude. This also is not to the same degree common in contemporary theology. Naturally it is important to bring out more fully and clearly the significance of this for a real understanding of the relationships of man to the Trinity and vice versa.

The objection, however, that no clear distinction is made between self-communication and the self-communication of God is hardly reasonable. If God is really God, i.e. absolute reality, with a personal spiritual nature, then self-communication must be the same as the self-communication of God. If God is Trinitarian and is really related to man and not merely by appropriation, then the communication of being and of self by God must also be Trinitarian. If in this self-communication he possesses as 'Father' a specific relationship to man, one can also speak quite naturally and without contradiction of the self-communication of the one God, as one can of the self-communication of the Father in his 'originality'.

The formula we proposed of 'distinct modes of subsistence' is of course no more than a formal abstraction which is of only limited use in making it easier to understand the religious life, and especially the prayer, of a Christian. The real content of the economy of salvation and of the immanent Trinity must be seen in the 'distinct modes of existence', if they are to be of any 'spiritual' assistance. In the traditional teaching of the Church and in theology, reference is made to 'persons', which means that there is a real distinction from the 'numerically' single reality of the one God. This distinction is brought together in a 'general concept' (i.e. person) in a manner which is quite unique and original. If this occurs in the mode of speech authorised by tradition, the new concept of 'mode of subsistence' is also be justified. Of course all the reservations and qualifications apply to it which one may reasonably make in the case of the concept 'person'.

To conclude our reflections on the mystery of the Trinity as it is presented in the faith and theology of the Church, we may point out in general terms the direction in which a contemporary theology of the Trinity can and should be developed in the future. It is at any rate certain that the identity of the economic and immanent Trinity must be taken seriously. Even if we are resolutely concerned out of fidelity to tradition to guard the deposit of faith as is demanded by contemporary conditions, we must start out from the fact that an interpretation of faith is prevalent in which the economic and immanent Trinity are not regarded as self-evidently identical. It is therefore easy to see why formulations are to be found today which do not appear to do justice to the basic thesis mentioned above, although this does not necessarily imply that the thesis itself has not been taken to heart.

It is not a question here of setting the immanent and economic Trinity in a narrower and clearer relationship, which nevertheless always assumes the prior existence of two separate realities. The goal of our efforts is rather to bring out a prior and original identity and unity of the two realities, in relation to which the immanent and economic Trinity offer developments, clarifications and aspects of this underlying unity. If this point is fully grasped, then it is no longer possible to assert that a 'speculative' doctrine of the immanent Trinity may (still) be possible but that it does not (any longer) arouse much interest. Such statements betray a basic misunderstanding, alluded to above, that a 'pure' dogma of the immanent Trinity can evolve which is totally different from the doctrine of the economic Trinity. In clarifying the *one* doctrine of the Trinity, as we have tried to do here and elsewhere, further advances can certainly be made in understanding the being of God in himself. In this endeavour it should not be taken as a foregone conclusion that the development of the doctrine of the immanent Trinity must be limited in its formulation of new insights to the concepts used by traditional scholastic theology. We may hope that any material could be pressed into service in the attempt to destroy once and for all the false conception that a 'speculative' doctrine of the immanent Trinity may perhaps be conceivable today, but that it is a completely idle and irrelevant undertaking, possessing neither spiritual nor religious interest to the modern Christian and theologian.

LIST OF SOURCES

THE FOUNDATION OF BELIEF TODAY
A paper given to preachers and catechists in the Bildungshaus Stift,
Zwettl in December, 1973. The hitherto unpublished text was revised
and expanded for publication.

EXPERIENCE OF THE SPIRIT AND EXISTENTIAL COMMITMENT
Originally composed as a contribution to the Festschrift for E. Schillebeeckx on his 60th birthday (1974). The text was revised and cross-
references added for publication here.

RELIGIOUS ENTHUSIASM AND THE EXPERIENCE OF GRACE
A paper given at the day conference of the Swiss Theological Society
in Berne in November, 1973. It was first published under the title,
'Das enthusiastisch-charismatische Erlebnis in Konfrontation mit der
gnadenhaften Transzendenzerfahrung' in: C. Heitmann and H.
Mühlen (editors), *Erfahrung und Theologie dès Heiligen Geistes* (Ham-
burg and Munich, 1974), pp. 64–80. The text was further revised and
in part expanded for publication here.

ANONYMOUS AND EXPLICIT FAITH
Originally published in, *StdZ* 192 (1974), pp. 147–152. In this edition
the footnotes were added in order to integrate the ideas into the
author's complete works.

FAITH BETWEEN RATIONALITY AND EMOTION

Originally a paper given at the Catholic Academy of Bavaria. It was first published in: K. Rahner (ed), *Ist Gott noch gefragt?* (Dusseldorf, 1973), pp. 125–144. For this edition the text was further revised and expanded.

THE 'SPIRITUAL SENSES' ACCORDING TO ORIGEN

This essay, published for the first time in German, was the author's first major theological work. It comes from the period of his theological training and yet in a remarkable way traces of later questions and of their possible solution can already be discerned in it. The original text was substantially shortened for this edition and the excessive number of footnotes considerably reduced, in order to fit the essay into this collection. For detailed references to the works of Origen one should consult the original French edition: 'Le début d'une doctrine des cinq sens spirituals chez Origène', *RAM* 13 (1932), pp. 113–145.

THE DOCTRINE OF THE 'SPIRITUAL SENSES' IN THE MIDDLE AGES: THE
    CONTRIBUTION OF BONAVENTURE

First published in French under the title, 'La doctrine des "sens spirituels" au Moyen-Age en particulier chez Saint Bonaventure', *RAM* 14 (1933), pp. 263–299; a larger, expanded section appeared in German under the title, 'Der Begriff der ecstasis bei Bonaventura', *ZAM* 9 (1934), pp. 1–19, and started a controversy with St. Grünewald, cf. *ZAM* 9 (1934), pp. 124–142 and 219–232. The essay has been included in this collection because of its fundamental importance for the author's later work in the philosophy of religion and because of the striking similarity of theme it bears to the questions which have principally occupied the author's attention over recent years (cf. the previous essays).

MODERN PIETY AND THE EXPERIENCE OF RETREATS

A shortened version was published under the title, 'Über den geistes-geschichtlichen Ort der ignatianischen Exerzitien heute', *GuL* 47 (1974), pp. 430–449. The text is based on a paper given to retreat-givers in Vienna.

REFLECTIONS OF A NEW TASK FOR FUNDAMENTAL THEOLOGY
Published in, *Estudios Eclesiasticos* 47 (1972), pp. 397–408 (Homenaje al P. Joaquin Salaverri S.J.).

THE ACCEPTANCE IN FAITH OF THE TRUTH OF GOD
First published as Thesis XVIII in: W. Kern and G. Stachel, (eds.) *Warum Glauben?* Begründung und Verteidigung des Glaubens in einundvierzig Thesen (Wurzburg, 1967), pp. 169–176, under the heading: 'Nicht das Weltbild der modernen Wissenschaft vermag dem Dasein letztlich Sinn zu geben, sondern erst die glaubende Annahme der geschichtlich uns zugesprochenen Wahrheit Gottes.' The text has been slightly revised for publication here.

THE OLD TESTAMENT AND CHRISTIAN DOGMATIC THEOLOGY
A paper given in Regensburg in 1972. It has been revised and expanded, and is published for the first time here.

ON THE 'HISTORY OF REVELATION' ACCORDING TO THE SECOND VATICAN COUNCIL
Originally a contribution to the Festschrift for R. Schnackenburg, *Neues Testament und Kirche* (Freiburg i. Br., 1974), pp. 543–549. It was published originally under the title, 'Kritische Anmerkungen zu Nr. 3 des dogmatischen Dekrets "Dei Verbum" des II Vaticanums'. The text was further revised and expanded for publication here.

THE ONE CHRIST AND THE UNIVERSALITY OF SALVATION
Previously unpublished.

THE HIDDENNESS OF GOD
A contribution to the Festschrift for Y. Congar, *Le service théologique dans l'Eglise* (Paris, 1974), pp. 249–268. Published for the first time in German.

AN INVESTIGATION OF THE INCOMPREHENSIBILITY OF GOD IN ST THOMAS
    AQUINAS

A slightly revised version of the essay in the collection, *Thomas von Aquin 1294–1974* (Munich, 1974), pp. 33–45. It appeared there under the title, 'Über die Unbegreiflichkeit Gottes bei Thomas von Aquin'.

THE MYSTERY OF THE TRINITY

The text is based on an explanatory note by the author for the study written by M. de França Miranda, cf. p. 255 of this volume, footnote 1. For this edition the essay has been shortened and footnotes and cross-references added, in order to fit it into the complete works of the author.

INDEX OF PERSONS

INDEX OF SUBJECTS